Student Resource Handbook

Mathematics
for
Elementary Teachers

A CONTEMPORARY APPROACH

Second Edition

Gary L. Musser
William F. Burger

OREGON STATE UNIVERSITY

Prepared by
Marcia L. Swanson
GREATER ALBANY PUBLIC SCHOOLS
AND
Karen A. Swenson
OREGON STATE UNIVERSITY

Macmillan Publishing Company
New York
Collier Macmillan Canada
Toronto
Maxwell Macmillan International
New York   Oxford   Singapore   Sydney

Copyright © 1991, Macmillan Publishing Company,
a division of Macmillan, Inc.

Printed in the United States of America

Macmillan Publishing Company
866 Third Avenue, New York, New York 10022

Collier Macmillan Canada, Inc.

Printing: 2 3 4 5 6 7   Year: 1 2 3 4 5 6 7

ISBN   0-02-418551-5

PREFACE

This handbook has been designed to illustrate and provide practice in the use of effective learning strategies for the mathematics classroom. These strategies are used to provide opportunities to gain understanding of the mathematical concepts and content of the elementary school program within the context of effective mathematics instruction. Students who use this handbook as a companion to the textbook *Mathematics for Elementary Teachers, A Contemporary Approach, Second Edition* by Gary Musser and William Burger will not only enhance their own learning, but will also begin to place that learning within the framework of the elementary classroom. This handbook may be used as part of a course focusing on mathematical content or on the methods of teaching mathematics, or perhaps in a course that combines the components of content and methods. In whatever situation, this handbook has features to enrich the classroom and study experiences. Each section can be identified by its unique icon. These key components are described in the following paragraphs.

Warm-up. Just as athletes or musicians need a time of warm-up before a competition or performance, a warm-up is also beneficial for students. This section allows students to engage in mathematical thinking and to focus on the task so that the learning time may be more productive. In this section, we provide an opportunity to review and apply the problem-solving strategies presented in the textbook cited above.

Hands-on Activities. Many new and revised activities are contained in this developmental phase of the second edition. It is through hands-on activities that mental images of a concept are developed. The purpose of this section is not only to teach "how" to perform the mathematical operations that are required, but also "why" to perform the operations based on an understanding of the concepts that underlie these operations.

These activities provide experience with a variety of materials and how they can be used in the elementary school classroom. And since research shows that prospective teachers use manipulatives in their teaching in the same manner in which they are taught, this experience is vital. In all of these activities, it is beneficial to approach them as a student just learning the concept. Imagine how an elementary school student would respond.

For each activity we have stated an objective. While there are many forms for writing objectives, it is important as future teachers to be aware of this aspect of any activity used. Some of the activities develop the concepts more quickly than would be practical in an elementary school classroom. Yet they do serve as a foundation for an expanded series of appropriate activities.

We have attempted to make this handbook as self-contained as possible. Some hands-on activities refer to materials cards. These are found at the back of the handbook and are numbered according to the activity (Materials Card 13.6 goes with Activity 6 of Chapter 13, for example). Some commercial materials are available and can be used if you have them. The multibase pieces in Chapters 2 and 4 can be replaced with Dienes blocks and the centimeter strips in Chapters 3 and 6 can be replaced with Cuisenaire rods. Other items used include cubes, dice, fraction bars, a metric tape, graph paper, and a protractor.

Mental Math. This section provides a chance to develop flexibility in thinking about mathematics. Students are encouraged to extend their ability to think about mathematics and to reason about the answer to mathematical problems. No paper and pencils allowed!

Exercises. In this section, students move from the concrete objects used in the hands-on section to visual representations and numerical problems. This section provides practice opportunities on the material presented in the textbook as well as the hands-on section of the handbook. These exercises are presented in creative formats which students find more interesting than usual pencil-and-paper exercises.

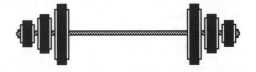

Self-Test. The self-test provides immediate feedback on student progress so that deficiencies can be recognized and corrected, and so that progress can be realized and supported. Students should use this section to self-prescribe further study as needed. The material included on the self-test is covered in the textbook chapter, but may go beyond the hands-on activities.

Solutions. This section provides a chance for students to verify results. Solutions and explanations (where appropriate) are included for all sections of the handbook chapter. Students should use this section only after having worked through the handbook activities so that the experience more closely matches the experiences of students in the elementary classroom.

Resource Articles. For students who wish to extend their learning, these articles are taken from professional journals used by classroom teachers. Use of such resources will develop and extend the student's repetoire of teaching ideas.

Directions in Education. Teachers face many important issues in designing mathematical instruction. Several current issues are briefly summarized in this section of each chapter. Possible questions and resources are included to help guide the exploration of these issues for their impact on future classrooms.

We hope that you will find this handbook to be both helpful and enjoyable. Approaching mathematics with a spirit of curiosity and enjoyment can do much to enhance learning. We have enjoyed preparing this material with you in mind and sincerely wish you success in making use of it.

In Appreciation . . .

We express our appreciation to the following for their assistance in preparing the Student Resource Handbook:

. . . to Gary Musser and Bill Burger for their faith in us in asking us to participate in this project and their support during its preparation,

. . . to Gary Ostedt and Bob Pirtle of Macmillan Publishing for their support of our ideas and expertise in producing these materials,

. . . to Lynn Trimpe for her thoughtful review of the materials and revision suggestions,

. . . to Nancy Swarat, Julie Borden, Heather Brown, Rosemary Troxel, and Marilyn Wallace for their assistance in proofreading and/or doing the computer entry of the material,

. . . to Steve Welsh for his artistic and technical contributions,

. . . to Susan Ellinwood, administrative officer of the Mathematics Department, for expediting matters when needed,

. . . to Charles Peckham and Rhonda Morgan of the Oregon State University Department of Printing for producing final pages on the Linotronic 300,

. . . to the people of Apple Computer, Adobe Systems, and Aldus Pagemaker for making desktop publishing with the Macintosh available,

. . . to Marcia's husband, Dennis, and children, Kelli and Craig, for their encouragement and sacrifice, and finally,

. . . to the elementary education students and faculty who have used the First Edition for their suggestions and contributions.

Marcia L. Swanson
Karen A. Swenson

CONTENTS

1

Introduction to Problem Solving

THEME:
1. **Understand the Problem**
2. **Devise a Plan**
3. **Carry Out the Plan**
4. **Look Back**

WARM-UP

Strategy Review: Guess and Test.
The guess and test strategy presented in Chapter 1 will help you solve these problems.

Hazel sold $65 worth of banquet tickets. Adult tickets cost $4 and student tickets cost $3. How many adult tickets did she sell?

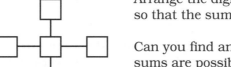

Arrange the digits 1, 2, 3, 4, and 5 in the boxes so that the sum is the same in both directions.

Can you find another arrangement? What sums are possible?

HANDS-ON ACTIVITIES

The activities in this chapter are designed to give you practice in using the problem-solving strategies presented in Chapter 1 of the text. See if you can name the strategy or strategies you find useful for solving each problem.

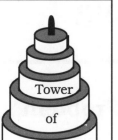

Tower

of

Hanoi

LEGEND:
Monks of
ancient Hanoi
needed to move
a tower of sacred
stones. The
stones were to
be kept on poles
at all times and
were so heavy
they could only
be moved one at
a time. Never
could a larger
stone be placed
on a smaller
one.

OBJECTIVE: **Use problem-solving strategies**

You Will Need: Materials Card 1.1

1. Place circles 3, 2, and 1 on peg A in that order.
   Your task is to move your stack to either peg B or C following
   these rules:

   Move only one circle at a time.
   Never put a larger circle on top of a smaller one.
   Circles must stay on a peg at all times—(except when being
   moved).
   Each time a circle is moved—count one move.

   What is the minimum number of moves required to transfer the
   stack to peg B or C?

2. Based on how many moves were required to move the 3 circles,
   how many do you think will be required to move 4 circles?

3. Repeat the activity using 4 circles; 5 circles; 6 circles.
   Keep a record of moves required using this chart:

Number of Circles	Number of Moves
3	
4	
5	
6	

4. How many moves would be required to move a stack built from 10 circles?   100 circles?
   n circles? Hint: Compare the number of moves to powers of 2: 2, 4, 8, etc...

5. What strategy or strategies did you try in solving this problem?

OBJECTIVE: **Use problem-solving strategies**

You Will Need: At least 3 pennies and 3 nickels, or other distinguishable small objects

1. Place pennies in the 3 squares on the left and nickels in the 3 squares on the right. Leave the center square empty.   Your task is to switch the positions of the coins. The coins may move forward either by a direct move or by jumping another coin. No backward moves.

    How many moves are required?

2. Try the activity using other numbers of coins. In each case, the center square is the only extra square used. For 1 coin per side use only 3 squares, for 2 coins per side, use only 5 squares, etc.

Number of Coins per Side	Number of Moves
1	
2	
3	
4	
n	

3. What problem-solving strategy did you find most useful in solving this problem?

OBJECTIVE: **Use problem-solving strategies**

You Will Need: A handful of toothpicks

1. Use 17 toothpicks to make this figure: Remove 6 toothpicks leaving 2 squares.

2. Use 12 toothpicks to make this figure: Reposition (do not remove) 3 toothpicks leaving 3 squares, all the same size.

3. Use 6 toothpicks to make 4 triangles.

4. Use 3 toothpicks to write 9. (No fair bending them.)

5. What problem-solving strategies did you find useful in solving these problems?

OBJECTIVE: **Use problem-solving strategies**

You Will Need: Materials Card 1.4

1. Find all the shapes that are rectangles two cubes wide. Write the number for each rectangle.

    _____ , _____ , _____ , _____ , _____ , _____

    What is special about these numbers ?

2. Find all the shapes that are not rectangles two cubes wide. Write the number for each shape.

    _____ , _____ , _____ , _____ , _____ , _____

    What is special about these numbers?

3. Choose two even-numbered shapes. Put them together. Record the shape and the addition equation.

    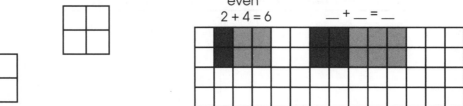

    even
    2 + 4 = 6   __ + __ = __

    Repeat four times. Record the answers and tell if they are odd or even. What do you notice about adding two even numbers?

4. Choose two odd-numbered shapes. Put them together. Record the shape and the addition equation. Repeat four times. Record the answers and tell if they are odd or even. What do you notice about adding two odd numbers?

    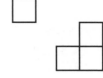

5. Choose one even-numbered shape and one odd-numbered shape. Put them together. Record the shape and the addition equation. Repeat 4 times. Record the answers and tell whether they are odd or even. What do you notice about adding one odd number and one even number?

    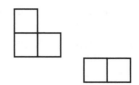

6. Write a statement that summarizes your findings in this activity.

OBJECTIVE: **Use problem-solving strategies**

You Will Need: Materials Card 1.5

1. Josephine the carpenter has been hired to patch a 2' by 12' hole on the side of a barn. She has only a 3' by 8' piece of plywood with which to make a patch. Since she wants to use as few pieces as possible, she wants to make only one cut. Show how Josephine can cut the plywood with only one cut to fill the 2' by 12' hole. Hint: The cut is not necessarily straight.

2. Now Josephine has another hole in the barn to repair. The hole is 10' by 10'. Josephine has a 9' by 12' piece of plywood with which to make the patch, but it has an 8' by 1' hole in the middle of it as shown:

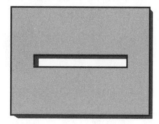

    Can it be cut into 2 pieces to fit the 10' by 10' hole?   Draw a picture of your solution.

3. What problem-solving strategies were most useful in solving these problems?

OBJECTIVE: **Use a calculator as a problem-solving tool**

You Will Need: A calculator

1. Multiply 11 by some two-digit numbers where the sum of the digits is less than 10. Record your results and make a conjecture.

   Explore what happens when the sum of the digits is not less than 10. Make a conjecture.

2. Divide some one-digit numbers by 9, some two-digit numbers by 99, and some three-digit numbers by 999. Record your results and make a conjecture.

3. The numbers 1, 1, 2, 3, 5, 8, 13, 21, 34, 55, 89, 144, ... form the Fibonacci sequence. Explain how the sequence 1/1, 1/2, 2/3, 3/5, 5/8, 8/13, 13/21, ... is derived from the first sequence.

   With your calculator, find the decimal form (in order) of the first 20 of the fractions. Record your results and make a conjecture.

   Repeat with the Fibonacci-like sequence beginning 1, 3, 4, 7, 11, ...

OBJECTIVE: **Use visual problem-solving strategies**

You Will Need: Materials Card 1.7 and scissors

1. Take the three unmarked pieces from
    Materials Card 1.7 and arrange them
    to form a square. Record your results
    to the right.

2. Cut a square or rectangle from scratch paper. First make a straight cut in any direction
    and then a second cut. Can you arrange the pieces back into the original shape? Make a
    third cut and share your pieces with a partner. Can he or she reassemble the pieces?

3. The next activity is best done with a group of four people. The first person takes the pieces
    marked A, the second person takes the pieces marked B, and so on. The object is for each
    person to assemble one square in front of them by following these rules:
    a. No talking at any time.
    b. You may pass any of your pieces to any other member of the group at any time.
    c. You may not ask for any piece from any other person (no talking, gesturing, etc...).

OBJECTIVE: **Explore game-playing strategies**

1. Find a partner to play the game "Force Out" with. Try to develop a strategy that will allow
    you to win.

    Force Out: A number is given. The players, in turn, subtract any single-digit number.
    The player who is forced to obtain zero loses.

2. Another game to try is this version of Reverse. The digits 1–9 are arranged in random
    order. The object of the game is to arrange the digits in increasing order from left to right.
    The only allowable operation is to "reverse the first n digits from the left" when $n = 2, ..., 9$.
    For example, 518432679 (reverse 6) $\rightarrow$ 234815679 (reverse 4) $\rightarrow$ 843215679 (reverse 8)
    $\rightarrow$ 765123489 (reverse 7) $\rightarrow$ 432156789 (reverse 4) $\rightarrow$ 123456789.

    a. Try to rearrange the sequence 468213957 in no more than 15 moves.
    b. Make up your own sequence to try.
    c. What strategy will always allow you to be successful in no more than 15 moves?

MENTAL MATH

How can you cut a cake into
8 pieces with exactly 3 cuts?

How can you cut a doughnut into 12 pieces with exactly 3 cuts?

EXERCISES

INTUITIVELY OBVIOUS?

The first step in problem solving involves understanding the problem. This includes reading carefully and thinking clearly. And, while intuition may give helpful insights, first impressions may need to be double-checked. For instance, consider these...

For each question on the following page, choose the correct answer and put the letter on the line preceding the question. Then, with a straightedge, follow the specific instructions given to connect those points on the diagram shown.

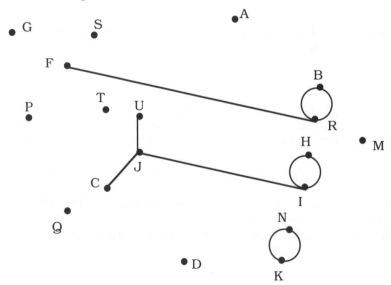

____1. How much dirt is there in a hole 5 meters long, 4 meters wide, and 2 meters deep?

     A. 40 cubic meters   B. no dirt

____2. Is it legal for a man to marry his widow's sister?

     R. yes   S. no

____3. From the bottom of a 24-foot well, a spider can climb up 4 feet each day, but slips back 2 feet each night. In how many days does he escape the well?

     F. 11 days   G. 12 days

____4. Wishing to get a long night's sleep, you go to bed at 8:00 in the evening and set the alarm (on a regular alarm clock) for 9:00 the next morning. How much sleep will you get?

     P. 13 hours   Q. 1 hour

____5. What is the fewest number of ducks if there are two ducks before a duck, two ducks behind a duck, and a duck in the middle?

     J. 5 ducks   K. 3 ducks

____6. Judy had a dozen apples in her office. She ate all but 5. How many were left?

     H. 5 apples   I. 7 apples

____7. Two U.S. coins have a total value of 30 cents. One coin is not a nickel. What are the two coins?

     T. quarter, nickel   U. not possible

____8. How many 3-cent stamps are there in a dozen?

     C. 12 stamps   D. 4 stamps

____9. A train leaves Chicago for Los Angeles, travelling at a rate of 125 kilometers per hour. Another train leaves Los Angeles an hour later, travelling at 75 kilometers per hour. When the two trains meet, which train is nearer to Los Angeles?

     M. faster one   N. neither one

Connect the letter answers to questions 1 through 5 in order. Lift your pencil. Now connect the answers to questions 6 through 9 in order. Can you build the figure you have drawn?

A MAZE OF PATTERNS

Looking for patterns is one of the strategies for problem solving. Many patterns have been known and studied for centuries, but for those who are new to patterns, it takes some practice to develop the skill. Try these...

DIRECTIONS:

Find the number to replace a letter in the pattern. Then, in the maze, shade in the path that connects the diamond containing that letter with the diamond containing the replacement number.

PASCAL'S TRIANGLE:

```
      1   1
    1   2   1
  1   3   3   1
1   4   E   4   1
  .     N   5   1
    .       C   6   1
      .         G   7   1
```

NUMERICAL SEQUENCES:

1, 4, 7, 10, O, G

1, 4, 9, 16, W

FIBONACCI SEQUENCE:

1, 1, 2, 3, 5, 8, K, W

TRIANGULAR NUMBERS:

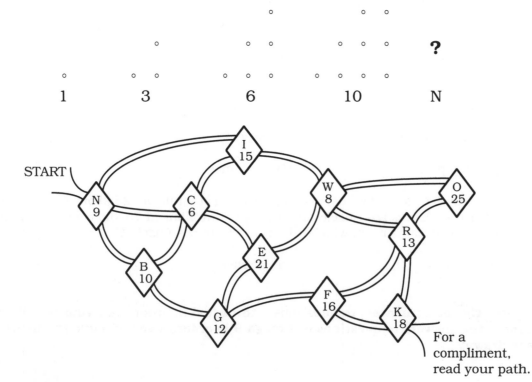

For a compliment, read your path.

SELF-TEST

A bottle and a cork together cost $1.00. If the bottle costs 90 cents more than the cork, how much does the cork cost? (Items 1 - 3)

1. In understanding the problem, each of the following statements is true *except*

   a. We know the combined cost of the bottle and cork is $1.
   b. We know the cork costs 10 cents.
   c. We know the bottle costs 90 cents more than the cork.
   d. We are asked to find the cost of the cork.

2. You decide to use the strategy of using a variable to solve this problem. Therefore, you let c represent the cost of the cork in cents. The cost of the bottle in cents is represented by

   a. $100 + c$ b. 90   c. $c + 90$ d. none of these

3. Proceeding to solve this problem, you find that the cost of the bottle is

   a. 95 cents   b. 90 cents   c. 10 cents   d. 5 cents

How can you bring exactly 2 liters of water from a pond when you have only a 4-liter pail and a 7-liter pail? (Items 4 -7)

4. In understanding the problem, each of the following statements is true *except*

   a. You have only two pails, one that holds 4 liters and the other 7 liters.
   b. You have no other container to hold water.
   c. You want to return with exactly 2 liters in one of the pails.
   d. You are not allowed to pour out any water.

5. What is the fewest number of steps in order to get exactly 3 liters in one pail? Consider each time you fill a pail or pour out a pail as a separate step.

   a. 1 step   b. 2 steps   c. 3 steps   d. more than 3 steps

6. The shortest solution to the problem involves

   a. filling up the 7-liter pail twice.   b. filling up the 4-liter pail five times.
   c. filling up the 4-liter pail four times.   d. none of these steps.

7. If, instead, you had a 6-liter pail and a 10-liter pail, which of the following exact amounts could you bring back?

   a. 3 liters   b. 5 liters   c. 8 liters   d. 9 liters

Given an *n*-gon (a polygon with *n* sides), draw all possible diagonals. How many diagonals are there? (Items 8 - 10)

8. In understanding the problem, each of the following statements is true *except*

   a. You are looking for the maximum number of diagonals.
   b. All possible segments are drawn connecting nonadjacent vertices.
   c. Each vertex of the *n*-gon will be an endpoint of only 2 diagonals.
   d. There are *n* vertices of the polygon.

9. Which of the following strategies could be used?
   (i) Solve a simpler problem - consider polygons with 3 sides, 4 sides, etc.
   (ii) Use a variable - let *s* be the number of vertices, then find the number of diagonals from each vertex, and the total number of diagonals.
   (iii) Make a list (table) - record the number of diagonals for 3-gon, 4-gon, etc.

   a. i and ii only   b. i and iii only   c. ii and iii only   d. all of i, ii, and iii

10. You set up the following chart and look for a pattern.

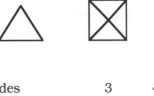

number of sides	3	4	5	6	7	8
number of diagonals from each vertex	0	1	2	3	4	—
total number of diagonals	0	2	5	9	—	—

Which of the following is *not* a valid conclusion to draw?

   a. The number of diagonals from each vertex of an *n*-gon is *n* - 3.
   b. The number of diagonals possible in an octagon (8 sides) is 20.
   c. The number of diagonals in an *n*-gon is an increase of (*n* - 2) over the number of diagonals in an (*n* - 1)-gon.
   d. The number of diagonals in an *n*-gon is the number of vertices, *n*, times the number of diagonals from each vertex, *n* - 3.

SOLUTIONS

Warm-up

One possible solution is that she sold 14 adult tickets. Can you find another solution?

One possible solution is: 5   Yes, possible sums are 8, 9, and 10.

                                4   1   3

                                    2

Hands-on Activities

Activity 1

1. 7 moves
2. Since you have to move the top 3 circles off to another peg, then move the bottom one to the third peg, and then move the pile of 3 back onto the 4th circle, it should take one more than twice the number of moves required for 3 circles.
3.

Number of circles	Number of moves
3	7
4	15
5	31
6	63

4. 1023, $2^{100} - 1$, $2^n - 1$
5. Look for a pattern and solve a simpler problem.

Activity 2

1. 15 moves
2.

Number of coins	Number of moves	
1	3	n-p-n
2	8	n-pp-nn-pp-n
3	15	n-pp-nnn-ppp-nnn-pp-n
4	24	n-pp-nnn-pppp-nnnn-pppp-nnn-pp-n
n	$n(n+2)$	

3. Again, you might look for a pattern.

Activity 3

1. The squares are not necessarily the same size.

2.

3. This figure will be three-dimensional.
4. Your numeral will look like this: IX
5. Guess and test, solve a simpler problem

Activity 4

1. 2, 4, 6, 8, 10, 12   They are all even numbers.
2. 1, 3, 5, 7, 9, 11   They are all odd numbers.
3. The sum is always an even number.
4. The sum is always an even number.
5. The sum is always an odd number.
6. The sum of two even numbers is even; the sum of two odd numbers is even; and the sum of an odd and an even number is odd.

Activity 5

1.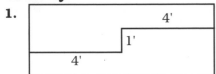

2.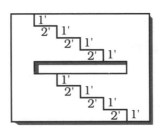

3. Drawing a picture and guess and test were probably useful.

Activity 6

1. If the two-digit number chosen is *ab*, then multiplying by 11 will give a three-digit number with hundreds digit *a*, tens digit, *a* + *b*, and ones digit *b*. If *a* + *b* > 9, then the 1 carries over to be added to the hundreds column.
2. $a/9 = 0.aaa...$ $ab/99 = 0.ababab...$ $abc/999 = 0.abcabc...$
3. Each number in the sequence is divided by the following number. These decimal numbers get closer and closer to the golden ratio which is $(\sqrt{5} - 1)/2 \approx 0.6180339...$ Each Fibonacci-like sequence leads to this result.

Activity 7

1.

Activity 8

1. Subtract a single-digit number to obtain a 1 as the ones digit.
2. Move 9 to the first position, then into place at the right end. Next move 8 to the first position and into place, etc. Other moves may do it more quickly in some instances.

Mental Math

The first cut through your cake could be horizontal as illustrated:

Cut the doughnut as shown:

Exercises

INTUITIVELY OBVIOUS?
1. B   2. S   3. F   4. Q   5. K   6. H   7. T   8. C   9. N

A MAZE OF PATTERNS
   Pascal's Triangle: E-6, N-10, C-15, G-21
   Numerical Sequences: O-13, G-16, W-25
   Fibonacci Sequence: K-13, W-21
   Triangular Numbers: N-15
   Pathway: NICE WORK!

Self-Test
1. b   **2.** c   **3.** a   **4.** d   5. b   **6.** a   **7.** c   **8.** c   **9.** d   **10.** d

RESOURCE ARTICLES

Barson, Alan, and Lois Barson. "Ideas." *Arithmetic Teacher* 35 (November 1987): 26-32. *Activities utilizing a variety of problem-solving strategies.*

Bush, William S., and Ann Fiala. "Problem Stories: A New Twist on Problem Posing." *Arithmetic Teacher* 34 (December 1986): 6-9. *Suggestions for writing problem-solving stories.*

Campbell, Patricia F. and Honi J. Bamberger. "Implementing the Standards: The Vision of Problem Solving in the Standards." *Arithmetic Teacher* 37 (May 1990): 14-17. *Ideas for teaching about, for, and via problem solving.*

Cemen, Pamela Byrd. "Developing a Problem-Solving Lesson." *Arithmetic Teacher* 37 (October 1989): 14-19. *Emphasizes questioning skills and outlines lessons structured around Polya's four stages of problem solving.*

Charles, Randall I. "The Role of Problem Solving." *Arithmetic Teacher* 32 (February 1985): 48-50. *Characteristics of problem solving that promote mathematical thinking.*

Day, Roger P. "A Problem-Solving Component for Junior High School Mathematics." *Arithmetic Teacher* 34 (October 1986): 14-17. *Suggestions for emphasizing the process of solving problems.*

Gilbert-Macmillan, Kathleen, and Steven J. Leitz. "Cooperative Small Groups: A Method for Teaching Problem Solving." *Arithmetic Teacher* 33 (March 1986): 9-11. *Instructional setting for improving students' problem-solving skills.*

Johnson, James E. "Do You Think You Might Be Wrong? Confirmation Bias in Problem Solving." *Arithmetic Teacher* 34 (May 1987): 13-16. *Activities involved in creating and relinquishing hypotheses.*

Knifong, J. Dan, and Grace M. Burton. "Understanding Word Problems." *Arithmetic Teacher* 32 (January 1985): 13-17. *General strategies for solving word problems.*

Krulik, Stephen, and Jesse A. Rudnick. "Developing Problem-Solving Skills." *Mathematics Teacher* 78 (December 1985): 685-692, 697-698. *Activities using "make an organized list" and "search for a pattern."*

Krulik, Stephen, and Jesse A. Rudnick. "Strategy Gaming and Problem Solving—an Instructional Pair Whose Time Has Come!" *Arithmetic Teacher* 31 (December 1983): 26-29. *Uses and adaptations of strategy games to develop problem-solving abilities.*

Leutzinger, Larry P. "Ideas." *Arithmetic Teacher* 34 (January 1987): 19-24. *Activities for interpreting story problems, drawing their own conclusions, and making guesses.*

O'Daffer, Phares G. "Problem Solving: Tips for Teachers." *Arithmetic Teacher* 32 (September 1984 through May 1985). *Spotlight on a different problem-solving strategy each month.*

Otis, Marlys Johnson, and Theresa Reardon Offerman. "How Do You Evaluate Problem Solving?" *Arithmetic Teacher* 35 (April 1988): 49-51. *Presents one approach and examples of evaluation.*

Rosenbaum, Linda, Karla Jeanne Behounek, Les Brown, and Janet V. Burcalow. "Step into Problem Solving with Cooperative Learning." *Arithmetic Teacher* 36 (March 1989): 7-11. *Suggestions for successfully using small, cooperative groups with primary-level pupils to solve word problems.*

Stimpson, Virginia C. "Using Diagrams to Solve Problems." *Mathematics Teacher* 82 (March 1989): 194-200. *Activities for grades 6-8 using diagrams to solve real-world problems and developing the concept of variable.*

Suydam, Marilyn N. "Research Report: Problem Solving." *Arithmetic Teacher* 31 (May 1984): 36. *Brief summary of research findings.*

Szetela, Walter. "The Problem of Evaluation in Problem Solving: Can We Find Solutions?" *Arithmetic Teacher* 35 (November 1987): 36-41. *Compares effectiveness of a variety of evaluation models.*

Van de Walle, John A., and Helen Holbrook. "Patterns, Thinking, and Problem Solving." *Arithmetic Teacher* 34 (April 1987): 6-12. *Pictorial and numeric patterns used to develop problem-solving thinking strategies.*

Van de Walle, John A., and Charles S. Thompson. "Let's Do It: Promoting Mathematical Thinking." *Arithmetic Teacher* 32 (February 1985): 7-13. *Activities to promote development of general problem-solving skills.*

Wheatley, Charlotte L., and Grayson H. Wheatley. "Problem Solving in the Primary Grades." *Arithmetic Teacher* 31 (April 1984): 22-25. *Activities to achieve problem-solving readiness in early childhood.*

Whitin, David J. "Problem Solving in Action: The Bulletin-Board Dilemma." *Arithmetic Teacher* 35 (November 1987): 48-50. *A real-life situation leads to problem solving.*

Wright, Jone Perryman, and Nancy Kight Stevens. "Improving Verbal Problem-solving Performance." *Arithmetic Teacher* 31 (October 1983): 40-42. *Suggestions for using language-experience approach to involve students in problem solving.*

DIRECTIONS IN EDUCATION

Mathematics as Communication - Mathematically Speaking

Young children develop language through verbal communication. When children use the language of the classroom to express their own ideas and thoughts, they invite the teacher "inside their head". They provide the teacher with a rich diagnostic tool through which the language of the classroom can be linked to what is already known by the student. Mathematical language allows students and teachers to express what is known and to use that knowledge base as the foundation for additional learning. The mathematics classroom can be as language rich as the reading/language arts classroom. Mathematical vocabulary can be placed on cards and displayed in the room as it is introduced. By keeping the language of mathematics visible and by encouraging the use of the new vocabulary in oral and written work in math, the teacher can set the stage for development of mathematical communication skills which empower students in the future study and application of mathematics.

Encouraging students to "speak mathematics" will:

- relate concrete materials, pictures, and graphic representations to mathematical ideas.

- allow students to evaluate and clarify their own thoughts about mathematics.

- connect their knowledge of the world around them to the mathematics of their classroom.

- extend their thinking about mathematics beyond pencil and paper skills.

- encourage students to experiment with and expand on mathematical ideas.

- develop comfort with the everyday use of mathematical vocabulary.

- encourage students to listen and respond to the ideas of others in the classroom.

- enhance the teacher's ability to assess student needs and to make sound instructional decisions.

Mathematical communication can be encouraged by:

- **Talking and listening.** This can be encouraged in small groups as well as with the whole class. When done in small groups, some debriefing with the whole class is advisable so that the teacher can question the students and clarify any misconceptions.

- **Writing.**   Students can explain the processes they used in problem solving, discuss individual feelings and attitudes toward mathematics, and create mathematical stories and problems to share with the class.

- **Representing.**   When students use manipulatives or pictorial representations in conjunction with oral or written language to explain mathematical ideas, meaning is clarified.

- **Reading.**   Children's literature is rich with books and stories which contain mathematical problems and which illustrate how other children have solved these problems. Children can use these stories as models to create their own mathematical stories for classmates to share. Interesting mathematics lessons can use children's literature as the starting point. This motivates student interest and involvement in the lesson.

As you think about mathematical communication, ask yourself:

- What is the role of the classroom teacher in encouraging such communication?

- Can I identify new vocabulary which should be developed in conjunction with a math concept?

- Can I develop a math lesson based on a piece of children's literature such as *Alexander, Who Used To Be Rich Last Sunday,* by Judith Viorst, New York: Atheneum, 1977.

- How is student learning enhanced by opportunities to communicate about mathematics either in writing or orally?

- What is the relationship between mathematical communication and
    - cooperative learning?
    - higher order thinking?
    - forming connections with the real world?

- How effectively do I speak mathematics?

To learn more:

Mathematical Sciences Education Board and National Research Council. *Everybody Counts: A Report to the Nation on the Future of Mathematics Education.* Washington, DC: National Academy Press, 1989: 57-59.

Small, Marian S. "Do You SPEAK MATH?" *Arithmetic Teacher* 37 (January 1990): 26-29.

2

Sets, Whole Numbers, and Numeration

THEME: Grouping and Place Value

WARM-UP

Strategy Review:
Use a Variable.
For these problems, you might find that using a variable will be helpful. See Chapter 1 if you need to review.

A total of 20 children and dogs are playing in the park. If you counted their legs, you would get 56 in all. How many children and how many dogs are there?

Sue has 2 brothers. She is 3 times as old as Michael, her youngest brother. The age of her other brother, Jon, is the difference between Sue's and Michael's ages. The sum of all their ages is 36. How old is Jon?

HANDS-ON ACTIVITIES

The activities in this chapter are designed to give you experience in working with the concepts of place value and regrouping. To make the experience more like that of your future students, you will be working in bases other than base ten with which you are already familiar.

OBJECTIVE: **Discover grouping in base three**

You Will Need: Materials Card 2.1

1. How many units comprise a long? _____

        a flat? _____   a block? _____

   How many longs comprise a flat? _____   a block? _____

   How many flats comprise a block? _____

2. What single piece can be exchanged for 3 units? _____

        for 3 flats? _____   for 3 longs? _____

3. These pieces are called **base three pieces**. Explain why.

UNIT

LONG

FLAT

BLOCK

OBJECTIVE: **Represent a number in base three**

You Will Need: Your base three pieces and a handful of paper clips or other objects

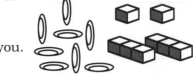

1. Place a pile of paper clips (or other small objects) in front of you. Make a pile of an equal number of units.

2. Make exchanges until the number of objects in the pile is represented using as few base three pieces as possible. Record the number in this chart:

B	F	L	U

3. Repeat parts 1 and 2 several times, using a different number of paper clips each time, and record the number of pieces on a chart.

OBJECTIVE: **Explore place value in base three**

You Will Need: Materials Card 2.3 and your base three pieces

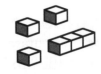

1. In this activity, you will have a growing pile of base three pieces. To start the pile, toss the die and put a unit on the pile for each dot on the die. Then look to see if you can make any exchanges, as in Activity 2.

2. Repeat tossing the die 9 more times, adding units to the pile each time and making exchanges.

3. How many blocks, flats, longs, and units are in your final pile? There should be no
    more than 2 of each. Record your results on the chart:

B	F	L	U

OBJECTIVE: **Make exchanges using place value**

You Will Need: Materials from Activity 3

1. Put three blocks in a pile.

2. Toss the die and remove a unit for each dot on the die. You will need to make some
    exchanges immediately.

3. Repeat 9 more times, removing from the resulting pile each time.

4. Record on a chart the blocks, flats, longs, and units left in the pile.

OBJECTIVE: **Write numerals to represent
                    base three pieces**

You Will Need: Your base three pieces

1. The numeral that describes these pieces
    is written 1022_3 (one block, no flats, two
    longs, two units). The subscript indicates
    a grouping by threes.

    What numeral describes these pieces?

2. Use your base three pieces to represent these numerals, and draw a picture of each.
    a. 1012_3 b. 1120_3 c. 112_3 d. 1102_3

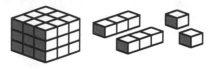

3. Using your drawings, arrange the numbers in part 2 from least to greatest. How can you
    arrange them by just looking at the numerals? Explain why.

Now think about base ten.

4. How many units would make up the longs, flats, and blocks in base ten?

5. A child writes 201 for 21 and 400,203 for 423. Show on these charts how 21 and 201 can be represented with base ten pieces.

B	F	L	U

B	F	L	U

How would you help a student see there is a difference between 201 and 21? Or between 400,203 and 423?

6. How could you show these base ten arithmetic problems to second graders using base ten pieces? Make a sketch to show your answer.

   a.   365
       + 486

                            b.   432
                              - 276

ACTIVITY 6

OBJECTIVE: **Use Venn diagrams to represent sets**

1. Place these numbers in the correct portion of the Venn Diagram:

2, 3, 4, 6, 8, 9, 10,
12, 14, 15, 16, 18, 20, 21, 22

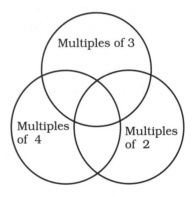

Why would this be a better diagram? Explain.

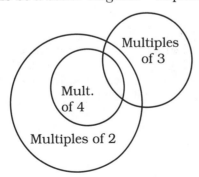

© Multiples of 4 are a subset of
    multiples of 2.
So, if $x \subseteq y$, then $x \cap y = x$
                    $x \cup y = y$

2. Write a description for the intersecting sets described by this diagram:

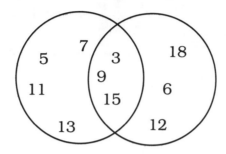

3. Draw a Venn diagram that will fit the following:

   A   Multiples of 6 less than 100
   B   Multiples of 15 less than 100
   C   Multiples of 3 less than 100

   Place the numbers 1 to 100 in your diagram.

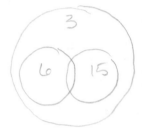

MENTAL MATH

Write the base 5 numeral that correctly represents the solution to each equation.

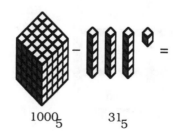

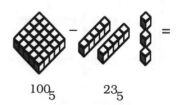

EXERCISES

HIDDEN MESSAGE

To find the hidden message, follow these directions:

- Choose any numeral in the left-hand column.

- Find its corresponding base ten expression in the right-hand column.

- Put the letter in the blank with the corresponding problem number in the message below.

- Keep making matches until you have discovered the message!

NUMERALS

1. 112_{12}
2. 320_4
3. 100010_2
4. 11111_2
5. 111_5
6. 111000_2
7. 200_7
8. 211_5
9. 70_8
10. 343_5
11. 124_8
12. $2T_{12}$
13. 2120_3
14. 51_6

BASE TEN

U	73
T	84
S	31
R	158
P	65
N	196
M	13
L	69
I	27
H	43
F	106
E	98
C	49
B	34
A	56

$$\overline{}_{12}\ \overline{}_{8}\ \overline{}_{4}\ \overline{}_{10}\ \overline{}_{5}\quad \overline{}_{9}\ \overline{}_{1}\ \overline{}_{7}\quad \overline{}_{2}\quad \overline{}_{3}\ \overline{}_{13}\ \overline{}_{6}\ \overline{}_{14}\ \overline{}_{11}!$$

MAZE CRAZE !

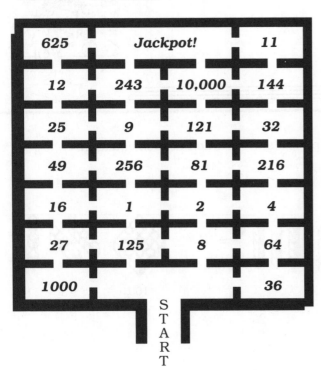

625	Jackpot!	11
12	243	10,000	144
25	9	121	32
49	256	81	216
16	1	2	4
27	125	8	64
1000		36

START

Each room in this maze contains a number. Twelve of these numbers are correct answers to the problems below.

In each problem, a particular digit in the numeral is underlined. Identify the base ten value of that place. Circle your answer in the maze.

(For $\underline{4}32_5$ you would circle 25.)

Keep doing problems until you can draw a path that goes *only* through rooms containing correct answers. (It might not go through all of the correct answers.)

$3\underline{6}1_9$ $3\underline{2}410_5$ $\underline{2}120_3$ $78T\underline{3}_{12}$

$1\underline{0}10111_2$ $56\underline{1}13_7$ $53\underline{1}402_6$

$100\underline{1}1_2$ $9\underline{T}1E_{12}$ $11\underline{2}2012_3$

$32\underline{2}130_4$ $2\underline{3}6797_{10}$

SELF-TEST

1. The number of different 1-1 correspondences possible between two three-member sets is

   a. 1 b. 2 c. 3 d. 6

2. Which of the following sets are equivalent, but not equal?

   a. {a, b, c}, {a, c, b} b. {a, b}, {1, 2} c. {a, b, c}, {a, c} d. {a, b, d, e}, {1, 2, 3, 4, 5}

3. If M = {a, b, c}, N = {b, c, d}, and P = {a, b, c, d}, which of the following is *false*?

   a. M ⊆ P b. N ⊂ P c. N ⊆ M d. None of a, b, or c.

4. If A and B are sets, A is a proper subset of B, and A is equivalent to B, then which must be true?

   a. B ⊆ A b. A = B c. B is an infinite set d. None of a, b, or c.

5. If A, B, and C are three sets, which of the following are equal sets?
   (Hint: Use a Venn Diagram.)
   (i) (A - B) ∪ (B - C) (ii) (A ∪ B) - C (iii) (A ∪ B) - (B ∩ C)

   a. i and ii b. i and iii c. ii and iii d. None of a, b, or c.

6. Which of the following sets would a child use to answer the question, "How many elements are in {a, b, c, d, e}?"?

   a. {0, 1, 2, 3, 4} b. {1, 2, 3, 4, 5} c. {2, 4, 6, 8, 10} d. None of a, b, or c.

7. The number for this set suggested by the grouping (in base 3) has

   a. A 1 in the third place from the right.
   b. A 1 in the second place from the right.
   c. No 1 in its numeral.
   d. None of a, b, or c.

8. How many longs are needed to represent 422 using as few base 6 pieces as possible?

   a. 5 b. 4 c. 2 d. None of a, b, or c.

9. How many zeros are required to be able to write $4 \cdot 8^7 + 6 \cdot 8^2 + 2$ in its standard base 8 representation?

   a. 6 b. 5 c. 4 d. None of a, b, or c.

10. When 983_{12} is changed into its *base 10* numeral, the hundreds digit is:

a. 1   b. 2   c. 7   d. None of a, b, or c.

SOLUTIONS

Warm-up

12 children and 8 dogs. Let x = number of children, then $20 - x$ = number of dogs. Then the number of legs = $2x + 4(20 - x) = 56$.

12 years old. Let x = Michael's age. Sue's age = $3x$ and Jon's age = $3x - x$ or $2x$. The sum of their ages is 36, so $3x + 2x + x = 36$.

Hands-on Activities

Activity 1
1. 3 units, 9 units, 27 units; 3 longs, 9 longs; 3 flats
2. A long, a block, a flat
3. Since 3 of one piece can be exchanged for the next larger piece.

Activity 2
Answers will vary. Check to be sure you are making exchanges when needed.

Activity 3
Answers will vary. Note: you must not have 3 pieces of any one size. Any 3 must be exchanged as in Activity 1.

Activity 4
Answers will vary.

Activity 5
1. 102_3

2.

	B	F	L	U
a.	1	0	1	2
b.	1	1	2	0
c.	0	1	1	2
d.	1	1	0	2

3. 112_3, 1012_3, 1102_3, 1120_3
    The numbers can be arranged from least to greatest by comparing the value of each place from left to right. Look at (a) and (b) for example: The first digit on the left is the same, but by checking the second digit from the left, we know that $1120_3 > 1012_3$.

4. 10 units would comprise a long, 100 units a flat, and 1000 units a block.

5. 2 longs and 1 unit; 2 flats, 0 longs and 1 unit
   Have the student work with the pieces to see that in 201 the 2 represents the number of flats and in 21 the 2 represents the number of longs, etc.

6. a. Have the students represent each number, add the pieces together, and make exchanges.
   b. Have the students represent 432 and then ask them to take away 276, making exchanges when necessary.

Activity 6

1. All multiples of 4 are also multiples of 2, so the second diagram is better.

2. Odds and multiples of 3

3. All multiples of 6 and 15 are also multiples of 3.

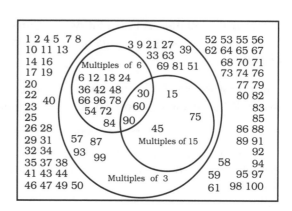

Mental Math

102_5 414_5 22_5

Exercises

HIDDEN MESSAGE		
1. 158	**6.** 56	**11.** 84
2. 56	**7.** 98	**12.** 34
3. 34	**8.** 56	**13.** 69
4. 31	**9.** 56	**14.** 31
5. 31	**10.** 98	
Bases Are A Blast!		

MAZE CRAZE !

Circle these answers: 9   125   27
1   32 49 216 2 144 81
64   10,000
The path through the maze is:
125, 1, 2, 81, 216, 32, 144, 10000, JACKPOT!
Remember: Use this pattern to determine the place value in any base (n for example)...n^5 n^4 n^3 n^2 n 1

Self-Test

1. d   **2.** b   **3.** c   **4.** c   **5.** b   **6.** b   **7.** b   **8.** b   **9.** b   **10.** d

RESOURCE ARTICLES

Arithmetic Teacher 35 (February 1988). *Focus issue on early childhood mathematics. Includes several articles on the process of learning place value and developing number sense.*

Beattie, Ian D. "The Number Namer: An Aid to Understanding Place Value." *Arithmetic Teacher* 33 (January 1986): 24-28. *Builds bridge between iconic representation of a number and its symbolic representation.*

Burton, Grace M. "Teaching the Most Basic Basic." *Arithmetic Teacher* 32 (September 1984): 20-25. *Explores the teaching of place value.*

Clements, Douglas H., and Leroy G. Callahan. "Number or Prenumber Foundational Experiences for Young Children: Must We Choose?" *Arithmetic Teacher* 31 (November 1983): 34-37. *Suggests a variety of activities with counting, simple addition, and subtraction.*

Frank, Alan R. "Counting Skills—A Foundation for Early Mathematics." *Arithmetic Teacher* 37 (September 1989): 14-17. *Discusses ways of teaching counting skills that are important to other mathematical learning.*

Harrison, Marilyn, and Bruce Harrison. "Developing Numeration Concepts and Skills." *Arithmetic Teacher* 33 (February 1986): 18-21, 60. *Activities for place value, multiples, and rounding.*

Nelson, Marvin N., H. Clifford Clark, and Marvin N. Tolman. "The Human Computer (Nudging Along Together)." *Arithmetic Teacher* 32 (March 1985): 24-25. *Understanding place value through number bases.*

Shaw, Jean M. "Let's Do It: A-Plus for Counters." *Arithmetic Teacher* 31 (September 1983): 10-14. *Using counters to develop number concepts and operations.*

Singer, Rita. "Estimation and Counting in the Block Corner." *Arithmetic Teacher* 35 (December 1987): 10-14. *Activities developing early number concepts and estimation.*

Strand, Susan. "Acting Out Numbers." *Arithmetic Teacher* 37 (January 1990): 6-9. *Use of base-ten-block skits in first grade to develop concept of place value.*

Suydam, Marilyn N. "Research Report: The Process of Counting." *Arithmetic Teacher* 33 (January 1986): 29. *Research findings on development of counting skills.*

Thompson, Charles S. "Number Sense and Numeration in Grades K-8." *Arithmetic Teacher* 37 (September 1989): 22-24. *Discusses content of NCTM Standards and describes activities to implement.*

Van de Walle, John, and Charles S. Thompson. "Let's Do It: Partitioning Sets for Number Concepts, Place Value, and Long Division." *Arithmetic Teacher* 32 (January 1985): 6-11. *Using manipulatives to develop number concepts, counting skills, and place value concepts.*

DIRECTIONS IN EDUCATION

Manipulative Materials — When I Do I Learn

Manipulative materials provide the opportunity for teachers to combine the child's natural curiosity and social interest with content learning. Lessons carefully structured to illustrate mathematical content through manipulatives allow children to become involved, investigate, and persist at activities in a stimulating and challenging environment.

What are manipulatives?

- Manipulative materials are concrete, "hands on" models which may be used to illustrate mathematical concepts.

- Manipulative materials are objects which appeal to a variety of senses — visual, aural or tactile — and which capture the attention of the learner.

- Manipulative materials are objects which **students** can touch, move, and rearrange — the materials may come from the students' own environment or may be designed specifically to represent mathematical ideas.

Reasons to use manipulatives:

- Manipulative materials can be used to make the abstract world of mathematics meaningful because they bridge the gap between concrete thinking and abstract content of mathematics.

- Students, particularly children, need physical involvement in order to add new ideas to their cognitive structure. Concrete experiences are necessary before the learner can think pictorially or abstractly.

- Manipulation leads to understanding and abstraction. Students who have had the opportunity to see and manipulate a variety of objects have clearer mental images and can represent abstract ideas more completely. Experiencing ideas to be learned through action can lead students to the use of associated symbols.

- Conceptual learning is maximized when learners are exposed to a concept through a variety of physical contexts.

- Research indicates that mathematical achievement is enhanced through the use of manipulatives.

- Manipulatives are fun!

Criteria for selection of manipulative materials:

- The materials should be a clear representation of the mathematical idea, appropriate for the students' developmental level, and as versatile as possible.

- Sufficient materials should be provided to accommodate individual student manipulation.

- The materials should be made to withstand normal use and handling by children and must also be safe for children to use.

- To increase student motivation and interest, the materials should be bright, precisely constructed and aesthetically pleasing.

- While still clearly portraying the concepts being taught, materials should be simple to operate and manipulate.

- Teachers should look for materials which can be distributed and collected with a minimum of time and which can be easily stored in the classroom.

- The initial cost as well as maintenance and replacement charges need to be considered. Also of concern will be the versatility and life durability of the materials.

- Teacher-made manipulatives may often be as effective as commercial ones.

Guidelines for the use of manipulatives:

- Teachers act as guides, asking frequent questions, probing and extending the student's understanding.

- A variety of manipulative materials should be provided.

- Provide time for free exploration when introducing new manipulatives.

- Be aware of irrelevant details of the manipulatives which may distract students.

As you think about manipulative materials, ask yourself:

- What materials can I think of to present fractions and their operations? number concepts? geometry and masurement concepts?

- What materials are appropriate for primary grades? upper grades? middle school?

- What are good sources of manipulatives?

To learn more:

Burns, Marilyn, and Bonnie Tank.   *A Collection of Math Lessons from Grades 1 through 3.* California: Marilyn Burns Education Associates, 1988.

Burns, Marilyn. *Mathematics with Manipulatives* videotapes for grades 3 through 6. California: Marilyn Burns Education Associates, 1988.

3

Whole Numbers – Operations and Properties

THEME:

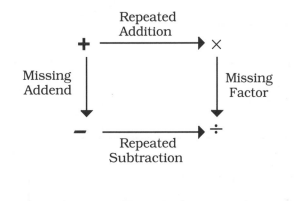

WARM-UP

Strategy Review:
Look for a Pattern.
In Chapter 1, the strategy of looking for a pattern was discussed. Try that strategy to solve these problems.

Fill in the blanks: 1, 1, 2, 3, 5, ___ , ___ '

Five people met at a business meeting. Each person shook hands with every other person exactly once. How many handshakes were exchanged altogether?

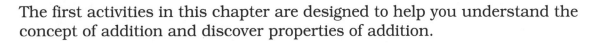

HANDS-ON ACTIVITIES

The first activities in this chapter are designed to help you understand the concept of addition and discover properties of addition.

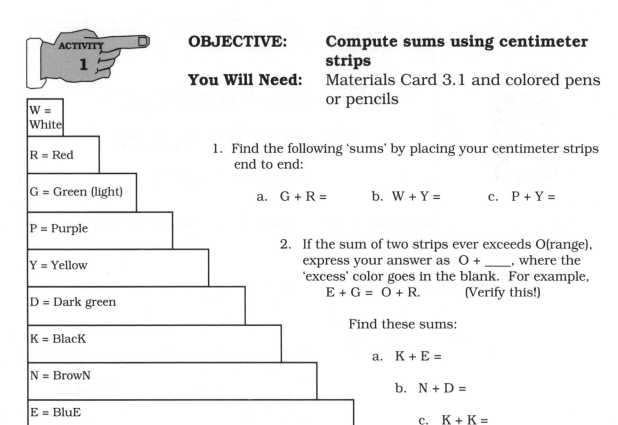

W = White

R = Red

G = Green (light)

P = Purple

Y = Yellow

D = Dark green

K = BlacK

N = BrowN

E = BluE

O = Orange

OBJECTIVE: **Compute sums using centimeter strips**

You Will Need: Materials Card 3.1 and colored pens or pencils

1. Find the following 'sums' by placing your centimeter strips end to end:

   a. G + R =   b. W + Y =   c. P + Y =

2. If the sum of two strips ever exceeds O(range), express your answer as O + ____, where the 'excess' color goes in the blank. For example, E + G = O + R.   (Verify this!)

   Find these sums:

   a. K + E =

   b. N + D =

   c. K + K =

3. Name pairs of strips that have sums of exactly O: ____+____ , ____+____ ,

   ____+____ , ____+____ , ____+____

OBJECTIVE: COMMUTATIVE
Discover properties of addition

You Will Need: Your centimeter strips

1. Compute using your centimeter strips.

   a. K + N =   b. N + K =
   c. Y + R =   d. R + Y =
   e. G + D =   f. D + G =

2. What relationship do you find between (a) and (b), (c) and (d), and (e) and (f)? Explain.

3. Fill in the portion of this
   table above the dotted line.

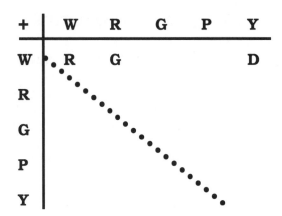

+	W	R	G	P	Y
W	R	G			D
R					
G					
P					
Y					

4. Use your discovery in part 2
   to complete the rest of the table.

Write a statement that explains the property of addition
that helps to simplify your task here.

OBJECTIVE: *ASSOCIATIVE*
                    Discover properties of addition

You Will Need: Your centimeter strips and the table
                     in Activity 2

1. Compute W + R. To this result add Y. We write this as (W + R) + Y where the parentheses
   tell you which part to add first. In summary, (W + R) + Y = _____ .

2. Now consider W + (R + Y). Which sum do you find first? Record your result. How does this
   result compare with part 1? *same*

3. Compute these sums.
   a. (P + R) + G   b. P + (R + G)
   c. (R + G) + Y   d. R + (G + Y)
   What do you notice?

Write a general statement that summarizes your findings.

The next activities in this chapter deal with the concept of subtraction.

OBJECTIVE: **Represent subtraction using a take-away approach**

You Will Need: Your centimeter strips

| Blue |
| Dark Green |

1. Take a blue and a dark green centimeter strip and put them side by side as shown. If the blue strip were shortened by taking away the length of the dark green, how long is the result E - D?

2. Use this take-away approach to find the following differences.
   a. N - G =   b. K - Y =   c. (O + Y) - N =

OBJECTIVE: **Represent subtraction using a missing addend**

You Will Need: Your centimeter strips

1. Solve the following:
   a. Y + ___ = O   O - Y = ___
   b. K + ___ = O + R   (O + R) - K = ___
   c. D + ___ = O + P   (O + P) - D = ___

2. In the first of each pair above, you were looking for the "missing addend." How did each addition problem relate to the subtraction problem?

3. Rewrite each of the following subtraction problems into its missing-addend equivalent and find the solution.
   a. N - R = ___   b. K - D = ___   c. (O + W) - Y = ___

4. The table to the right is the one you should have obtained in Activity 2. Using the missing-addend approach and this table, find the following differences.

   a. N - Y = ____   b. O - Y = ____

   c. K - P = ____   d. P - R = ____

   Use your centimeter strips to check your results.

+	W	R	G	P	Y
W	R	G	P	Y	D
R	G	P	Y	D	K
G	P	Y	D	K	N
P	Y	D	K	N	E
Y	D	K	N	E	O

The concepts of '**greater than**' and '**less than**' are explored in the next activity.

ACTIVITY 6

OBJECTIVE: Describe 'greater than' and 'less than' using addition

You Will Need: Your centimeter strips

1. Order the following strips from smallest to greatest.

    Y   O   N   P   D

2. Complete the following:

    a. Y + ____ = N   Y is _____ (shorter, longer) than N.
    b. Y + ____ = O   O is _____ (shorter, longer) than Y.
    c. N + ____ = O   R is _____ (shorter, longer) than O.

3. Since Y + G equals N, what do we know is true of the relationship between Y and N? between G and N?

    > Explain how addition can be used to order two strips; that is, how addition can be used to show that one strip is longer than another.

4. Insert the correct symbol (>, <, or =) in each of the following:

    a. Y + N____P + D   b. P + O____N + D   c. P + Y____D + N

The next set of activities in this chapter will be helpful in understanding the concept of multiplication and for discovering properties of multiplication. The results may seem simple to you, but try thinking as a student just introduced to the idea.

OBJECTIVE: **Use a set model for multiplication**

You Will Need: Materials Card 3.7

1. Make 3 groups of 4 squares.

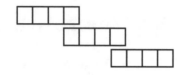

How many squares are there altogether?_____
This shows that $3 \times 4 = 12$.

2. Use squares to represent these products. Record.

   a. $6 \times 3 =$ _____   b. $3 \times 9 =$ _____   c. $8 \times 5 =$ _____

3. Take 24 squares. Find and record four multiplication facts that can be shown about 24.

   a. _____ × _____ = 24   b. _____ × _____ = 24

   c. _____ × _____ = 24   d. _____ × _____ = 24

OBJECTIVE: **Use an array model for multiplication**

You Will Need: Materials from Activity 7

1. Make an array of squares that has 5 rows and 7 columns as pictured.
    This represents 5×7.
    How many squares are in the array?_____
    Record: $5 \times 7 =$ _____

2. Make arrays of squares to represent these products.
    Record:
    a. $2 \times 8 =$ _____   b. $6 \times 7 =$ _____
    c. $4 \times 9 =$ _____   d. $5 \times 8 =$ _____

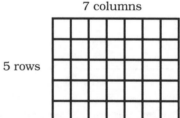

7 columns

5 rows

OBJECTIVE: **Discover properties of multiplication**

You Will Need: Materials from Activity 7

1. Make one array with 3 rows and 5 columns and a second array with 5 rows and 3 columns.
    Record: $3 \times 5 =$ _____ $5 \times 3 =$ _____

    What do you observe about these two results?

2. Use squares and your shortcut from part 1 to solve these multiplication problems:

    a. $9 \times 3 =$ ____   b. $3 \times 9 =$ ____   c. $8 \times 7 =$ ____   d. $7 \times 8 =$ ____

Write a general statement to explain your results.

3. Make 4 arrays, each 2 by 3. We will represent this as $4 \times (2 \times 3)$, where the product in parentheses represents the dimensions of the array. How many squares are there altogether?____
    Record: $4 \times (2 \times 3) =$ ____

    Now make 3 arrays, each 4 by 2. This could be represented as $3 \times (4 \times 2)$ or, by commutativity, $(4 \times 2) \times 3$.
    How many squares are there altogether?____   Record: $(4 \times 2) \times 3 =$ ____

    Compare the statements and their results:
       $4 \times (2 \times 3) =$ ____ $(4 \times 2) \times 3 =$ ____

4. Write two multiplication equations using the numbers 2, 5, and 6.

    ____ $\times$ (____ $\times$ ____) = ____   (____ $\times$ ____) $\times$ ____ = ____

    What do you notice about the solution to each equation?

Write a general statement to explain your results.

5. Make an array that has 2 rows and 5 columns. Extend this array by adding to it an array with 2 rows and 3 columns. How many squares are there altogether?____
    Record $(2 \times 5) + (2 \times 3) =$ ____

    How many rows are in the final array? ____   How many columns?____   How does the number of columns relate to the original arrays that were combined?
    Record: $2 \times (5 + 3) =$ ____

    Compare the statements and their results:
       $(2 \times 5) + (2 \times 3) =$ ____ $2 \times (5 + 3) =$ ____

Write a general statement to explain your results.

The final activities in this chapter deal with the concept of division.

OBJECTIVE: **Use a set model for division**

You Will Need: Materials from Activity 7

1. Take 24 squares. Divide the squares into groups of 6. How many groups of 6 are there?_____   This shows 24 ÷ 6 using a set of objects.

2. Take 40 squares. Compute 40 ÷ 8 by dividing the 40 squares into groups of 8. How many groups are there?_____   Record: 40 ÷ 8 = _____

3. Use squares to solve these division problems. Record:

   a. 48 ÷ 3 = _____   b. 52 ÷ 4 = _____   c. 68 ÷ 4 = _____   d. 72 ÷ 12 = _____

OBJECTIVE: **Use an array model for division**

You Will Need: Materials from Activity 7

1. Take 45 squares. Make an array that has 5 rows. How many columns does the array have?_____ Record: 45 ÷ 5 = ___

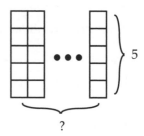

2. Find these quotients by making arrays. Record:
   a. 56 ÷ 7 = _____   b. 48 ÷ 6 = _____   c. 49 ÷ 7 = _____

3. Use 24 squares. Make an array that has 3 rows. Here are two division equations shown by your array: 24 ÷ 3 = 8   24 ÷ 8 = 3

   Make two different arrays (not having 3 rows or columns), using 24 squares. Write the two division equations for each array.
   a. _____ ÷ _____ = _____   and   _____ ÷ _____ = _____

   b. _____ ÷ _____ = _____   and   _____ ÷ _____ = _____

OBJECTIVE: **Find remainders**

You Will Need: Materials from Activity 7

1. Use 26 squares. Make an array that has 7 rows. How many columns are in the array?_____   Are any squares left over?_____   How many?_____
   Record: 26 ÷ 7 = _____remainder_____

2. Use 20 squares. Make arrays to solve these problems:

    a. 20 ÷ 6 = _____ remainder _____
    b. 20 ÷ 3 = _____ remainder _____
    c. 20 ÷ 7 = _____ remainder _____

3. Use squares to make a 3 by 5 rectangle.

    The rectangle shows this division problem:
    $$3\overline{)15}\,\,^{5}$$

4. Use 26 squares. Make a rectangle to solve: $6\overline{)26}$
   How long is the rectangle?_____ How wide?_____
   How many squares are left over?_____

   We record the problems this way:
   $$\begin{array}{r} 4 \\ 6\overline{)26} \\ -24 \\ \hline 2 \end{array}$$

5. Use 21 squares. Make rectangles to solve these problems. Record:

    a. $5\overline{)21}\,\,^{r}\underline{}$
        -20

    b. $4\overline{)21}\,\,^{r}\underline{}$
        $-\underline{}$

    c. $2\overline{)21}$

MENTAL MATH

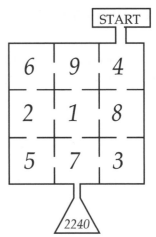

Add as you trace the correct path through each maze.
You may pass through each square only once.
You must obtain the result in the triangle.

Multiply as you trace the correct path through this maze. You may pass through each square only once.

START

3	5	1
7	4	6
8	2	9

26

START

11	16	14
15	18	12
13	17	9

104

START

6	9	4
2	1	8
5	7	3

2240

EXERCISES

Proper-T-Practice

Each of the following computations could be simplified by applying one of the properties listed at the right below. For each computation, identify the property or properties used and place the code letter on the line in front of the computation.

<u>Properties of Whole Numbers</u>

___1.   (96 + 56) + 44 = 196

___2.   (56 × 29) + (56 × 71) = 5600

___3.
      } 132 + (51 + 68) = 251
___4.

___5.   4 × (250 × 29) = 29000

___6.   21 + (39 + 0) = 60

___7.   (121 × 49) - (21 × 49) = 4900

___8.
      } 8 × (57 × 125) = 57000
___9.

__10.   (56 × 1) × 4 = 224

__11.   (46 × 27) + (54 × 27) = 2700

(C)   commutativity for addition

(M)   associativity for addition

(E)   identity for addition

(H)   commutativity for multiplication

(A)   associativity for multiplication

(I)   identity for multiplication

(T)   distributivity for multiplication
         over addition

(S)   distributivity for multiplication
         over subtraction

Now unscramble these 11 code letters to identify a subject that is an art and a tool, as well as a science.

— — — — — — — — — — —

Want Ads

Needed: Doctors who know how to operate.
Tools Available: 3, 5, 6, 7, 9
Skills required: +, -, ×, ÷, and ( )

First of all, you are to choose three different tools to complete the following operations successfully. Remember that multiplication and division are done before addition and subtraction, unless grouping symbols indicate otherwise. There may be several correct answers.

9 + 6 - 5 = 10	☐ × ☐ ÷ ☐ = 2
☐ × ☐ - ☐ = 9	☐ × ☐ - ☐ = 15
☐ + ☐ × ☐ = 21	(☐ + ☐) × ☐ = 60

Now that you are getting proficient, you choose four different tools as well as any of the operations (don't forget parentheses can be used). Fill in the triangles with tools (numbers given above) and place operations and parentheses between the triangles to make a correct equation.

▽△▽△ = 17	▽△▽△ = 12
▽△▽△ = 20	▽△▽△ = 16
▽△▽△ = 19	▽△▽△ = 53

SELF-TEST

1. Using the set union definition of the addition of whole numbers, which of the following pairs of sets could be used to show that 2 + 4 is 6?

   a. {a, b} and {b, c, d, e}   b. {2} and {4}
   c. {x, y} and {x, y, z, w}   d. {1, 3} and {2, 4, 6, 8}

2. Which of the following is *not* an example of the commutative property?

   a. (3 + 4) + 5 = 5 + (3 + 4)   b. 9 + 8 = 8 + 9
   c. (2 + 4) + (5 + 6) = (5 + 6) + (2 + 4)   d. (6 + 3) + 2 = 6 + (3 + 2)

3. Which of the following properties is *not* used in the computation below?

   a. Distributivity
   b. Associativity
   c. Commutativity
   d. None of a, b, or c.

   $$5(37 + 43) = 5(30 + (7 + 43))$$
   $$= 5(30 + (7 + 43))$$
   $$= 5(30 + 50)$$
   $$= 5 \cdot 30 + 5 \cdot 50$$

4. Which statement is *false* ? W is the set of whole numbers.

   a. $a - 0 = a$ for all $a \in W$ b. $a - b = b - a$ for some $a, b \in W$
   c. $(a - b) - c = a - (b - c)$ for all $a, b, c \in W$ d. $a - b \in W$ for some $a, b \in W$

5. Using this addition table find (A - B) - C.

   a. A   b. B   c. C   d. D

+	A	B	C	D
A	A	B	C	D
B	B	C	D	A
C	C	D	A	B
D	D	A	B	C

6. Which two of the following models represent the same multiplication problem?

   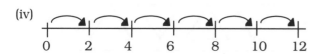

   (i) xxxx
        xxxx
        xxxx

   (ii) [number line: 0, 6, 12 with two arcs]

   (iii) (xxx xxx) (xxx xxx)

   (iv) [number line: 0, 2, 4, 6, 8, 10, 12 with six arcs]

   a. i and ii   b. ii and iv   c. ii and iii   d. iii and iv

7. Which of the following does *not* model division?

    a. There are n objects. You can place them in m equivalent piles. How many will be in each pile?
    b. There are n objects. You can place the objects in a rectangular array with m rows. How many columns are there?
    c. There are n objects. You can make m piles. How many objects will each pile contain?
    d. There are n objects. You can make piles of m objects each. How many piles will you obtain?

8. If a divided by b gives a quotient of c and a remainder d, then

    a. $ac + d = b$ b. $bc = a + d$
    c. $bc = a - d$ d. $ac - d = b$

9. The quotients $6 \div 3$ and $3 \div 6$ can be used to show that

    (i) Division of whole numbers is *not* associative.
    (ii) Division of whole numbers is *not* commutative.
    (iii) The whole numbers are *not* closed under division.

    a. i only   b. iii only   c. i and iii only   d. ii and iii only

10. Which of these is *false*?
    a. $3^4 \cdot 3^5 = 3^3 \cdot 3^6$ b. $4^2 = 2^4$
    c. $5^6 \div 5^2 = 5^{6+2}$ d. $4^3 \cdot 6^3 = (4 \cdot 6)^3$

SOLUTIONS

Warm-up
8, 13   10 handshakes

Hands-on Activities

Activity 1
1. a. Y   b. D   c. E
2. a. O + D   b. O + P   c. O + P
3. E + W, N + R, K + G, D + P, Y + Y

Activity 2
1. a. O + Y   b. O + Y   c. K   d. K   e. E   f. E
2. The results are the same when pieces being added are reversed in order.

3. Row 1: P, Y; Row 2: P, Y, D, K; Row 3: D, K, N; Row 4: N, E; Row 5: O

4. The first column has the same entries as the first row, etc.

$a + b = b + a$ This is called the commutative property of addition.

Activity 3

1. G, N, N

2. R + Y, N; It is the same.

3. a. E   b. E   c. O   d. O

The order in which three pieces are added does not change the result.

Activity 4

1. G

2. a. Y   b. R   c. K

Activity 5

1. a. Y, Y   b. Y, Y   c. N, N

2. The subtraction problem A - B is equivalent to asking what missing addend needs to be added to B to get the result A.

3. a. R + ___ = N, D   b. D + ___ = K, W   c. Y + ___ = O + W, D

4. a. G   b. Y   c. G   d. R

Activity 6

1. $P < Y < D < N < O$

2. a. G, shorter   b. Y, longer   c. R, shorter

3. $Y < N$, $G < N$

If two strips form a third strip, then each of the two is less than the third.

4. a. >   b. =   c. <

Activity 7

1. 12

2. a. 18   b. 27   c. 40

3. a. 4, 6   b. 3, 8   c. 2, 12   d. 1, 24

(Your answers may be in a different order.)

Activity 8

1. 35

2. a. 16   b. 42   c. 36   d. 40

Activity 9

1. 15, 15   They are the same.

2. a. 27   b. 27   c. 56   d. 56

$a \times b = b \times a$ This is called the commutative property of multiplication.

3. 24, 24, 24, 24, 24, 24   The grouping of the factors changes, but the results are the same.

4. $2 \times (5 \times 6) = 60$ and $(2 \times 5) \times 6 = 60$; Equal

$a \times (b \times c) = (a \times b) \times c$ This is called the associative property of multiplication.

5. 16, 2, 8, it is the sum of 5 and 3, 16, 16, 16. When a sum is multiplied by a factor, you get the same result as multiplying each addend by the factor and then adding the results.

$a \times (b + c) = a \times b + a \times c$ This is called the distributive property of multiplication over addition.

Activity 10
1. 4
2. 5, 5
3. a. 16   b. 13   c. 17   d. 6

Activity 11
1. 9, 9
2. a. 8   b. 8   c. 7
3. a. 24 ÷ 4 = 6 and 24 ÷ 6 = 4
  b. 24 ÷ 2 = 12 and 24 ÷ 12 = 2 (Your answers may be in a different order.)

Activity 12
1. 3, Yes, 5, 3, 5
2. a. 3, 2   b. 6, 2   c. 2, 6
4. 6, 4, 2
5. a. 4, 1   b. 5, 1   c. 10, 1

Mental Math
3, 5, 1, 6, 9, 2;   14, 16, 11, 15, 18, 17, 13;   4, 8, 1, 2, 5, 7

Exercises

Proper-T-Practice
1. M   **2.** T   **3-4.** M, C   **5.** A   **6.** E   **7.** S   **8-9.** A, H
10. I   **11.** T   **MATHEMATICS**

Want Ads (There may be more than one correct answer.)

	3 × 6 ÷ 9 = 2
3 × 5 - 6 = 9	3 × 7 - 6 = 15
6 + 3 × 5 = 21	(3 + 7) × 6 = 60
5 + 6 + 9 - 3 = 17	3 × 5 + 6 - 9 = 12
5 × 6 - 3 - 7 = 20	(3 + 5) × (9 - 7) = 16
5 × 6 ÷ 3 + 9 = 19	3 × 6 + 5 × 7 = 53

Self-Test
1. d **2.** d **3.** c **4.** c **5.** b **6.** c **7.** c **8.** c **9.** d **10.** c

RESOURCE ARTICLES

Baroody, Arthur J. "Children's Difficulties in Subtraction: Some Causes and Cures." *Arithmetic Teacher* 32 (November 1984): 14-19. *Analyzes children's informal subtraction strategies.*

Campbell, Melvin D. "Basic Facts Drill—Card Games." *Arithmetic Teacher* 36 (April 1989): 41-43. *Describes games to practice and reinforce basic facts for students of differing abilities.*

Feinberg, Miriam M. "Using Patterns to Practice Basic Facts." *Arithmetic Teacher* 37 (April 1990): 38-41. *Activities at the semiconcrete level to help students memorize and integrate basic facts.*

Greene, Gary. "Math-Facts Memory Made Easy." *Arithmetic Teacher* 33 (December 1985): 21-25. *Instructional strategies to help students learn addition and subtraction facts.*

Hendrickson, A. Dean. "Verbal Multiplication and Division Problems: Some Difficulties and Some Solutions." *Arithmetic Teacher* 33 (April 1986): 26-33. *Examples of situations requiring multiplication and/or division.*

Huinker, DeAnn M. "Multiplication and Division Word Problems: Improving Students' Understanding." *Arithmetic Teacher* 37 (October 1989): 8-12. *Presents instructional strategy to develop understanding of the operations involved in word problems using a part-whole relationship.*

Madell, Rob. "Children's Natural Processes." *Arithmetic Teacher* 32 (March 1985): 20-22. *How children in grades K-3 add and subtract.*

Mahlios, Jan. "Word Problems: Do I Add or Subtract?" *Arithmetic Teacher* 36 (November 1988): 48-52. *Introducing word problems involving addition and subtraction using a part-part-whole concept.*

Quintero, Ana Helvia. "Children's Conceptual Understanding of Situations Involving Multiplication." *Arithmetic Teacher* 33 (January 1986): 34-37. *Activities to help students understand the concept of multiplication.*

Remington, Jim. "Introducing Multiplication." *Arithmetic Teacher* 37 (November 1989): 12-14, 60. *Activities developing the concept of multiplication.*

Rightsel, Pamela S., and Carol A. Thornton. "72 Addition Facts Can Be Mastered by Mid-Grade 1." *Arithmetic Teacher* 33 (November 1985): 8-10. *Sequence of activities presented.*

Swart, William L. "Some Findings on Conceptual Development of Computational Skills." *Arithmetic Teacher* 32 (January 1985): 36-38. *A case for conceptual rather than mechanized approach.*

Talton, Carolyn F. "Let's Solve the Problem Before We Find the Answer." *Arithmetic Teacher* 36 (September 1988): 40-45. *Suggestions for helping students determine whether word problems involve combining, separating, or comparing.*

Thompson, Charles S., and A. Dean Hendrickson. "Verbal Addition and Subtraction Problems: Some Difficulties and Some Solutions." *Arithmetic Teacher* 33 (March 1986): 21-25. *Presents different context for verbal addition and subtraction problems.*

Thompson, Charles S. and John Van de Walle. "Let's Do It: Modeling Subtraction Situations." *Arithmetic Teacher* 32 (October 1984): 8-12. *Manipulative to abstract variations of take-away and comparison subtraction problems.*

Thornton, Carol A. "'Look Ahead' Activities Spark Success in Addition and Subtraction Number-Fact Learning." *Arithmetic Teacher* 36 (April 1989): 8-11. *Activities emphasizing extensions to counting as prerequisites to addition and subtraction.*

DIRECTIONS IN EDUCATION ▤

Developmentally Appropriate Practices – I Think I Can!

In his book, *Insult to Intelligence*, Frank Smith suggests that young students enter school as "explorers". They are eager to join the "Learners' Club" – to be accepted by the learners and to be like the learners. By the time these children enter school they are already accomplished learners, having attained an understanding of the language and culture within which they live. To maintain this positive attitude toward learning, schools must match the activities provided to the developmental needs of children.

For young children, the partitioning of school subjects into discrete subsets of knowledge further divided into discrete skills and facts is not developmentally appropriate. A focus on skill acquisition is frequently based in correcting student failure rather than celebrating student success. Because the domains of a child's development are interwoven, a sense of failure in one domain (cognitive) may also invade into the development of the others (physical, social, emotional). It is essential for teachers of primary grade children to understand developmentally appropriate practices which extend learning, and also foster feelings of success and a lifelong love of learning.

What are some components of a developmentally appropriate classroom for young children?

The National Association for Education of Young Children (NAEYC) has identified guidelines for developmentally appropriate practices:

- Curriculum goals are designed to promote physical, social, emotional, and intellectual growth. Both curriculum and instruction are responsive to individual differences with a focus on the development of self-esteem, and positive attitudes toward learning.

- Instruction is designed to encourage the "explorer" in every child. The environment is created with materials which are concrete, real, and relevant to children's lives. These materials are arranged in ways to invite interest and participation.

- Interaction with peers in small cooperative groups promotes communication while the children engage in work or play.

- Math content is integrated with other relevant projects as children use math through exploration, discovery, and solving meaningful problems.

- Social skills are developed which enable the child both to interact appropriately with others and to become a self-manager.

- Teachers build on children's internal motivation to make sense of the world and to acquire competence.

- Parents are involved as partners in the learning process. This involvement enhances the home/school transition for students and allows parents to reinforce and support the learning process at home.

- Evaluation of student work is done by the student in combination with the teacher and/or peers. The purpose of the evaluation is to guide students to see alternatives, improvements, and solutions.

- Student progress is reported to parents in narrative form based on observational records rather than as letter or numerical grades.

- Children are allowed to progress through the curriculum at their own appropriate pace. The curriculum is adapted to meet the needs of the child. The child is not asked to adapt to the demands of the curriculum.

As you think about developmentally appropriate practices, ask yourself:

- Do I have an adequate understanding of the development that typically occurs in the lives of primary grade children?

- How can I plan instruction which addresses required curriculum yet provides for individual student differences?

- Am I aware of instructional materials and manipulative equipment which will meet the needs for concrete exploration and involvement by the learner?

- What traits might be typical of a lifelong learner? What can I do in the classroom to develop and enhance these traits?

- How can I focus on individual accomplishments rather than on comparison against the group or against an established norm?

- At what age can symbols begin to replace concrete objects as students think about problems?

To learn more:

Bredekamp, Sue (Ed.). *Developmentally Appropriate Practice in Early Childhood Programs Serving Children From Birth Through Age 8, Expanded Edition.* Washington, DC: National Association for Education of Young Children, 1987.

Smith, Frank. *Insult to Intelligence.* New York: Arbor House, 1986.

4

Whole Number Computations — Mental, Electronic, and Written

THEME: Understanding Algorithms

WARM-UP

Strategy Review: Make a List.
The strategy of making a list was presented in Chapter 1. It will be useful in solving these problems.

How many ways can you make change for 35 cents using only nickels, dimes, or quarters?

What possible scores can you get by hitting the target with 3 darts?

HANDS-ON ACTIVITIES

Calculators are widely available and commonly used in today's world and classrooms. To understand how and when to use calculators, it is important to know how they operate and what their capabilities and limitations are. Further, different calculators have different features. The first activities help you explore the features of the calculators available for your use.

OBJECTIVE: **Explore features of your calculator**

You Will Need: A calculator

1. What is the source of power for your calculator? How do you turn the calculator and/or the display on and off?

2. a. Enter the digits 1, 2, 3, etc. until the display is full. How many digits does the display hold? What happens if you try to enter more digits?

    b. Enter a change of sign $\boxed{+/-}$ or $\boxed{+ \leftrightarrow -}$. Does that alter the number of digits displayed?

    c. Clear the display ($\boxed{\text{ON/C}}$ or $\boxed{\text{ON/AC}}$ should do that). Next enter a decimal point followed by the digits 1, 2, 3, etc. until the display is filled. How many digits to the right of a decimal point will your calculator hold?

    d. What is the largest positive number your calculator will hold in its display? What is the smallest positive number?

3. You have already seen that $\boxed{\text{ON/C}}$ or $\boxed{\text{ON/AC}}$ is one way to clear the calculator display. This "All Clear" key is generally the most comprehensive way to clear the calculator because it clears more than just the display.   Other keys that may appear on your calculator include $\boxed{\text{CE}}$, meaning "clear entry" or $\boxed{\text{CE/C}}$ or $\boxed{\text{Backspace}}$.

    a. Using those keys which appear on your calculator, try to find ways to make the following corrections without starting again.

Actual Problem	Your Mistaken Keystrokes	Correction
256×719	256×716	
538×923	538×623	
762×516	$762 + 516$	

    b. For those keys on your calculator, summarize what each clears.

4. Does your calculator have a memory? Hint: Look for keys like $\boxed{M+}$, $\boxed{x \leftrightarrow M}$, or $\boxed{STO}$.

    a. To store a number, enter a number, say 100, and press $\boxed{M+}$, $\boxed{x \leftrightarrow M}$, or $\boxed{STO}$. What does your display look like?

    Is there an M displayed to indicate there is a nonzero number in memory?

    Enter the number 55 and store it. What is now displayed?

    b. To recall the number stored in memory, press $\boxed{MRC}$, $\boxed{MR}$, or $\boxed{RCL}$.

    Next, do some simple calculations like 25 $\boxed{\times}$ 32 $\boxed{=}$ and 478 $\boxed{+}$ 918 $\boxed{=}$.

    Now recall the memory. Has it remembered the number that was in memory?

    c. Eventually you will probably want to start a new computation in memory and/or clear out memory entirely (so that the M is no longer displayed). Find at least two ways to clear the memory on your calculator. Describe the ways.

    d. After entering the following, predict what has been stored in memory. Check your prediction by pressing recall.

    3 $\boxed{\times}$ 5 store   Prediction: _____   Check: _____

    3 $\boxed{\times}$ 5 $\boxed{=}$ store   Prediction: _____   Check: _____

    e. Begin a new computation by entering 60 into memory. Then enter the number 45 and press $\boxed{M+}$ or $\boxed{SUM}$. Now recall the contents of memory. What has happened?

    f. Enter the number 15 and press $\boxed{M-}$ or press $\boxed{+/-}$ and $\boxed{M+}$. What happens to the contents of memory?

    Compute the following using the memory.

    $(5 \times 6) + (10 \times 13) - (7 \times 9)$

ACTIVITY 2

OBJECTIVE: **Explore operations of your calculator**

You Will Need: A calculator

1. a. Enter each of the following keystroke sequences on your calculator and describe what happens.

   | AC | + | 3 | = | = | = |

   | 3 | + | = | = | = | = |

   | 3 | + | 3 | = | = | = |

   | 5 | + | 3 | = | = | = |

   If any of these produce a sequence counting by 3, your calculator has an automatic constant feature. If not you may have to use 3 [+] 3 [+] 3, etc.

   b. How can you get your calculator to reproduce the following sequences? List the keystroke sequences.

   5, 10, 15, 20, . . .

   8, 16, 24, 32, . . .

   3, 8, 13, 18, . . .

   c. How can you get your calculator to count by the even numbers? By the odd numbers?

2. a. Record the results your calculator gives to the following expressions:

   4 [+] 6 [×] 3 [=]   12 [×] 2 [-] 3 [×] 5 [=]

   b. Does your calculator give the results 30 and 105?
   Some do. To get these results, in what order did the calculator perform the operations? (Watching the display as you slowly enter the operations may give you a clue.)

   Calculators that perform operations in this manner, namely as the operations are entered, have what is called **arithmetic logic**.

   c. Does your calculator give the results 22 and 9?
   If so, in what order were the operations performed to get these results?

   Calculators that perform operations according to the usual mathematical convention for order of operations (innermost parentheses, exponents, multiplication and division, and finally addition and subtraction) have **algebraic logic**.

d. Which kind of logic does your calculator have?

e. Since parentheses have the highest priority, calculators often have $\boxed{(}$ and $\boxed{)}$ keys. Insert parentheses as needed in the following expressions to obtain the result shown.

$12 \div 3 + 3 \times 5 = 19$ $25 + 20 \div 5 - 2 \times 4 = 21$

$12 \div 3 + 3 \times 5 = 10$ $25 + 20 \div 5 - 2 \times 4 = 1$

$12 \div 3 + 3 \times 5 = 35$ $25 + 20 \div 5 - 2 \times 4 = 60$

$25 + 20 \div 5 - 2 \times 4 = 28$

Verify using your calculator.

f. How could you obtain the results above without using parentheses (on a calculator with either arithmetic or algebraic logic)?

3. Sometimes you will try to do an operation that your calculator cannot do. What happens, for example, when you enter the following?

12 $\boxed{\div}$ 0 $\boxed{=}$ 25 $\boxed{+/-}$ $\boxed{\sqrt{\ }}$

What is wrong with the operations you tried to do?
Which clearing key on your calculator do you need to use to clear out the result?

4. In Activity 1, you discovered how many digits can be displayed on your calculator. What happens when the results of a computation are either too large or too small? Perform the following calculations to find out.

98989898 $\boxed{\times}$ 19191919 $\boxed{=}$ 0.0000003 $\boxed{\times}$ 0.0000005 $\boxed{=}$

a. Does your calculator give you an error message for overflow or underflow?

b. Does your calculator give answers like $\boxed{1.8998 \quad ^{15}}$ and $\boxed{1.5 \quad ^{-13}}$?
These answers are expressed in **scientific notation** and represent the product of a decimal number between 1 and 10 (10 not included) and a power of 10. For example, $\boxed{1.8998 \quad ^{15}}$ means 1.8998×10^{15} or $1,899,800,000,000,000$ and $\boxed{1.5 \quad ^{-13}}$ means 1.5×10^{-13} or 0.00000000000015. Notice that these are only approximate results to the original problems.

c. How could you use your calculator to find the exact answer for $98,989,898 \times 19,191,919$? Hint: Recall what you know about place value and the usual multiplication procedure.

OBJECTIVE: **Combine mental math and estimation with the calculator**

You Will Need: A calculator and a partner

1. Given below are sequences of operations. Mentally decide what number needs to be put in the blank to obtain the number given on the next line. Use a calculator to verify your solutions.

   a. 52361 - _____

       50361 - _____

       50360 - _____

       50300 ÷ _____

         503 + _____

        6503

   b.   78 - _____

        70 ÷ _____

         7 × _____

     70000 + _____

     70200 ÷ _____

       7020

   c. Make up some similar sequences and have your partner do them.

2. The beginnings of several problems are given below. Estimate the remaining whole number so that the result will fall within the given range. Check your estimate with a calculator and adjust as necessary. Can you find solutions in fewer tries than your partner?

Start	Range (inclusive)	List estimates tried
a. 36 + ____	(80, 90)	_____
b. 374 - ____	(235, 245)	_____
c. 27 × ____	(1200, 1300)	_____
d. 134 × ____	(2000, 2500)	_____
e. 856 ÷ ____	(20, 30)	_____
f. 2406 ÷ ____	(90, 120)	_____

3. Play the following game with your partner or in a larger group. If desired, a 10-second time limit can be established for responses.

   The first player enters a two-digit number and passes the calculator to the second player. The first player then calls out a new two-digit number. The second player must obtain the new number by adding to or subtracting from the number displayed. The second player then passes on the calculator and calls out a new number.

ACTIVITY 4

OBJECTIVE: **Explore and reinforce concepts using a calculator**

You Will Need: A calculator and a partner

Do the following activities with a partner.

1. One person enters a number into the calculator, say 751.98, and hands it to the other person, asking them to change one of the digits, say 5, to a 0 by subtracting an appropriate number. That person identifies verbally what is being subtracted. Exchange roles and repeat. As a variation, you could ask the other player to change the chosen digit to something other than 0, say change the 5 to a 2.

2. One player selects a "secret" two-digit number. He or she then performs a sequence of operations, known to both players, and hands the result to the second player. The object for the second player is to determine the original number.

    For example, ___ $\times$ 2 $=$ $+$ 15 $=$ $\div$ 3 $=$ 19.

    (Note: You might be able to omit $=$ depending on your calculator's logic.)

3. Using the digits 2, 3, 4, 6, 9, complete the following exercises so that you have the largest possible answers and the smallest possible answers.

    a. Largest possible answers

    b. Smallest possible answers

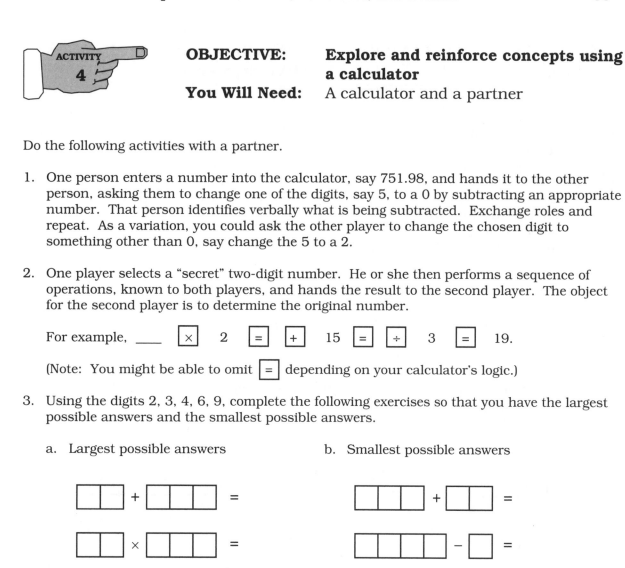

    c. Choose 5 different digits and repeat parts (a) and (b).

In mathematics, **algorithms** are the mechanical 'how-to-do-it' part of the curriculum. For example, the step-by-step procedures you follow as you add a column of numbers or do a long division problem are algorithms. In Chapter 3, we looked at the 'concepts' of addition, subtraction, multiplication, and division—that is, the basic ideas of what is happening when we perform these operations. The following activities will help you gain further insight into 'how-to-do' these operations.

OBJECTIVE: **Use the chip abacus to add and subtract in base 3**

You Will Need: Materials Card 4.5

For many of these activities you will be using a **chip abacus.** The chip abacus consists of a sheet of paper with lines drawn as shown.

The columns represent the various place values—depending on the base. Numbers are represented by putting chips in the appropriate columns.

Example:

10^2	10	1

327 is represented as [diagram] on a base ten abacus.

Notice that the chips used in each column are the same. They do not represent different values because of their shape and size as did longs and flats. Here they represent different values because of where they are placed.

1. Write the base three numerals that are represented by these diagrams:

    a.

3^3	3^2	3	1

    _____

    b.

3^3	3^2	3	1

    _____

    c.

3^3	3^2	3	1

    _____

2. Represent these numerals on your chip abacus.

    a. 221_3 b. 120_3 c. 12_3 d. 1002_3

3. Your chip abacus can be used to find a sum such as $112_3 + 212_3$. First represent both numbers on the abacus.

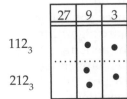

27	9	3	1

112_3

212_3

add →

27	9	3	1

record →

    1 1 add ones
      2 add threes
 1 0   add nines
_____

Then exchange as needed in the columns.

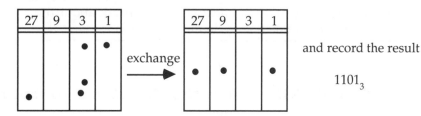

and record the result

1101_3

Compute these on your chip abacus. Record the intermediate steps.

a. $212_3 + 22_3$ b. $121_3 + 21_3 + 12_3$

4. The chip abacus can also be used to find a difference such as $211_3 - 12_3$

| Represent the first number | 27 | 9 | 3 | 1 | Exchange if necessary to be able to take away from ones ⟶ | 27 | 9 | 3 | 1 | Repeat in threes column | 27 | 9 | 3 | 1 |

$$\begin{array}{r} 211_3 \\ -\ 12_3 \\ \hline \end{array}$$

$$\begin{array}{r} 0\ \ 11 \\ 2\ \not{1}\ \not{1}_3 \\ -\ \ 1\ \ 2_3 \\ \hline 2_3 \end{array}$$

$$\begin{array}{r} 1\ \ 10\ \ 11 \\ \not{2}\ \not{1}\ \not{1}_3 \\ -\ \ \ 1\ \ 2_3 \\ \hline 1\ \ 2\ \ 2_3 \end{array}$$

Compute these on your chip abacus. Record the intermediate steps.

a. $1212_3 - 221_3$ b. $1111_3 - 212_3$

5. How could you do these addition and subtraction problems without your abacus? Did you use an algorithm? If so, how is the algorithm related to how you usually add or subtract?

6. Compute the following without using your abacus:

a. $\begin{array}{r} 1221_3 \\ +\ 2122_3 \\ \hline \end{array}$ b. $\begin{array}{r} 2211_3 \\ -\ 1212_3 \\ \hline \end{array}$

Check your answers using your abacus.

We can also look more closely at the operation of multiplication by using the chip abacus. As you do the next activities, think about the algorithm *you* use to do multiplication.

OBJECTIVE: **Use the chip abacus to multiply in base 3**

You Will Need: Materials from Activity 5

1. Show 121_3 on your abacus.

2. Put two *more* 121_3's on your abacus and simplify (no column should have more than two chips after simplification).

3. Compare your results with 121_3. How are they alike? How are they different?

4. The result obtained in part 2 was three times 121_3, or $10_3 \times 121_3$. Can you suggest a shortcut for multiplying any number (in base 3) by 10_3? by 100_3?

5. Find the product $2_3 \times 102_3$, by putting 102_3 on your abacus twice and then simplifying (making exchanges).

$$2_3 \times 102_3 = \underline{\hspace{2cm}}$$

6. Now see if you can combine what you have learned in parts 4 and 5 to do the following computation. Hint: Associativity and commutativity will help you simplify.

$$20_3 \times 102_3 = (2_3 \times 10_3) \times 102_3 = \underline{\hspace{2cm}}$$

7. Now use distributivity to do this problem:

$$21_3 \times 102_3 = (20_3 + 1_3) \times 102_3 = (20_3 \times 102_3) + (1_3 \times 102_3) =$$

Check this problem using your abacus if you need to. How is this related to the usual multiplication algorithm?

8. Combine what you have learned in this activity to find these products:

   a. $12_3 \times 111_3 = \underline{\hspace{1.5cm}}$ b. $21_3 \times 21_3 = \underline{\hspace{1.5cm}}$

   c. $21_3 \times 201_3 = \underline{\hspace{1.5cm}}$ d. $12_3 \times 120_3 = \underline{\hspace{1.5cm}}$

ACTIVITY 7

OBJECTIVE: **Explore the multiplication algorithm using base ten pieces**

You Will Need: Materials Card 4.7

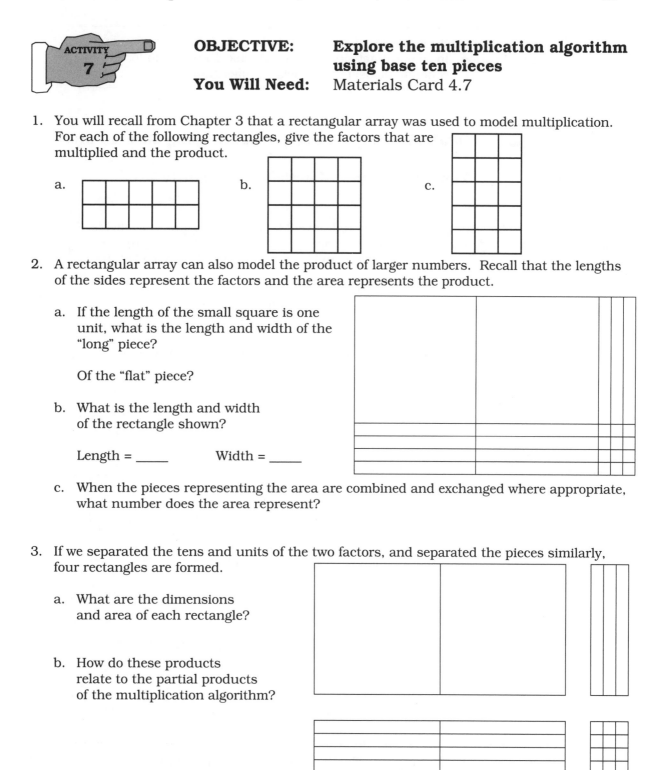

1. You will recall from Chapter 3 that a rectangular array was used to model multiplication. For each of the following rectangles, give the factors that are multiplied and the product.

   a.   b.   c.

2. A rectangular array can also model the product of larger numbers. Recall that the lengths of the sides represent the factors and the area represents the product.

   a. If the length of the small square is one unit, what is the length and width of the "long" piece?

      Of the "flat" piece?

   b. What is the length and width of the rectangle shown?

      Length = _____   Width = _____

   c. When the pieces representing the area are combined and exchanged where appropriate, what number does the area represent?

3. If we separated the tens and units of the two factors, and separated the pieces similarly, four rectangles are formed.

   a. What are the dimensions and area of each rectangle?

   b. How do these products relate to the partial products of the multiplication algorithm?

4. Build rectangles to compute the following products. Show how the rectangles relate to the usual algorithm.

   a. 52×14 b. 26×34 c. 17×24

We have looked at models for algorithms in addition, subtraction, and multiplication. In the next activity we will use base 10 pieces to look at a concrete model for the division algorithm.

ACTIVITY 8

OBJECTIVE: **Find quotients using base 10 pieces**

You Will Need: Materials from Activity 7

1. Represent 23 in base 10 pieces. You should have 2 longs and 3 units. Now divide those pieces into two equal piles. Each pile has _____longs and _____units. Are there any units left over?_____ How many?_____ Leftover units are called the **remainder**.

    $23 \div 2 =$ _____longs_____units, remainder_____ or $23 \div 2 = 11$, remainder 1

2. Divide the pieces representing 23 into 3 equal piles. Why is this problem more difficult than $23 \div 2$?

    $23 \div 3 =$ ____longs____units, remainder____

3. Represent 376 in base 10 pieces. Now divide the pieces into 3 piles.
    Hint: Always begin with the largest pieces and work down to the units.

    Record: $376 \div 3 =$____flats___longs___units, remainder____

4. Perform these computations using your base 10 pieces.

    a. $1042 \div 5 =$ __f __l __u, r__   b. $572 \div 3 =$ __f __l __u, r__

    c. $76 \div 12 =$ __l __u, r__   d. $95 \div 6 =$ __l __u, r__

    Explain how this method is like the standard division algorithm.

The chip abacus provides a manipulative for addition and multiplication. As an alternative to the standard algorithm, it may be easier to do, but it requires more time or space to perform the computation. In the next activities, we will look at other methods for addition and multiplication, using a **lattice**.

OBJECTIVE: **Use a lattice to add in base 3**

1. Examine this addition procedure:

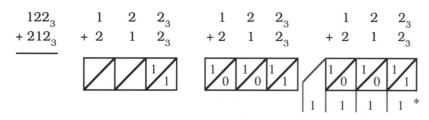

*This sum was obtained by adding down the "diagonals".

2. Is this a correct procedure?   Try it on these. Remember that no subscript indicates base ten.

   a. $2 \quad 1 \quad 2_3$
       $+ 2 \quad 2 \quad 2_3$

   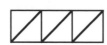

   _____sum

   b. $5 \quad 4 \quad 3$
        $+ 6 \quad 5 \quad 4$

   _____sum

   c. $5 \quad 9 \quad 9$
       $+ 9 \quad 4 \quad 2$

   _____sum

Is this a correct procedure in all three cases?

Show how this relates to the standard addition algorithm you usually use.

OBJECTIVE: **Use the lattice method for multiplication**

1. Examine this multiplication method:

    34×56

$4 \times 6 = 24$

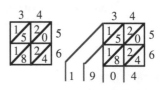

By adding down the diagonals and carrying, we see that $34 \times 56 = 1904$.

2. Try this method again.

$19 \times 35 =$ $72 \times 38 =$

3. Try this method with 3-digit numbers.

$165 \times 219 =$ $327 \times 408 =$

Use the notion of place value to explain why this method works.

MENTAL MATH

Find the correct path to the calculator.

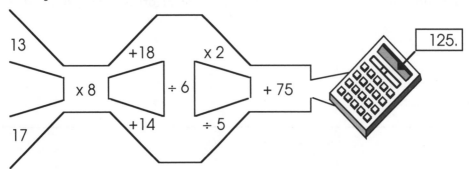

EXERCISES

Worm Work

In going through my great-grandmother's attic recently, I found the following homework page. However, over the years, hungry worms have done their share of damage. Repair the damage by finding the missing digits.

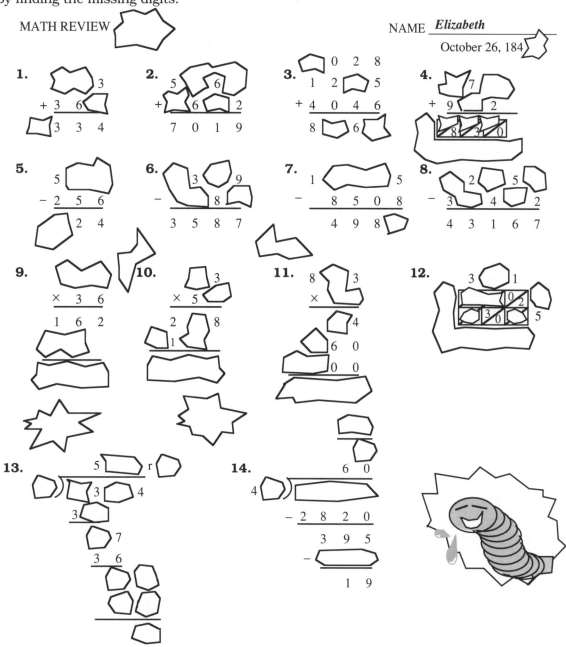

MATH REVIEW

NAME *Elizabeth*

October 26, 184█

P.S. The year this paper was written was a perfect square. What year was it?

CALCULATOR CAPERS

What did the old woman who lived in a shoe admire most about her husband? Put your head and calculator together to discover the answer. Complete the problems below and discover the patterns. Find the answers that replace the boxes on the calculator keys below. Find the same number in the calculator display given and shade that portion.

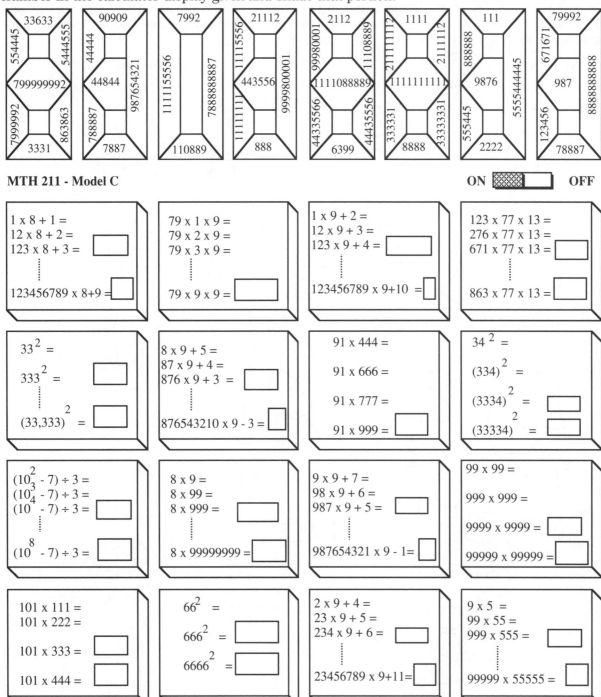

MTH 211 - Model C   ON ▨▨▨☐ OFF

Now turn the page upside down to find the answer.

SELF-TEST

1. Which of the following computations can be simplified using distributivity?

   a. 34(17 + 83)   b. 20(5 × 163)   c. 17 + (13 + 42)   d. 27 × 7 + 27 × 3

2. Which of the following illustrates the left-to-right addition method for finding 35 + 41?

   a. 30 + 40 + 5 + 1   b. 30 + 5 + 40 + 1
   c. 5 + 1 + 30 + 40   d. None of a, b, or c.

3. Fill in the correct values for this intermediate
   addition algorithm. Then find the sum of the
   numbers in the three boxes.

   a. 6   b. 5
   c. 7   d. None of a, b, or c.

   ```
       4 8 9 2
     + 7 6 5 9
     ─────────
           1 1
         1 □ 0
       □ 4 0 0
     1 1 □ 0 0
   ```

4. In performing this subtraction problem, we eventually express 50,000 as

   a. 4000 + 900 + 90 + 9   b. 40000 + 900 + 90 + 10
   c. 40000 + 9000 + 900 + 90 + 9   d. None of a, b, or c.

   ```
       5 0 0 0 0
     −   2 3 9 2
   ```

5. The subtraction problem at the right was done
   by the *subtract-from-the-base* algorithm. The
   3 in the answer was obtained by calculating

   a. (10 - 9) + 2   b. 12 - 9
   c. □ , where 9 + □ = 12   d. None of a, b, or c.

   ```
       2
     3̸ 2
     −  9
     ────
     2 3
   ```

6. Find the indicated product by
   completing the lattice to the right.

   a. 15,125   b. 14,125
   c. 15,200   d. 15,225

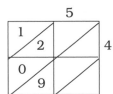

7. Fill in the correct values for this intermediate multiplication algorithm.
   Then find the sum of the numbers in the four boxes.

   a. 13   b. 15
   c. 17   d. None of a, b, or c.

   ```
        274
      ×  38
      ─────
         32
        560
      □□00
       □20
       2100
      □000
   ```

8. In the division problem to the right, the # sign represents various numbers. What is the value of y?

    a. 2   b. 5
    c. 7   d. None of a, b, or c.

$$
\begin{array}{r}
47\ \overline{|\ \#\ \#\ \#\ y\,} \\
-\ \#\ \#\ \#\ \#\quad 30 \\
\hline
\#\ \#\ \# \\
-\ \#\ \#\ \#\quad 10 \\
\hline
\#\ \#\ \# \\
-\ \#\ \#\ \#\quad\ 6 \\
\hline
1\ 3
\end{array}
$$

9. Find the remainder for 6,289,214 divided by 92,365.

    a. 68   b. 8,394   c. 571,555   d. None of a, b, or c.

10. Which of the following are equal?

    (i) $37_8 + 124_8$ (ii) $354_8 - 152_8$ (iii) $32_8 \times 5_8$

    a. i and ii   b. i and iii   c. ii and iii   d. None of a, b, or c.

SOLUTIONS

Warm-up
6 ways   3, 7, 11, 12, 15, 16, 20, 21, 25, 30

Hands-on Activities

Activity 1
Answers will vary

Activity 2
1. b. $5 + 5 = = = \ldots$ $8 + 8 = = = \ldots$ $3 + 5 = = = \ldots$
    c. $2 + 2 = = = \ldots$ $1 + 2 = = = \ldots$
2. e. Solutions for calculators with algebraic logic:
    $12 \div 3 + 3 \times 5 = 19$ $25 + 20 \div 5 - 2 \times 4 = 21$
    $12 \div (3 + 3) \times 5 = 10$ $(25 + 20) \div 5 - 2 \times 4 = 1$
    $(12 \div 3 + 3) \times 5 = 35$ $(25 + 20) \div (5 - 2) \times 4 = 60$
                                            $((25 + 20) \div 5 - 2) \times 4 = 28$
    f. $12 \div 3$ store $3 \times 5 =$ M+ recall 25 store $20 \div 5 =$ M+ $2 \times 4 =$ M- recall
        $3 + 3$ store $12 \div$ recall $\times 5 =$ $25 + 20 = \div 5 =$ store $2 \times 4 =$ M- recall
        $12 \div 3 + 3 = \times 5 =$ $5 - 2 =$ store $25 + 20 = \div$ recall $\times 4 =$
                                            $25 + 20 = \div 5 - 2 = \times 4 =$
3. Division by zero and square roots of negative numbers are not defined for the set of real numbers.

4. c.

```
                        9898   9898
                     ×  1919   1919
                        1899   4262   (9898 × 1919)
                 1899   4262   0000   (98980000 × 1919) - find product, then add zeros
                 1899   4262   0000   (9898 × 19190000)
          1899   4262   0000   0000   (98980000 × 19190000)
          1899   8061   0423   4262
```

Activity 3
1. a. 2000, 1, 60, 100, 6000   b. 8, 10, 10000, 200, 10
2. a. 44-54   b. 129-139   c. 45-48   d. 15-18   e. 29-42   f. 21-26

Activity 4
3. a. 963 + 42 = 1005 (or exchange 6 and 4, 3 and 2)
         94 × 632 = 59,408   6432 × 9 = 57,888   964 - 23 = 941
      b. 236 + 49 = 285 (or exchange 3 and 4, 6 and 9)
         2346 - 9 = 2337   2 × 3469 = 6938   249 × 36 = 8964

Activity 5
1. a. 212_3 b. 1010_3 c. 1201_3
2. a. 0, 2, 2, 1 chips   b. 0, 1, 2, 0 chips   c. 0, 0, 1, 2 chips   d. 1, 0, 0, 2 chips
3. a. 1011_3 b. 1001_3
4. a. 221_3 b. 122_3
5. Use the usual addition or subtraction algorithm, regrouping by 3's
6. a. 11120_3 b. 222_3

Activity 6
2. 1210_3
3. Multiplying by 3 has shifted 121_3 one place to the left.
4. Shift the numeral one place to the left. For 100_3, shift two places left.
5. 211_3
6. 2110_3
7. $2110_3 + 102_3 = 2212_3$. In base ten we would similarly multiply 21 × 102 as 20 × 102 + 1 × 102.
8. a. 2102_3 b. 1211_3 c. 11221_3 d. 2210_3

Activity 7
1. a. 2 × 5 = 10   b. 4 × 4 = 16   c. 5 × 3 = 15
2. a. 10, 1, 10, 10   b. 23, 14   c. 322
3. a. 10 × 20 = 200, 10 × 3 = 30, 4 × 20 = 80, 4 × 3 = 12
      b. They are the same.
4. a. 728   b. 884   c. 408

Activity 8
1. 1, 1   Yes, 1, 1, 1, 1
2. You need to exchange longs for units.   0 longs 7 units, remainder 2
3. 1, 2, 5 r 1
4. a. 2, 0, 8 r 2   b. 1, 9, 0 r 2   c. 0, 6 r 4   d. 1, 5 r 5
      We start from the left dividing up the bigger pieces first and proceed to the right.

Activity 9

2. Yes   a. 1211_3 b. 1197   c. 1541   Yes, it avoids some carrying.
Places are added, then regrouped diagonally instead of vertically.

Activity 10

2. 19×35—   Row 1: 0, 3, 2, 7   Row 2: 0, 5, 4, 5   Product: 665
    72×38—   Row 1: 2, 1, 0, 6   Row 2: 5, 6, 1, 6   Product: 2736
3. 165×219—   Row 1: 0, 2, 1, 2, 1, 0   Row 2: 0, 1, 0, 6, 0, 5
                      Row 3: 0, 9, 5, 4, 4, 5   Product: 36135

    327×405—   Row 1: 1, 2, 0, 8, 2, 8   Row 2: 0, 0, 0, 0, 0, 0
                      Row 3: 2, 4, 1, 6, 5, 6   Product: 133416

Places are multiplied, then regrouped diagonally. For example, in the product 327×408 the intersection of the "3" column and the "4" row represents $300 \times 400 = 120000$.

Mental Math

17, 8, 14, 6, 2, 75

Exercises

Worm Work

  1. 973 + 361 = 1334   **2.** 5367 + 1652 = 7019
  3. 3028 + 1295 + 4046 = 8369   **4.** 978 + 962 =

= 1940

  5. 580 - 256 = 324
  6. 4369 - 782 = 3587
  7. 13495 - 8508 = 4987   **8.** 82659 - 39492 = 43167

9.
```
    27
  × 36
   162
    81
   972
```

10.
```
     43
   × 56
    258
    215
   2408
```

11.
```
   873    or    823
   ×  8         ×  8
    24          24
   560         160
  6400        6400
  6984        6584
```

12.

13.
```
     562 r2
  6) 3374
     30
     37
     36
     14
     12
      2
```

14.
```
          68
           8
          60
  47) 3215
    - 2820
       395
     - 376
        19
```

Calculator Capers

Top Row:	987, 987654321, 6399, 1111, 1111111111, 671671, 863863
Second Row:	110889, 1111088889, 7887, 7888888887, 90909, 11115556, 1111155556
Third Row:	3331, 33333331, 7992, 799999992, 8888, 8888888888, 99980001, 9999800001
Bottom Row:	33633, 44844, 443556, 44435556, 2112, 211111112, 554445, 5555444445

           hIS ShOES

Self-Test

1. d **2.** a **3.** b **4.** d **5.** a **6.** d **7.** d **8.** b **9.** b **10.** c

RESOURCE ARTICLES

Abel, Jean, Glenn D. Allinger, and Lyle Andersen. "Popsicle Sticks, Computers, and Calculators: Important Considerations." *Arithmetic Teacher* 34 (May 1987): 8-12. *Use of teaching aids to help students learn the concept and algorithm for division.*

Barson, Alan, and Lois Barson. "Ideas." *Arithmetic Teacher* 35 (October 1987): 27-32. *Activity pages to enable students to practice estimation, skip counting, place value, and computation, all with the use of a calculator.*

Bates, Tom, and Leo Rousseau. "Will the Real Division Algorithm Please Stand Up?" *Arithmetic Teacher* 33 (March 1986): 42-46. *Approaches and applications of the division algorithm.*

Beattie, Ian D. "Modeling Operations and Algorithms." *Arithmetic Teacher* 33 (February 1986): 23-28. *Rationale for using manipulatives.*

Broadbent, Frank W. "Lattice Multiplication and Division." *Arithmetic Teacher* 34 (January 1987): 28-31. *Extends lattice method to division.*

Cheek, Helen Neely, and Melfried Olson. "A Den of Thieves Investigates Division." *Arithmetic Teacher* 33 (May 1986): 34-35. *Activity using distributive connotation of division.*

Ewbank, William A., and John L. Ginther. "Subtraction Drill with a Difference." *Arithmetic Teacher* 31 (January 1984): 49-51. *Collection of number games and puzzles to supplement textbook.*

Grossman, Anne S. "A Subtraction Algorithm for the Upper Grades." *Arithmetic Teacher* 32 (January 1985): 44-45. *Subtraction by the equal addition method.*

Haigh, William E. "The Only Way To Do It Is To Undo It." *Arithmetic Teacher* 31 (November 1983): 24-25. *Illustrates relationship between inverse operations.*

Hall, William D. "Division with Base-Ten Blocks." *Arithmetic Teacher* 31 (November 1983): 21-23. *Provides transition from manipulatives to written division algorithm.*

Kamii, Constance, and Linda Joseph. "Teaching Place Value and Double-Column Addition." *Arithmetic Teacher* 35 (February 1988): 48-52. *Presents an approach based on Piaget's theory.*

Lessen, Elliott I., and Carla L. Cumblad. "Alternatives for Teaching Multiplication Facts." *Arithmetic Teacher* 31 (January 1984): 46-48. *Suggests alternative sequence to teaching multiplication facts.*

Markovits, Zvia, Rina Hershkowitz, and M. Bruckheimer. "Estimation, Qualitative Thinking, and Problem Solving." *Mathematics Teacher* 80 (September 1987): 461-468. *Activities for grades 6-9 using estimation.*

Meyer, Ruth A., and James E. Riley. "Multiplication Games." *Arithmetic Teacher* 33 (April 1986): 22-25. *Variety of games for drill and practice of multiplication.*

Pearson, Eleanor S. "Summing It All Up: Pre-1900 Algorithms." *Arithmetic Teacher* 33 (March 1986): 38-41. *Algorithms for operations.*

Pereira-Mendoza, Lionel. "Using English Sentences and Pictures for Practice in Mathematics." *Arithmetic Teacher* 32 (September 1984): 34-38. *Game for self-checking practice with addition and subtraction.*

Reys, Barbara J. "Estimation and Mental Computation: It's 'About' Time." *Arithmetic Teacher* 34 (September 1986): 22-23. *Develops difference between mental computation and estimation with teaching suggestions.*

Reys, Barbara J., and Robert E. Reys. "Implementing the Standards: Estimation-Direction from the Standards." *Arithmetic Teacher* 37 (March 1990): 22-25. *Suggestions and examples for developing estimation abilities.*

Reys, Robert E. "Estimation." *Arithmetic Teacher* 32 (February 1985): 37-41. *Discusses characteristics of mathematical thinking involved in estimation.*

Reys, Robert E. "Testing Mental-Computation Skills." *Arithmetic Teacher* 33 (November 1985): 14-16. *Suggestions for testing mental-computation skills in the classroom.*

Richbart, Lynn A. "Fun and Arithmetic Practice with Days and Dates." *Arithmetic Teacher* 32 (January 1985): 48. *Practice in dividing, multiplying, adding, subtracting, and using simple algebraic expressions.*

Schoen, Harold. "Front-End Estimation." *Arithmetic Teacher* 34 (February 1987): 28-29. *Describes four steps of front-end estimation.*

Singer, Rita. "Estimating and Counting in the Block Corner." *Arithmetic Teacher* 35 (January 1988): 10-14. *Examples of class use of estimation in kindergarten.*

Sowder, Judith T. "Mental Computation and Number Sense." *Arithmetic Teacher* 37 (March 1990): 18-20. *Developing number sense through emphasis on mental computation.*

Watson, Charles D., and Judy Trowell. "Let Your Fingers Do the Counting." *Arithmetic Teacher* 36 (October 1988): 50-53. *Suggestions for selecting and introducing calculators to primary children.*

Young, Jerry L. "Uncovering the Algorithms." *Arithmetic Teacher* 32 (November 1984): 20. *Method for diagnosing students' problems with applying algorithms.*

DIRECTIONS IN EDUCATION

Estimation/Mental Math — It's About . . .

Estimation and the ability to perform mental computation are useful, practical skills. We all make estimates each time we answer questions such as the following:

- How long will it take to drive to the airport?
- Do I have enough cash to buy everything I need?
- How much food should I prepare for dinner?
- How much money should I budget for extras?
- How many people were at the ball game?
- How much wallpaper should I order?

Some studies have found that adults use estimation in 75% of the non-occupational calculations they perform. With increasing reliance on calculators for exact computation, the skill of estimation to predict or assess the results displayed on the calculator is essential.

Much of classroom instruction in mathematics is focused on exact computation and on arriving at the "right answer". Students often receive little or no instruction and practice in the skills of estimation and approximation. Should it simply be left to chance that students will learn effective techniques to use mathematics in the ways common to mainstream society?

Estimation is the process used in answering such questions as, "About how many...?" or "About how much...?" **Mental math** is the process of performing exact computations mentally.

Reasons to teach estimation and mental math:

- They are basic skills in the application of mathematics.
- They provide a form of self-checking skills to take into the real world.
- They comprise an experiential background from which errors can be explained.
- Number sense is reinforced and enhanced through practice in estimation.
- Experience with estimation helps students to understand mathematical concepts.
- Estimation encourages flexibility in reasoning about numbers.
- Students develop a "feel" for very large or very small numbers and for measurements through experiences with estimation.
- Estimation enhances problem-solving skills and the ability to use certain problem-solving strategies.
- Estimation activities aid in the development of a positive attitude toward mathematics by helping to eliminate the "right answer syndrome."

What kinds of estimation skills should be taught?

- Skills dealing with relative size:
  - Understanding of the concepts of greater-than, less-than and betweenness.
  - A "feel" for numbers and orders of magnitude.

- Skills dealing with measurement:
  - Ability to use units of measure.
  - Ability to measure a given object using a given unit.
  - Ability to match an object or entity to a given measurement.
  - Ability to check estimates by using measuring devices.

- Skills dealing with questions of computation:
  - Understanding place value which permits leading-digit estimates.
  - Rounding skills used in conjunction with addition, subtraction, multiplication and division.
  - Averaging skills which provide for grouping of similar numbers in a problem.
  - Using a reference point to determine if an answer will be over or under that specified point.
  - Finding a range of answers. This skill is particularly useful in assessing the reasonableness of results.

The one remaining ingredient required to insure the success of efforts to include estimation and mental math in the mathematics program is that of **teacher commitment.** Time must be devoted to such study on a regular basis. The use of estimation and mental math must be interwoven with the use of pencil-and-paper skills. The teacher should learn to model these skills for the class and to encourage the use of these skills by the students.

As you think about estimation and mental math, ask yourself:

- How often and in what settings do I use estimation or mental math?

- Do I rely on paper-and-pencil skills when a mental calculation might be more efficient?

- Can I think of ways to incorporate estimation or mental math in my lessons?

To learn more:

Hope, Jack A., Larry Leutzinger, Barbara J. Reys, and Robert E. Reys. *Mental Math in the Primary Grades.* Palo Alto, CA: Dale Seymour Publications, 1988. Also available are *Mental Math in the Middle Grades* and *Mental Math in Junior High.*

Reys, Robert E., Paul R. Trafton, Barbara J. Reys, and Judy Zawojewski. *Computational Estimation, Grades 6, 7, 8.* Palo Alto, CA: Dale Seymour Publications, 1987.

Seymour, Dale. *Developing Skills in Estimation, Books A and B.* Palo Alto, CA: Dale Seymour Publications, 1981.

Zweng, Marilyn, editor. *Estimation, Approximation and Mental Math.* 1986 Yearbook of the National Council of Teachers of Mathematics: Reston, Virginia.

5 Number Theory

THEME: Composing and Decomposing with Primes

WARM-UP

Strategy Review:
Solve a Simpler Problem.
To solve these problems, begin by solving a simpler version first. See Chapter 1 for a review of this strategy.

A restaurant has 23 square tables that seat 1 person on each side. How many people can be seated at a banquet if one long, rectangular table is made by pushing the 23 tables together?

Craig and 6 of his friends have telephones. Each friend talks with every other friend exactly once each day. How many phone calls are made each day?

HANDS-ON ACTIVITIES

What is a factor? The numbers 2 and 3 are **factors** of 6 because 2 × 3 = 6. The list of all the factors of 6 is 1, 2, 3, and 6. In order to deal with the concepts in this chapter, you need to have a clear understanding of factors. Activity 1 will help you understand factors.

73

OBJECTIVE: **Investigate factors**

You Will Need: Squares from Materials Card 3.7

1. Use 12 squares.   Make a 3 by 4 rectangle.   The numbers 3 and 4 are called factors of 12.

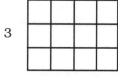

3

4

Use the 12 squares again. Make a 2 by 6 rectangle. 2 and 6 are also factors of 12.

Use the 12 squares again. Make a 1 by 12 rectangle. 1 and 12 are also factors of 12.
Record all the factors of 12:

_____ , _____ , _____ , _____ , _____ , _____

2. Use 15 squares. Find all of the factors of 15 by making rectangles.
Record the factors of 15:

_____ , _____ , _____ , _____

3. Find all of the factors of each number by making rectangles.   Record.

a.   4 _____   b.   9 _____

c. 18 _____   d. 20 _____

e. 25 _____   f. 36 _____

4. Which numbers in part 3 have an odd number of factors?

_____ , _____ , _____ , _____

What is the special name for these numbers?

_____

When two numbers have the same factor or factors, they are said to have
common factors. Both 4 and 6 have 2 as a factor. Therefore, 2 is a
common factor of 4 and 6. Activity 2 will give you more information about
common factors.

ACTIVITY 2

OBJECTIVE: **Find the greatest common factor**

You Will Need: Materials from Activity 1

1. Make 3 different rectangles, using 16 squares for each rectangle.
   Record:

   _____ by _____ , _____ by _____ , _____ by _____

   Record the factors of 16: _____ , _____ , _____ , _____ , _____

2. Make 4 different rectangles, using 24 squares for each rectangle.
   Record:

   _____ by _____ , _____ by _____ , _____ by _____ , _____ by _____

   Factors of 24: _____ , _____ , _____ , _____ , _____ , _____ , _____ , _____

3. List the factors that 16 and 24 have in common:

   _____ , _____ , _____ , _____

   These factors are called the **common factors** of 16 and 24.
   Which of these factors is the largest? _____
   This is called the **greatest common factor (GCF).**

4. Find the common factors of 15 and 20. Record: _____ , _____

   What is the greatest common factor of 15 and 20? _____

5. Find the greatest common factor of each pair of numbers:

   a. 12 and 18 _____   b. 8 and 12 _____

   c. 9 and 12 _____   d. 12 and 24 _____

   CHALLENGE: Find the greatest common factor of 12, 16, and 20.

   The **multiples** of a number are found by multiplying that number by
   the counting numbers. For example, the multiples of 3 are 3, 6, 9, 12 . . .
   Activity 3 will give you additional practice in finding multiples.

OBJECTIVE: **Investigate multiples**

You Will Need: Materials from Activity 1

1. Make a 4 by 1 rectangle. How many squares are in the rectangle?_____
    4 is called a multiple of 4.

    Now make a 4 by 2 rectangle. How many squares are in the rectangle?_____
    8 is also a multiple of 4.

    Now make a 4 by 3 rectangle. How many squares are in the rectangle?_____
    12 is also a multiple of 4.

2. Make 6 more rectangles with 4 squares on one side. Use the rectangles to find six more
    multiples of 4.

    Record: _____ , _____ , _____ , _____ , _____ , _____

3. Make rectangles to find six multiples of each number.

    a. 3 _____   b. 7 _____

    c. 5 _____   d. 6 _____

When two numbers have the same number as a multiple, they are said
to have a **common multiple**. You can always find a common multiple
by multiplying the two numbers together, but it is important to know how
to find the **least common multiple (LCM)**. Activity 4 will help you
understand common multiples.

OBJECTIVE: **Find least common multiples**

You Will Need: Materials Card 5.4

1. For each multiple of 2, shade in the triangle in the upper left corner of the box in the grid
    on Materials Card 5.4 (2 and 4 have been done for you). For each multiple of 3, use
    vertical lines to shade in the triangle in the upper right corner of the box (3 and 6 have
    been done for you). Using different colored pencils will be helpful.

List the common multiples (those with both a solid and striped triangle) of 2 and 3 less than 100:

Which number is the least common multiple of 2 and 3?_____

2. For all of the multiples of 4 use horizontal lines to shade in the triangle in the lower left corner of the box.

   Use dots to shade in the lower right corner of the box for each multiple of 6.

   List the common multiples of 4 and 6 less than 100:

   What is the least common multiple of 4 and 6?_____

3. Find the least common multiple for each pair of numbers.
   Hint: Instead of shaded triangles, use bits of paper to cover the multiples of 3, then 5.

   a. 3 and 5 _____   b. 4 and 7 _____

   c. 9 and 6 _____   d. 2 and 8 _____

   What can you say about the bits of paper and the common multiples?

   the least common multiples?

4. Find the least common multiple for each group of numbers.

   a. 2, 3, and 5 _____   b. 3, 6, and 8 _____

   c. 3, 4, and 7 _____   d. 2, 5, and 9 _____

Some numbers have exactly 2 factors; these numbers are called **prime** numbers. Numbers that have more than two factors are called **composite** numbers. This activity will demonstrate a method for finding prime and composite numbers.

OBJECTIVE: **Find prime and composite numbers**

You Will Need: Materials from Activity 1

1. Make a rectangle using 3 squares. Draw your rectangle here:

   Can you make a different rectangle with 3 squares?_____
   The dimensions of the rectangle are the factors of 3. Record the factors of 3: _____ , _____

2. Make two different rectangles using 4 squares in each rectangle. (Remember: A square is also a rectangle.) Draw your rectangles here:

   Record the factors of 4: _____ , _____ , _____

3. Make all of the different rectangles that can be made for each number. Record all of the factors for each number here:

   a. 18_____   b. 27_____

   c. 23_____   d. 29_____

   Circle each number for which you could make only one rectangle.

   > The numbers you have circled are **primes** because they have exactly two factors, themselves and 1. (The number 1 is not prime because it has only one as a factor.)

4. On the next grid, cross out 1 and circle 2. Then cross out all the multiples of 2. Now circle 3 and cross out all the multiples of 3. What is the next number that has not been crossed out? _____ Circle it and cross out all of its multiples.

   Continue in this manner until all of the numbers on the grid are circled or crossed out.

1	2	3	4	5	6	7	8	9	10
11	12	13	14	15	16	17	18	19	20
21	22	23	24	25	26	27	28	29	30
31	32	33	34	35	36	37	38	39	40
41	42	43	44	45	46	47	48	49	50
51	52	53	54	55	56	57	58	59	60
61	62	63	64	65	66	67	68	69	70
71	72	73	74	75	76	77	78	79	80
81	82	83	84	85	86	87	88	89	90
91	92	93	94	95	96	97	98	99	100

> The circled numbers are the primes less than 100. List them here:

5. The numbers on the grid, except 1, that are crossed out are called composite numbers because they have more than two factors. Take 6 for example. Build as many different rectangles as you can using 6 squares. Draw your rectangles here:

   Did you find two different rectangles?_____

   Record the factors of 6:   _____ , _____ , _____ , _____

   6 is a composite number because it has more than two factors. Which of these factors are prime numbers? _____ , _____

   6 can be written as the product of primes: $2 \times 3 = 6$

6. Build as many different rectangles as you can using 10 squares. Draw your rectangles.

   Is 10 a composite number?_____

   Record the factors of 10:   _____ , _____ , _____ , _____

   Write 10 as the product of primes: _____ × _____ = 10

7. Build as many different rectangles as you can using 30 squares. Record your rectangles.

   Is 30 a composite number?_____

   What are the factors of 30?

   _____ , _____ , _____ , _____ , _____ , _____ , _____ , _____

   Write 30 as the product of primes: _____ × _____ × _____ = 30

8. Write these composite numbers as products of primes.

   a. 14 = _____ × _____   b. 15 = _____ × _____

   c. 12 = _____ × _____ × _____   d. 16 = _____ × _____ × _____ × _____

   e. 50 = _____ × _____ × _____   f. 24 = _____ × _____ × _____ × _____

   > Can every composite number be written as the product of primes?_____
   > If two people each correctly factor the same number into prime factors, how will their factorizations be alike?
   >
   > How might they differ?

MENTAL MATH

OBSERVE THIS PATTERN:

Begin with a hexagon.

 = 1

Surround it with hexagons.

2

Count the number of hexagons.

3

The sum is a prime.

$$\frac{+\ 2}{7}$$

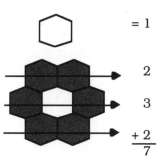

Add another ring of hexagons.

$$\begin{array}{r} 3 \\ 4 \\ 5 \\ 4 \\ +\ 3 \\ \hline \end{array}$$

What is this sum?
Is it a prime?
What will be the sum for the next figure? Will it be a prime?
If you continue the pattern, adding 2 more rings, will the sum be a prime?

EXERCISES

STAINED GLASS DISCOVERY

This exercise is divided into four frames. In each frame, shade each region that contains a number divisible by the given number. You should find 7 of these regions in each frame.

Divisible by 3

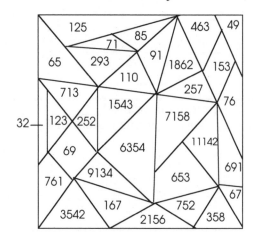

Divisible by 9

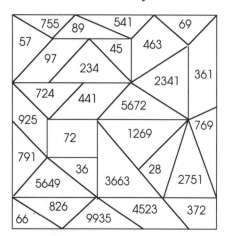

Divisible by 8   Divisible by 6

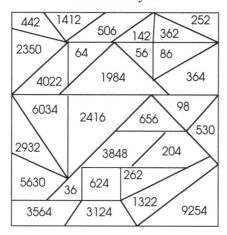   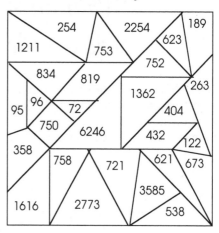

Which one is the swan?_____   the cat?_____   the profile of a man's head?_____
the whale?_____

A TIMELY TAIL

DIRECTIONS: A special message is written in code at the bottom of the page. To decode it, determine what number should replace each letter in the factor trees below. Each time this number appears in the code, write the letter above it.

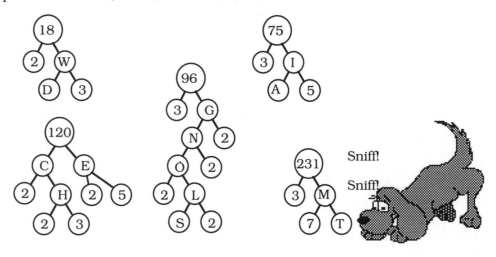

5   9 - 5 - 11 - 12 - 6 - 3 - 8 - 32   25 - 2   5   3 - 8 - 32

11 - 6 - 5 - 11   12 - 5 - 16   11 - 10 - 4 - 4   11 - 25 - 77 - 10

                                                                                              !

What do Alexander the Great and Smokey the Bear have in common?

DIRECTIONS: Find the greatest common factor or least common multiple for the numbers given on the left. Draw a straight line connecting each problem with its answer. Each line will cross a number and a letter, as the first problem indicates. Wherever the number appears in the code below, fill in the letter.

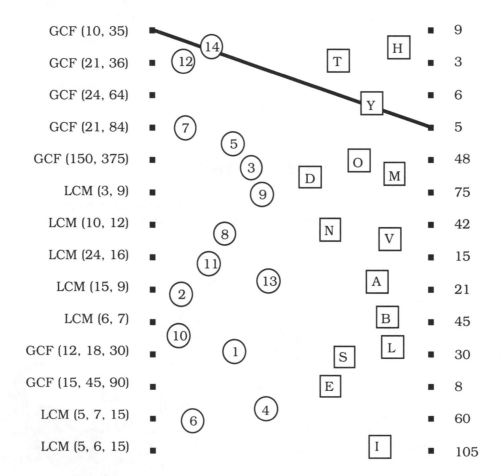

GCF (10, 35)		9
GCF (21, 36)		3
GCF (24, 64)		6
GCF (21, 84)		5
GCF (150, 375)		48
LCM (3, 9)		75
LCM (10, 12)		42
LCM (24, 16)		15
LCM (15, 9)		21
LCM (6, 7)		45
GCF (12, 18, 30)		30
GCF (15, 45, 90)		8
LCM (5, 7, 15)		60
LCM (5, 6, 15)		105

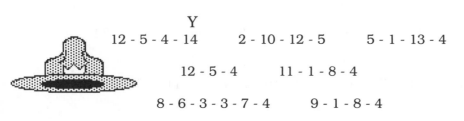

Y
12 - 5 - 4 - 14   2 - 10 - 12 - 5   5 - 1 - 13 - 4

12 - 5 - 4   11 - 1 - 8 - 4

8 - 6 - 3 - 3 - 7 - 4   9 - 1 - 8 - 4

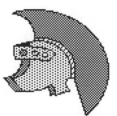

SELF-TEST

1. Which of a, b, or c is *false?*

    a. 68 is a multiple of 17
    b. 111 is a prime
    c. 19 is a divisor of 76
    d. None of a, b, or c is false.

2. Which of the following does *not* divide 1357924860?

    a. 9   b. 4   c. 6   d. 8

3. Given the following prime factor tree, the sum of the unknown prime factors is:

    a. 22   b. 18   c. 15   d. 4

    312
    2
    2

4. If $a = 2^7 \cdot 3^3 \cdot 5^2$, which of the following is *false?*

    a. 15 divides a b. 12 divides a c. 21 divides a d. 75 divides a

5. By the fundamental theorem of arithmetic, if $2^4 \cdot 6^3 \cdot 3^5 = 2^7 \cdot 3^x$, then x must be

    a. 5   b. 8   c. 12   d. None of a, b, or c.

6. 144 is the LCM for which pair of numbers below?

    a. 36, 16   b. 27, 24   c. 12, 18   d. None of a, b, or c.

7. Find the *sum* of the GCF and the LCM of 8, 22, and 46.

    a. 1518   b. 2530   c. 1024144   d. 2026

8. The LCM is $2^2 \cdot 3^3 \cdot 5^2 \cdot 13$ and the GCF is $2^2 \cdot 3^2 \cdot 13$. One number is 1404, what is the *sum* of the digits of the other number?

    a. 9   b. 8   c. 7   d. None of a, b, or c.

9. If p and q are primes (but neither is 2), then

    a. $2p$ is prime
    b. $p + q$ is prime
    c. $p + q$ is composite
    d. $p + q$ is an odd number

10. The number of divisors of 425 is

    a. 6   b. 8   c. 4   d. 3

SOLUTIONS

Warm-up

48 people. 1 table = 4 seats, 2 tables = 6 seats, 3 tables = 8 seats, etc.
21 calls (To count them, label the callers A, B, C, D, E, F, G.)

    AB AC AD AE AF AG
    BC BD BE BF BG
    CD CE CF CG
    DE DF DG
    EF EG
    FG

Hands-on Activities

Activity 1
1. 1, 2, 3, 4, 6, 12
2. 1, 3, 5, 15
3. a. 1, 2, 4   b. 1, 3, 9   c. 1, 2, 3, 6, 9, 18   d. 1, 2, 4, 5, 10, 20
    e. 1, 5, 25   f. 1, 2, 3, 4, 6, 9, 12, 18, 36
4. 4, 9, 25, 36, Square numbers

Activity 2
1. 1 by 16, 2 by 8, 4 by 4,   1, 2, 4, 8, 16
2. 1 by 24, 2 by 12, 3 by 8, 4 by 6,   1, 2, 3, 4, 6, 8, 12, 24
3. 1, 2, 4, 8   GCF = 8
4. 1, 5   GCF = 5
5. a. 6   b. 4   c. 3   d. 12   CHALLENGE = 4

Activity 3
1. 4, 8, 12
2. Answers may vary—possibly 16, 20, 24, 28, 32, 36
3. Answers may vary—possibly 3, 6, 9, 12, 15, 18;   7, 14, 21, 28, 35, 42;
    5, 10, 15, 20, 25, 30;   6, 12, 18, 24, 30, 36

Activity 4
1. 6, 12, 18, 24, 30, 36, 42, 48, 54, 60, 66, 72, 78, 84, 90, 96   LCM = 6
2. 12, 24, 36, 48, 60, 72, 84, 96   LCM = 12
3. a. 15   b. 28   c. 18   d. 8
    Two bits of paper on a square indicates common multiple. First one to occur is LCM.
4. a. 30   b. 24   c. 84   d. 90

Activity 5

1. 1 by 3, No other rectangle can be made. 1, 3
2. 1 by 4 and 2 by 2; 1, 2, 4
3. a. 1, 2, 3, 6, 9, 18   b. 1, 3, 9, 27   c. 1, 23   d. 1, 29
   23 and 29 should be circled.
4. 5;
   2, 3, 5, 7, 11, 13, 17, 19, 23, 29, 31, 37, 41, 43, 47, 53, 59, 61, 67, 71, 73, 79, 83, 89, 97
5. 1 by 6 and 2 by 3;   Yes;   1, 2, 3, 6;   2 and 3
6. 1 by 10 and 2 by 5;   Yes;   1, 2, 5, 10; $2 \times 5 = 10$
7. 1 by 30, 2 by 15, 3 by 10, and 5 by 6; Yes;
   1, 2, 3, 5, 6, 10, 15, 30; $2 \times 3 \times 5 = 30$
8. a. 2×7 b. 3×5 c. $2 \times 2 \times 3$ d. $2 \times 2 \times 2 \times 2$ e. $2 \times 5 \times 5$ f. $2 \times 2 \times 2 \times 3$
   Yes;   They will contain the same prime factors. The factors may be listed in a different order.

Mental Math

The sum is 19, a prime. The next sums are 37, a prime, 61, a prime, and 91, not a prime.

Exercises

STAINED GLASS DISCOVERY

Divisible by 3: 123, 252, 69, 6354, 7158, 11142, 153; the cat.
Divisible by 9: 234, 441, 72, 36, 3663, 1269, 45; the swan.
Divisible by 8: 64, 56, 1984, 2416, 656, 3848, 624; the profile of a man's head.
Divisible by 6: 834, 96, 750, 72, 6246, 1362, 432; the whale.

A TIMELY TAIL

18: W = 9, D = 3   75: I = 25, A = 5   96: G = 32, N = 16, O = 8, L = 4, S = 2
120: C = 12, H = 6, E = 10   231: M = 77, T = 11
A watchdog is a dog that can tell time!

What do Alexander the Great and Smokey the Bear have in common?
GCF (21, 36) = 3   LCM (15, 9) = 45
GCF (24, 64) = 8   LCM (6, 7) = 42
GCF (21, 84) = 21   GCF (12, 18, 30) = 6
GCF (150, 375) = 75   GCF (15, 45, 90) = 15
LCM (3, 9) = 9   LCM (5, 7, 15) = 105
LCM (10, 12) = 60   LCM (5, 6, 15) = 30
LCM (24, 16) = 48
They both have the same middle name.

Self-Test

1. b   **2.** d   **3.** b   **4.** c   **5.** b   **6.** a   **7.** d   **8.** a   **9.** c   **10.** a

RESOURCE ARTICLES

Beattie, Ian D. "Building Understanding with Blocks." *Arithmetic Teacher* 34 (October 1986): 5-11. *Activities illustrating concrete forms of factors and multiples.*

Bezuszka, Stanley J. "A Test for Divisibility by Primes." *Arithmetic Teacher* 33 (October 1985): 36-38. *General divisibility algorithm for prime numbers.*

Brown, G. W. "Searching for Patterns of Divisors." *Arithmetic Teacher* 32 (December 1984): 32-34. *Practice in examining divisors.*

Dearing, Shirley Ann, and Boyd Holtan. "Factors and Primes with a T square." *Arithmetic Teacher* 34 (April 1987): 34. *Technique for finding all factors of a number.*

Dockweiler, Clarence J. "Palindromes and the 'Law of 11'." *Arithmetic Teacher* 32 (January 1985): 46-47. *Classifying numbers through palindromes.*

Edwards, Flo McEnery. "Geometric Figures Make the LCM Obvious." *Arithmetic Teacher* 34 (March 1987): 17-18. *An approach using geometric figures to find LCM and GCF.*

Ewbank, William A. "LCM—Let's Put It in Its Place." *Arithmetic Teacher* 35 (November 1987): 45-47. *Discusses when and how LCM should be taught.*

Hopkins, Martha H. "Number Facts - or Fantasy." *Arithmetic Teacher* 34 (March 1987): 38-42. *Shares past and present beliefs about specific numbers.*

Lamb, Charles E., and Lyndal R. Hutcherson. "Greatest Common Factor and Least Common Multiple." *Arithmetic Teacher* 31 (April 1984): 43-44. *Strategies for avoiding misconceptions about GCF and LCM and computational algorithms.*

Litwiller, Bonnie H., and David R. Duncan. "Pentagonal Patterns in the Addition Table." *Arithmetic Teacher* 32 (April 1985): 36-38. *Activities and patterns involving the addition table.*

DIRECTIONS IN EDUCATION

Learning Styles — I'll Learn It My Way

If students don't learn in the way I teach, then I must teach in the way they learn.

Individual learning styles are as diverse as individual faces or personalities. Although teachers accomodate many differences in their classrooms, they consistently expect students to adapt their learning styles to the teaching style of the classroom teacher. Some advocates of learning styles theory would suggest that the teacher assess and accommodate every student's learning style on an individual basis.

Classroom attributes which may require modification to address needs of individual students include temperature, lighting, noise level, movement patterns, grouping patterns and the ways in which information is transmitted. By considering the number of variables and the number of students in a single classroom, a teacher may find a significant number of modifications to take into account. It is, however, essential that the classroom teacher find a practical way to manage instruction which provides for the diverse learning styles within every classroom.

Students learn constantly at both the conscious and unconscious levels in our classrooms. If learning styles are not accommodated so that meaningful, comprehensive learning can occur, the brain simply engages in personally meaningful activity. However, the personally meaningful activity may not necessarily be related to the lesson or to what the teacher hopes to teach.

What are some of the traits which make up the individual's learning style?

- **Perceptual preferences:**
  - Auditory learners need to hear information.
  - Visual learners need to see and to use visual instructional resources.
  - Tactile learners need to touch and manipulate objects.
  - Kinesthetic learners need to involve the large muscles of the body as they learn.

- **Instructional environment preferences** (which may change as children develop) include:
  - The need for strong light versus soft light.
  - The need for quiet versus sound.
  - A preference for warm or cool temperatures.
  - The need for formal versus informal seating arrangements.

- **Sociological preferences** (which may also change as the child matures) include:
  - Students who are motivated by interaction with their peers.
  - Students who wish to learn directly from their teachers.
  - Students who learn best by themselves with appropriate resources.

- **Time-of-day preferences:**
  - Some students are morning people who can deal with complex ideas as soon as they arrive at school.
  - Some students are night owls who start to come alive around lunch time. (These students are often known as underachievers!)

- **Mobility needs:**
  - Some students flourish in an activity-based learning environment.
  - Some students are quite content to be seated passively for long periods of time.

- Brain research suggests a strong correlation between learning styles and **hemisphericity**. In addition, hemisphericity may determine a preference for:
  - A concrete, linear presentation of information in small incremental steps which lead to understanding.
  - A holistic approach which begins with the broad concept and then focuses on the details.

How can learning styles be accommodated in the classroom?

- Remember that most children can master the required content, but their learning style will dictate how they master it.

- Present information more than once and in more than one way to increase the appropriateness of instruction for individuals.

- Provide an environment rich in instructional materials which address the needs of various learning styles.

- Recognize that there is not one best learning style.

- Realize that you will tend to teach in a style that matches your own learning style preferences. Know your own style and become aware of how often you design instruction to fit yourself.

As you think about learning styles, ask yourself:

- How would I describe my own learning style?

- How can I teach so that the needs of students with various learning styles are met?

To learn more:

Dunn, Rita, Jeffrey S. Beaudry, and Angela Klavas. "Survey of Research on Learning Styles." *Educational Leadership* 46 (April 1989): 50-58.

Dunn, Rita, K. Dunn, and G.E. Price. *Learning Styles Inventory.* Lawrence, Kansas: Price Systems, 1985.

6

Fractions

THEME: Understanding Fractions and their Operations

WARM-UP

**Strategy Review:
Draw a Picture.**
You may find these problems easier to solve if you draw a picture to help you visualize the problem. This strategy was introduced in Chapter 1.

A sleepy snail wants to climb to the top of a sunflower 10 feet tall so that he can check out the snails in the neighbor's yard. Each day he climbs up 3 feet, but at night he slides back down 2 feet as he sleeps. How many days will it take him to reach the top of the sunflower?

The South High football team wears consecutive numbers starting with 1.   If they form a circle in numerical order, number 1 is directly across from number 17. How many players are on the team?

HANDS-ON ACTIVITIES

The first activities explore ways of representing fractions. We will use both an area model and a measurement model. For the first activity, let's look at a representation using area.

OBJECTIVE: **Use an area model to represent fractions**

You Will Need: Materials Card 6.1

Place the whole circle in front of you. This will represent the value 1.

1. Find the two pieces of equal size that will exactly cover the circle. Each of these pieces is called one half of the circle, written 1/2, since it is one of two equal-sized pieces comprising the whole circle. Label them.

2. If you are sharing pizza with a friend who cuts the pizza as pictured and gives you piece B, have you received 1/2 of the pizza? Why or why not?

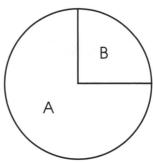

3. Find the three pieces of equal size that exactly cover the circle. What would these pieces be called? Label them.

4. Students, asked to cover the whole circle with three pieces, cover it as shown. Do the pieces they used represent 1/3? Why or why not?

a. 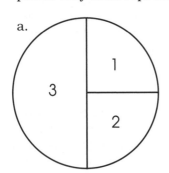 b. 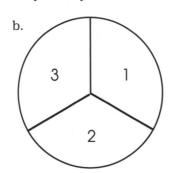 c.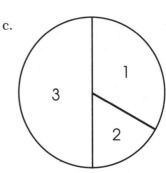

5. Continue in this manner until all the pieces are labelled. What are the fractions represented by the other pieces?

OBJECTIVE: **Describe the meaning of numerator and denominator**

You Will Need: Materials Card 6.2

1. In writing the fraction 1/3, we see that two numbers are involved, each having a particular meaning.

   a. The 3 is called the **denominator**. What does the 3 represent?

   b. The 1 is called the **numerator**. What does the 1 represent?

   c. What would the fraction 2/3 represent?

2. In the fraction 5/12, into how many equal-sized pieces is the whole divided? _____

   How many are shaded? _____ Find the piece that represents 5/12.

3. Identify the fraction represented by the shaded portion of the fraction strips.

   a. [strip] _____   b. [strip] _____

   c. [strip] _____   d. [strip] _____

4. Find the fraction strips that represent the following fractions. Describe what you are looking for in each case.

   a. 7/12   b. 4/6   c. 1/4   d. 9/12

5. If you were given a fraction strip, like the one pictured, that did not have any subdivisions marked, how would you determine what fractional amount of the bar was shaded?

As we further explore the representation of fractions, the next activity
uses a linear measurement model.

OBJECTIVE: **Use different amounts as a whole**

You Will Need: Centimeter strips from Materials Card 3.1

As we have explored fractions thus far we have seen that a whole is divided into a certain number of equal-sized pieces, as designated by the denominator. Of those pieces, a certain number is shaded or considered, as designated by the numerator. There is a third part that is important to consider - what is the whole?

1. For this part, let an ORANGE represent the whole number 1. Place an ORANGE strip in front of you. Now find the strip that represents 1/2 by putting together 2 identical strips of another color that measure the same length as an ORANGE. For example:

ORANGE	
YELLOW	YELLOW

Since ORANGE is equal to 1, YELLOW is equal to ____. Now use your centimeter strips to find the value of:

a. RED = _____   b. WHITE = _____

2. Now let BROWN be equal to the whole number 1. What color represents each of these fractions:

a. 1/2 = _____   b. 1/8 = _____

c. 1/4 = _____   d. 1 1/4 = _____

How did you solve (d) above? Hint: Use a BROWN and your answer to (c).

Now find the strips that are equal to these values, (BROWN = 1):

e. 1 1/8 = ____   f. 3/4 = ____   g. 3/8 = ____

3. Use BLUE as the unit. Find the value of these strips:

a. WHITE = _____   b. LIGHT GREEN = _____

4. Complete the following.

a. WHITE = 1/2 of _____   b. RED = 1/2 of _____

c. _____ = 1/2 of BROWN   d. _____ = 1/2 of DARK GREEN

e. Why do these different colors all represent 1/2?

5. Complete the following:

   a. RED = _____ of DARK GREEN   b. RED = _____ of BROWN

   c. RED = _____ of YELLOW   d. RED = _____ of LIGHT GREEN

   e. How can RED represent all these different fractions?

6. Which different fractions can the following picture represent? Explain how.

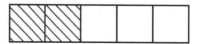

OBJECTIVE: **Solve a problem using the area model for fractions**

You Will Need: Materials Card 6.4

1. Determine what fractional part of the large square is represented by each of these pieces:

   a. large triangle = _____   b. medium triangle = _____
   c. small triangle = _____   d. small square = _____
   e. parallelogram = _____   f. large square = _____

2. Which 3 different pieces have the same area (represent the same fractional part of the large square)?

   _____ _____ _____

3. Repeat part 1 with the large triangle being the "whole".

We have looked at several ways to represent fractions. The following activities
will address the concept of **equivalent fractions**—fractions
that represent the same relative amount.

OBJECTIVE: **Find equivalent fractions**

You Will Need: Circle pieces from Activity 1

1. Lay the circle in front of you.
    Find the piece that is 1/3 of the circle.
    Now find two pieces that exactly cover the piece labelled 1/3.
    What is each of these pieces labelled?_____
    We can say that 1/3 is equivalent to two _____pieces — or that 1/3 = 2/6.

2. Find the piece that is 1/2 of the circle. How else could you cover the same amount of the circle, using equal-sized pieces?

    _____ = 1/2   _____ = 1/2   _____ = 1/2

3. Now use this procedure to find fractions equivalent to the following:

    a. 2/3   b. 1/4   c. 3/3   d. 3/4   e. 4/8   f. 5/6

    Why is the last problem difficult with these pieces?

OBJECTIVE: **Represent equivalent fractions**

You Will Need: Materials from Activity 2

1. a. What fraction is represented
        by the fraction strip shown?

    b. Divide each of the subdivisions shown into 2 equal-sized pieces. Now what fraction
        is represented?

    c. Are these two fractions equivalent? Why or why not?

    d. When you subdivided the parts by 2, what happened to the number of parts the
        denominator represented?   the numerator represented?

2. a. Using the same fraction strip, divide each subdivision into 3 equal-sized pieces. Now what fraction is represented?

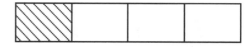

   b. How have the numerator and denominator been changed?

   c. Is this fraction equivalent to the fractions in part 1?

> Summarize how you can write another fraction equivalent to *a/b*.

3. Using your fraction strips, group them into sets that represent the same relative amount. Record the equivalent fractions. Using your conclusion to part 2, verify the equivalence of the fractions you have listed.

OBJECTIVE: **Recognize equivalent fractions**

You Will Need: Fraction strips from Activity 2
2-4 people (to make it more fun)

1. Arrange the following fraction strips face down in a random 4 by 5 array on the table:

    1/2,   1/3,   2/3,   1/4,   2/4,   3/4,   1/6,   2/6,   3/6,   4/6,

    5/6,   6/6,   2/12,   3/12,   4/12,   6/12,   8/12,   9/12,   10/12,   12/12

2. The object of the game is to collect pairs of fraction strips that represent the same relative amount.

3. The players take turns turning over two fraction strips. If the two represent the same amount, the player keeps the strips and chooses two more. If they do not represent the same amount, the strips are placed face down in the same location and it becomes the next player's turn.

4. After all possible matches have been made (the last pair will not match), the player with the most strips is the winner.

OBJECTIVE: **Use manipulatives to add fractions**

You Will Need: Circle pieces from Activity 1
Materials Card 6.8

1. You and your friends are again at the pizza parlor.

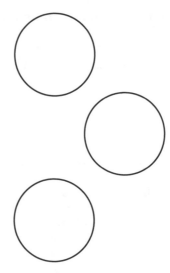

   a. One pizza had a 1/6 piece left.
      Represent that on the circle.

   b. Another pizza had 2/6 pieces left.
      Represent that amount.

   c. To take the leftover pizza home, you
      combine it in a single container.
      Represent that amount. How much
      pizza will you take home? Explain.

2. Represent the following problems with your circle pieces and find the solution.

   a. 1/4 + 2/4   b. 3/8 + 2/8   c. 1/6 + 5/6

3. What is unique about each of these sums?

> Summarize how to add fractions with the same denominator.

4. Suppose instead that you have half of one pizza and one third of another. Represent the two amounts and the combined amount.

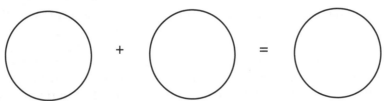

Since you have described a method for adding fractions with the same denominator, it would be much easier if we had equal-sized pieces to deal with.

   a. What sized piece can you find that will cover both the 1/2 and 1/3 portions?

b. How many of these pieces will cover the 1/2 portion? _____ the 1/3 portion? _____

c. How many does it take to cover the combination? _____
   In other words, 1/2 + 1/3 =   /   +   /   =   /

5. Now use your method in part 4 to solve these problems:

   a.  = _____   b. 3/4 + 1/8 = _____   c. 3/6 + 1/3 = _____

   d. 1/2 + 1/4 = _____   e. 5/8 + 1/2 = _____

6. Now test yourself. Construct the die on Materials Card 6.8. Roll the die three times. Pick up the pieces indicated by each roll. Use the method in part 4 to compute the sum on each turn. Repeat 4 times. Record the rolls and sum on each turn.

   a. ___ + ___ + ___ = ___   b. ___ + ___ + ___ = ___

   c. ___ + ___ + ___ = ___   d. ___ + ___ + ___ = ___

   Were you able to use the method in part 4 for all of your sums? _____ Why might you encounter difficulties with this method? Hint: Look at a problem like 1/3 + 1/4 + 1/8.

Now let's look at a model for the operation of subtraction with fractions.

 **OBJECTIVE:**   **Use the take-away model for subtraction**

You Will Need: Circle pieces from Activity 1

1. Place the circle in front of you. For the problem 7/8 - 1/4, place 7 of the 1/8-pieces on the circle as illustrated:

   1/8 sections ——

   Now take away enough pieces to cover the 1/4-piece (see above). How many 1/8-pieces remain on the circle?_____ We can say seven 1/8-pieces take away one 1/4-piece equals _____1/8-pieces or 7/8 - 1/4 = _____.

2. Use your pieces to solve these problems:

   a. 5/6 - 1/3 = _____   b. 5/8 - 1/2 = _____   c. 3/8 - 1/8 = _____   d. 5/6 - 1/4 = _____

   Why is (d) a difficult problem to do using this method?

OBJECTIVE: **Add and subtract fractions**

You Will Need: Fraction strips from Activity 2
                      2-4 people (to make it more fun)

1. Arrange all the fraction strips face down on the table.

2. The object of the game is to collect pairs of fraction strips whose sum represents one whole bar.

3. The players take turns turning over two fraction strips. If the sum of the strips is 1, the player keeps the strips and chooses two more.   If the sum is not 1, the strips are placed face down in the same location and it becomes the next player's turn.

4. After all matches have been made, the player with the most strips is the winner.

We have worked with the operations of addition and subtraction. In these next activities we will be looking at models for multiplication of fractions.

OBJECTIVE: **Use manipulatives to multiply fractions**

You Will Need: Circle pieces from Activity 1

1. Recall that repeated addition was one approach we used to describe multiplication.

    a. How would you represent 3×5 using this approach?

    b. How could you represent $3 \times 1/4$ using this approach and your circle pieces?

2. Represent the following products using your circle pieces. State the result.

    a. $3 \times 1/8$ b. $5 \times 1/6$ c. $9 \times 1/4$

3. Represent 1/3 of the circle shown. What sized piece would cover half of the represented portion? _____

    In other words,
    $1/2$ of $1/3$ = $1/2 \times 1/3$ = _____ .

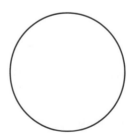

4. Represent 1/2 of the circle shown. What amount would represent 2/3 of the represented portion?
    Hint: Temporarily consider the 1/2
    to represent the "whole".

    2/3 of 1/2 = 2/3 × 1/2 = ____

5. Using your circle pieces represent the following products.

    a. 1/2 × 1/4   b. 1/2 × 3/4   c. 1/3 × 3/6

OBJECTIVE: **Use the area model to multiply fractions**

You Will Need: Square pieces of scratch paper

1. Another approach we used to represent multiplication of whole numbers was the rectangular area model. Give the product represented by the following rectangles.

    a.    b.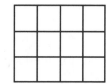

2. This area model can be extended to solve problems like 1/3 × 1/4. Take a square piece of scratch paper. The length of the side will be 1.

    First fold the square lengthwise into quarters as illustrated:

    Fold in   Fold in   You have now
    half   half   divided the
                                             again   square into
                                                                                      fourths.

    Now, without unfolding the quarters, fold into thirds in the opposite direction, as illustrated:

    Fold up   Fold   Now color or
    one third   again   shade the top only.

    Unfold the paper. It should look like this:

    What fractional portion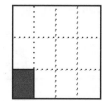
    of the square is shaded? _____

We can see that 1/3 of 1/4 = 1/12 because the paper is divided into 12 equal sections and one of those is shaded. So, 1/3 × 1/4 means 1/3 of 1/4.

3. Try the paper folding method to solve these problems. Draw a picture to show the unfolded square.

   a. $1/2 \times 1/4 =$ _____   b. $1/3 \times 1/3 =$ _____

4. Will the paper folding method also work to solve these problems?_____

   a. $1/2 \times 2/3 =$ _____   b. $2/3 \times 1/4 =$ _____

   What adjustments must you make to do these problems?
   Hint: Unfold before refolding or coloring.

   Draw a picture to show your square in each case.

5. a. What is $2/3 \times 3/4$?___
       Draw a picture to show the unfolded square for this problem.

    b. Notice when the paper is opened up that there are two rectangles, (1) the shaded rectangle, and (2) the entire rectangle (square), that have been divided into smaller, equal-sized parts. In one direction the square has been divided into 3 lengths and in the other into 4 lengths. How many parts was the entire square divided into? _____ In the usual multiplication algorithm, where do we see 3×4?

    c. Of this whole the part we are considering has been shaded. In one dimension you shaded two (of the three parts), and in the other you shaded three (of the four parts) so the shaded region is 2 by 3 or contains 6 parts. In the usual algorithm, where do we see 2×3?

   > Summarize how the usual fraction
   > multiplication algorithm is modelled by folding paper.

   The final activities deal with division of fractions. First, we will use the centimeter strips to look at a model for representing division of fractions.

OBJECTIVE: **Use manipulatives to divide fractions**

You Will Need: Centimeter strips from Activity 3

1. First, let's look back at our division model for whole numbers. If we have 12 people, for example, and wish to form teams of 2, we would ask, "**How many** teams of 2 can we make from 12 people?" The result would be 12 ÷ 2 or 6 teams.

   For each of the following division problems, state the appropriate question to ask (such as, "How many REDs are there in a PURPLE?") and give the result.

   a. BLUE ÷ LIGHT GREEN

   b. BROWN ÷ RED

   c. ORANGE ÷ YELLOW

2. Next, let's consider what happens when we have 14 people and wish to form teams of 3. Again we would ask, "How many teams could be formed?" We could form 4 teams, but we have some people left over, which is similar to reporting 14 ÷ 3 = 4 r 2. On the other hand, since we are talking about the number of teams, we could consider how much of a team the two people form, which is 2/3. Thus we could report that 14 ÷ 3 = 4 2/3. Notice that the divisor, a team of 3, is the unit whole we use in naming the fraction.

   Find the quotient for the following division problems. State remainders in fractional form.

   a. BLACK ÷ LIGHT GREEN   b. ORANGE ÷ PURPLE   c. (ORANGE + RED) ÷ YELLOW

3. Now, we are going to change teams again. This time we want to play football with 11 members on a team, and we only have 8 people. It is quite obvious that we do not even have one team. Instead of asking, "How many teams can we form?", it would be more appropriate to ask, "**How much** of a team do we have?" Of the 11 "equal" parts of the team we have 8, so the answer would be 8/11, or 8 ÷ 11 = 8/11.

   For each of the following division problems, state the appropriate question to ask (such as, "How much of a PURPLE is a RED?") and give the result.

   a. RED ÷ YELLOW

   b. LIGHT GREEN ÷ DARK GREEN

   c. PURPLE ÷ (ORANGE + RED)

4. a. When is it most appropriate to ask the question, "How many . . .?" ?

   b. When is it most appropriate to ask the question, "How much . . .?" ?

5. For each of the following division problems, state the appropriate question to ask and give the result.

   a. ORANGE ÷ RED

   b. YELLOW ÷ BLUE

   c. RED ÷ DARK GREEN

   d. (ORANGE + BROWN) ÷ BLACK

6. Let ORANGE + RED = 1. Find pieces which represent the lengths involved in the problems given. Then find the quotient.

   a. 5/6 ÷ 1/4   b. 3/4 ÷ 1/6

   c. 2/3 ÷ 5/6   d. 5/12 ÷ 2/3

   e. 1 1/4 ÷ 1/3   f. 1/2 ÷ 1 3/4

OBJECTIVE: **Use manipulatives to divide fractions**

You Will Need: Fraction strips from Activity 2

1. We can use fraction strips to divide fractions, much like we did in the last activity. For example, let's do 7/12 ÷ 1/3.

   a. Find the pieces representing 7/12 and 1/3. How many 1/3's are in 7/12? _____

   b. Is there any amount left over? _____ If so, what part of the divisor, 1/3, is the leftover?

2. Using your fraction strips, find the following quotients.

   a. 5/6 ÷ 1/3   b. 1 2/3 ÷ 1/4

   c. 1/4 ÷ 9/12   d. 1/2 ÷ 1 1/4

3. a. Using your fraction strips, find the result of 1/3 ÷ 1/4. Picture your process and result.

   b. Find bars to represent 1/3 and 1/4 which have the same size subdivisions. Rewrite the problem using these strips and find the result.

   1/3 ÷ 1/4 = _____ ÷ _____ = _____

   c. How do results from parts a and b compare?

   ┌───┐
   │   │
   │   State a general procedure for dividing fractions.   │
   │   │
   │   │
   │   │
   └───┘

4. Find the following quotients using your general procedure.

   a. 5/8 ÷ 1/4   b. 1 1/4 ÷ 2/3   c. 1 5/6 ÷ 2/5

   d. 1/3 ÷ 5/12   e. 2/3 ÷ 3/4   f. 1 3/8 ÷ 2 5/6

MENTAL MATH

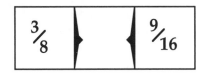

THE RANGE GAME

Use the digits 1 through 9 to see how many fractions you can find within the given range. Example: 3/8 < 1/2 < 9/16 . Write your fractions here:

$$\frac{3}{8} \quad \text{〉} \quad \text{〈} \quad \frac{9}{16}$$

Now, play the game with a partner. Score 1 point for each correct fraction, lose 1 point for each error. Play until one person gets 10.

EXERCISES

THE MOUSE RACE

These hungry mice have spied a chunk of cheese. To reach the cheese, they must find a path from their current location that travels through equivalent fractions. Which two mice will go hungry?

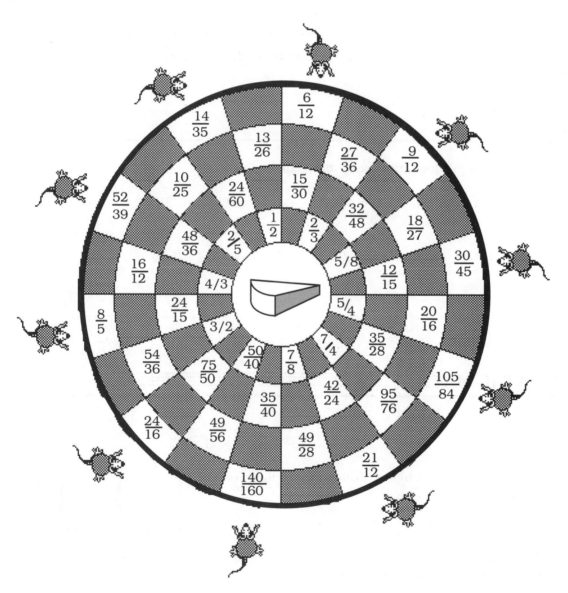

YOU CAN'T FIT A SQUARE PEG INTO A ROUND HOLE!

DIRECTIONS: Use the fractions given on the left to fill in the missing holes on the right. The results should give true equations across and down.

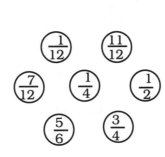

$$\left(\frac{1}{6}\right) + \bigcirc + \bigcirc = \left(1\right)$$

$$+ \quad + \quad + \quad +$$

$$\left(\frac{7}{12}\right) + \bigcirc + \left(\frac{5}{6}\right) = \left(\frac{5}{3}\right)$$

$$+ \quad - \quad | \quad |$$

$$\bigcirc + \left(\frac{5}{12}\right) - \bigcirc = \bigcirc$$

$$|| \quad || \quad || \quad ||$$

$$\left(\frac{5}{3}\right) + \bigcirc - \left(\frac{5}{12}\right) = \left(\frac{11}{6}\right)$$

Given fractions: $\frac{1}{12}$, $\frac{11}{12}$, $\frac{7}{12}$, $\frac{1}{4}$, $\frac{1}{2}$, $\frac{5}{6}$, $\frac{3}{4}$

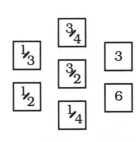

Given: $\frac{3}{4}$, $\frac{1}{3}$, 3, $\frac{3}{2}$, $\frac{1}{2}$, 6, $\frac{1}{4}$

$$\boxed{24} \times \square \times \square = \boxed{9}$$

$$\times \quad \times \quad \times \quad \times$$

$$\square \times \boxed{24} \times \boxed{\tfrac{1}{12}} = \square$$

$$\times \quad \times \quad \times \quad \times$$

$$\square \times \square \times \boxed{24} = \boxed{2}$$

$$|| \quad || \quad || \quad ||$$

$$\boxed{9} \times \square \times \boxed{1} = \boxed{54}$$

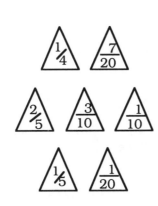

Given triangles: $\frac{1}{4}$, $\frac{7}{20}$, $\frac{2}{5}$, $\frac{3}{10}$, $\frac{1}{10}$, $\frac{1}{5}$, $\frac{1}{20}$

$$\triangle_{\tfrac{1}{2}} + \triangle + \triangle = \triangle_{1}$$

$$+ \quad + \quad |$$

$$\triangle + \triangle - \triangle_{\tfrac{3}{20}} = \triangle_{\tfrac{1}{2}}$$

$$+ \quad + \quad |$$

$$\triangle + \triangle - \triangle = \triangle_{0}$$

$$|| \quad || \quad ||$$

$$\triangle_{1} \quad \triangle_{\tfrac{1}{2}} \quad \triangle_{0}$$

SELF-TEST

1. Which of the following diagrams does *not* represent the same number as the other two?

   a. A
   b. B
   c. C
   d. None of a, b, or c.

   A.  B.   C.

2. Which of the following is *not* in simplest form?

   (i) 45/64   (ii) 108/135   (iii) 369/492

   a. i and ii   b. ii and iii   c. ii only   d. None of a, b, or c.

3. If 12/40 = 15/*a*, then the sum of the digits in *a* is

   a. 5   b. 6   c. 8   d. None of a, b, or c.

4. What is the reciprocal of 2 3/8?

   a. 8/19   b. 19/8   c. 2 8/3   d. 22/4

5. Compute, write in simplest form, and then add your numerator and denominator.

   a. 328   b. 82   1/10 + 13/18
   c. 164   d. None of a, b, or c.

6. This model is used to represent:

   a. 2/5 × 3/4   b. 6/8 × 3/4
   c. 2/6 × 3/4   d. 2/5 × 6/15

   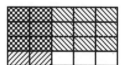

7. 1 1/3 ÷ 5/6 =

   a. 8/5   b. 1 2/5   c. 1/15   d. None of a, b, or c.

8. Which of the following is *not* helpful
   in simplifying this computation?   (5/7 · 13/19) · 7/5

   a. Commutativity for multiplication   b. Associativity for multiplication
   c. Inverse for multiplication   d. Distributivity

9. If the following numbers are arranged from least
   to greatest, which one will be in the middle?   3/7, 2/9, 5/13, 7/11, 5/12

   a. 3/7   b. 5/12   c. 5/13   d. 7/11

10. Which of these fractions is between 7/15 and 8/13 ?

    a. 3/5   b. 2/5   c. 2/3   d. None of a, b, or c.

SOLUTIONS

Warm-up

He will climb out on day number 8.   There are 32 players on the team.

Hands-on Activities

Activity 1
2. No, the pieces are not equal-sized.
3. 1/3
4. a. No, the pieces are not equal-sized.   b. Yes, equal-sized pieces.   c. No, not equal-sized.
5. 1/4, 1/6, 1/8

Activity 2
1. a. The number of equal-sized pieces that make up a whole.
    b. The number of pieces shaded or considered.
    c. Two of three equal pieces are present.
2. 12, 5   **3.** a. 5/6   b. 0/4 = 0   c. 3/8   d. 6/6 = 1
4. a. A piece with 12 subdivisions, 7 of which are shaded.
    b. A piece with 6 subdivisions with 4 shaded.
    c. A piece with 4 subdivisions with 1 shaded.
    d. A piece with 12 subdivisions with 9 shaded.
5. You need to find a length into which both the whole bar and the shaded portion can be divided evenly. If the shaded area does not evenly divide the whole bar, try one half of the shaded area, then 1/3 and 1/4, etc. Eventually one of these lengths will also divide the whole bar evenly.

Activity 3
1. 1/2   a. 1/5   b. 1/10
2. a. PURPLE   b. WHITE   c. RED   d. ORANGE   e. BLUE   f. DARK GREEN   g. LIGHT GREEN
3. a. 1/9   b. 1/3
4. a. RED   b. PURPLE   c. PURPLE   d. LIGHT GREEN   e. The size of the whole is different.
5. a. 1/3   b. 1/4   c. 2/5   d. 2/3   e. The size of the whole is different.
6. If the square is the whole, the bar represents 2. If 2 squares is the whole, the bar represents 1. If 3 squares is the whole, the bar represents 2/3. If 4 squares is the whole, the bar represents 2/4 and if 5 squares is the whole, the bar represents 2/5.

Activity 4
1. a. 1/4   b. 1/8   c. 1/16   d. 1/8   e. 1/8   f. 1
2. Medium triangle, small square, and parallelogram
3. a. 1   b. 1/2   c. 1/4   d. 1/2   e. 1/2   f. 4

Activity 5
1. 1/6, 1/6   **2.** 2/4, 3/6, 4/8
3. a. 4/6   b. 2/8   c. 6/6, 4/4, 2/2   d. 6/8   e. 1/2, 3/6
  f. There are no divisions of the circle that exactly cover 5/6 from these pieces.

Activity 6
1. a. 1/4   b. 2/8   c. Yes, they cover the same part of the whole.
  d. Both were multiplied by 2.
2. a. 3/12   b. Multiplied by 3   c. Yes
  Multiply both the numerator and denominator by the same nonzero value.
3. 1/6 = 2/12   1/4 = 3/12   1/3 = 2/6 = 4/12   1/2 = 2/4 = 3/6 = 6/12

Activity 8
1. a. 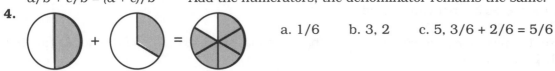 1/6   b. 2/6   c. 3/6 = 1/2

2. a. 3/4   b. 5/8   c. 6/6 = 1
3. The denominators are the same.
  $a/b + c/b = (a + c)/b$ Add the numerators; the denominator remains the same.
4.

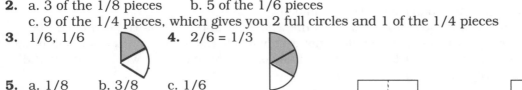

a. 1/6   b. 3, 2   c. 5, 3/6 + 2/6 = 5/6

5. a. 3/8   b. 7/8   c. 5/6   d. 3/4   e. 9/8 = 1 1/8
6.   Answers will vary. You don't have a piece available as a common denominator.

Activity 9
1. 5, 5, 5/8   **2.** a. 3/6 or 1/2   b. 1/8   c. 2/8 or 1/4   d. 7/12 There are no 1/12 pieces.

Activity 11
1. a. 5 + 5 + 5   b. 1/4 + 1/4 + 1/4
2. a. 3 of the 1/8 pieces   b. 5 of the 1/6 pieces
  c. 9 of the 1/4 pieces, which gives you 2 full circles and 1 of the 1/4 pieces
3. 1/6, 1/6   **4.** 2/6 = 1/3

5. a. 1/8   b. 3/8   c. 1/6

Activity 12
1. a. 2 × 3   b. 3 × 4   **2.** 1/12   **3.** a. 1/8   b. 1/9
4. Yes   a. 2/6   b. 2/12   Partially unfold the square before
folding in the opposite direction.

5. a.

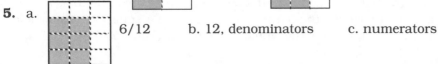 6/12   b. 12, denominators   c. numerators

  The product of the numerators represents the subdivisions of the shaded area and is the
  numerator of the result. The product of the denominators represents the subdivisions of
  the whole square and is the denominator of the result.

Activity 13

1. a. How many LIGHT GREEN in BLUE? 3
   b. How many RED in BROWN? 4
   c. How many YELLOW in ORANGE? 2
2. a. 2 1/3   b. 2 1/2   c. 2 2/5
3. a. How much of a YELLOW is RED? 2/5
   b. How much of a DARK GREEN is LIGHT GREEN? 1/2
   c. How much of (ORANGE + RED) is PURPLE? 1/3
4. a. When the divisor is smaller than the number being divided.
   b. When the divisor is larger than the number being divided.
5. a. How many? 5   b. How much? 5/8   c. How much? 1/3
   d. How many? 2 4/7
6. a. ORANGE ÷ LIGHT GREEN = 3 1/3   b. BLUE ÷ RED = 4 1/2
   c. BROWN ÷ ORANGE = 4/5   d. YELLOW ÷ BROWN = 5/8
   e. (ORANGE + YELLOW) ÷ PURPLE = 3 3/4
   f. DARK GREEN ÷ (ORANGE + ORANGE + WHITE) = 6/21 = 2/7

Activity 14

1. a. 1   b. Yes, 3/4
2. a. 2 1/2   b. 6 2/3   c. 1/3   d. 2/5
3. a. 4/3 = 1 1/3
   b. 4/12 ÷ 3/12 = 4/3 = 1 1/3
   c. They are the same.

   Obtain a common denominator,
   then divide the numerators.

   1 Leftover piece is 1/3 of divisor

   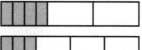

4. a. 5/2 = 2 1/2   b. 15/8 = 1 7/8   c. 4 7/12   d. 4/5
   e. 8/9   f. 33/68

Mental Math

Answers will vary.

Exercises

THE MOUSE RACE

6/12 = 13/26 = 15/30 = 1/2   14/35 = 10/25 = 24/60 = 2/5
52/39 = 16/12 = 48/36 = 4/3   24/16 = 54/36 = 75/50 = 3/2
140/160 = 49/56 = 35/40 = 7/8   21/12 = 49/28 = 42/24 = 7/4
105/84 = 95/76 = 35/28 = 5/4   30/45 = 18/27 = 32/48 = 2/3
Hungry Mice are 8/5 and 9/12.

YOU CAN'T FIT A SQUARE PEG INTO A ROUND HOLE!

Round Holes:	Square Holes:	Triangular Holes:
First row: 3/4, 1/12	First row: 3/4, 1/2	First row: 1/10, 2/5
Second row: 1/4	Second row: 3/2, 3	Second row: 3/10, 7/20
Third row: 11/12, 1/2, 5/6	Third row: 1/4, 1/3	Third row: 1/5, 1/20, 1/4
Fourth row: 7/12	Fourth row: 6	

Self-Test

1. b **2.** b **3.** a **4.** a **5.** b **6.** a **7.** a **8.** d **9.** b **10.** a

RESOURCE ARTICLES

Beede, Rudy B. "Dot Method for Renaming Fractions." *Arithmetic Teacher* 33 (October 1985): 44-45. *Ideas at manipulative level leading to abstract.*

Bezuk, Nadine S. "Fractions in the Early Childhood Mathematics Curriculum." *Arithmetic Teacher* 35 (February 1988): 56-60. *Discusses important components in developing an understanding of fractions.*

Curcio, Frances R., Francine Sicklick, and Susan B. Turkel. "Divide and Conquer: Unit Strips to the Rescue." *Arithmetic Teacher* 35 (December 1987): 6-12. *Activities building the proper understanding of dividing fractions.*

Edge, Douglas. "Fractions and Panes." *Arithmetic Teacher* 34 (April 1987): 13-17. *Activities using window panes to extend knowledge of fractions.*

Ettline, J. Fred. "A Uniform Approach to Fractions." *Arithmetic Teacher* 32 (March 1985): 42-43. *A look at two common student difficulties in computing with fractions.*

Greenwood, Jay. "Problem Solving with Fractions." *Mathematics Teacher* 82 (January 1989): 44-50. *Activities for grades 5-9 focusing on a complete definition of fractions to solve problems.*

Ott, Jack M. "A Unified Approach to Multiplying Fractions." *Arithmetic Teacher* 37 (March 1990): 47-49. *Using "of" meaning of multiplication to develop multiplication with fractions.*

Payne, Joseph N., and Ann E. Towsley. "Implementing the Standards: Implications of NCTM's Standards for Teaching Fractions and Decimals." *Arithmetic Teacher* 37 (April 1990): 23-26. *Building conceptual foundation and meaningful computational procedures.*

Post, Thomas, and Kathleen Cramer. "Children's Strategies in Ordering Rational Numbers." *Arithmetic Teacher* 35 (October 1987): 33-35. *Presents research and activities for ordering fractions.*

Rees, Jocelyn Marie. "Two-sided Pies: Help for Improper Fractions and Mixed Numbers." *Arithmetic Teacher* 35 (December 1987): 28-32. *Presents concrete model and teaching suggestions for improper fractions.*

Steiner, Evelyn E. "Division of Fractions: Developing Conceptual Sense with Dollars and Cents." *Arithmetic Teacher* 34 (May 1987): 36-42. *An eight-level monetary model for division of fractions.*

Van de Walle, John, and Charles S. Thompson. "Let's Do It: Fractions with Fraction Strips." *Arithmetic Teacher* 32 (December 1984): 4-9. *Fraction concept tasks.*

Zawojewski, Judith S. "Ideas." *Arithmetic Teacher* 34 (December 1986): 18-25. *Activities using region model for fractions.*

DIRECTIONS IN EDUCATION

Cooperative Learning - Together We Can

Cooperative learning is a teaching model which provides for heterogeneous grouping of students within the classroom. By using this instructional strategy, the classroom teacher can combine the teaching of social skills with the teaching of content area goals and objectives. It is a strategy which must be carefully planned by the teacher so that the students need only concern themselves with being totally involved in the accomplishment of the task at hand. The lesson will usually begin with instruction required to accomplish both the content objective and the social skill. The students then participate in the group activity. The lesson ends with a discussion of both the content objective and the social skill.

Reasons to use cooperative learning:

- Cooperative learning is supported by research as an effective teaching strategy.
- Student involvement with the learning is enhanced.
- It reduces the tracking of students into ability groups.
- Cooperative learning promotes higher level reasoning and communication skills.
- It enhances problem solving skills and increases retention of learning over time.
- Skills are used in a real world setting.
- It enhances self esteem by promoting acceptance of and by peers.
- It values individual contributions to the group task.
- Cooperative learning is fun!

Cooperative learning means more than just learning and working together in groups - it has 5 essential elements:

- **Positive Interdependence** - activities are structured in such a way that individual success is enhanced by group success. The objective is a feeling of "We're in this thing together" rather than a feeling of "We win, you lose" or of "Everyone for themselves."

- **Individual Accountability** - each person is responsible for his/her own learning within the cooperative group. It is the task of the teacher to clarify the criteria for success so that learners can monitor their own progress toward the goal.

- **Face to Face Interaction** - students must be seated in such a way that they are literally face to face as they participate in the cooperative activity. Materials should be provided in group sets rather than individual sets to promote this interaction.

- **Collaborative Skills** - in addition to an academic goal, each lesson has a collaborative goal which provides for use of a previously learned skill or for instruction about the use of a new skill. It is generally wise to pair difficult academic goals with previously learned social skills and to pair difficult new social skills with previously introduced academic goals.

- **Group Processing** - the success of any cooperative learning classroom is closely linked to the quality of the debriefing which occurs after each lesson. It is during the debriefing that academic understandings are clarified and that social skills are refined. The debriefing should deal first with the academic content of the lesson and then with the social skill being practiced.

Cooperative skills which enhance the classroom environment and enrich the teaching/learning process:

- Communication skills such as active listening, asking good questions, clarifying, giving constructive criticism.

- On-task skills such as staying with the group, encouraging everyone, and using manipulatives in helpful ways.

- Skills which check and redirect the group's activities such as knowing when to ask for help, summarizing the group's progress, and checking the solution to a problem.

As you think about cooperative learning, ask yourself:

- What is my role as a teacher in planning and presenting a successful cooperative lesson?

- What kinds of learning objectives work best in cooperative groups?

- Are there some kinds of learning objectives which may not be appropriate for cooperative groups?

- How often should students be engaged in cooperative activities in an average week?

- Which types of students will benefit the most from cooperative grouping in the classroom?

To learn more:

Glaser, William. *Control Theory in the Classroom.* New York: Harper & Row, 1986.

Johnson, David W., Roger T. Johnson, Edythe Johnson Holubec, and Patricia Roy. *Circles of Learning: Cooperation in the Classroom.* USA: Association for Supervision and Curriculum Development, 1988.

Slavin, Robert E. *Cooperative Learning.* New York: Longman, 1983.

7

Decimals, Ratio, Proportion, and Percent

THEME: Fractions

Decimals ⟷ Percent

WARM-UP

Strategy Review:
Use Indirect Reasoning.
In Chapter 4, the strategy of using indirect reasoning was explained. Use that strategy to help you in solving these problems.

Three baseball players, Chuck, Mark, and Paul, play for Chicago, Montreal, and Philadelphia. No player's city starts with the same letter as his name. Paul has never been to Chicago. Who plays for Philadelphia?

Ann, Amy, Alice, and Angie like apples, apricots, asparagus, and anchovies. Ann hates vegetables. One of Alice's friends loves all kinds of fish. Amy can't eat crunchy food because she wears braces. Angie loves green food. Amy has never met Alice. Who likes anchovies?

HANDS-ON ACTIVITIES

Decimals give us a convenient way to represent fractions. The first activities in this chapter will introduce you to decimals as well as their numerals, names, and operations.

OBJECTIVE: **Extend place value system to decimals**

You Will Need: Base ten pieces from Materials Card 4.7, Materials Card 7.1

1. Originally when we used the base ten pieces, the small cube represented 1 (that's why we called it a unit). What did the following pieces represent? Explain why.

   Long =   Flat =   Block =

   Complete the chart:

Piece:	B	F	L	U
Value:				1

2. With our understanding of fractions as representing equivalent parts of a whole or a relative amount, we can extend the place value system. For example, let the flat represent our whole or unit amount of 1. What do the following pieces represent? Explain why.

   Block =   Long =   Small cube =

   Complete the chart:

Piece:	B	F	L	U
Value:		1		

3. In working with fractions, we found that the whole could vary. If we let the block represent our whole or the unit amount of 1, what do the following pieces represent? Explain why.

   Long =   Small Cube =   Flat =

   Complete the chart:

Piece:	B	F	L	U
Value:	1			

4. Review the charts that you have completed.

    a. As you move from right to left, how are the values of the adjacent columns related?

    b. How are the values of the adjacent columns related as you move from left to right?

    c. If moving from any column to the column on its left is described as "grouping by tens," how would you describe moving from any column to the column on its right?

    d. Use your observations to extend the place value chart to the right. Label the missing place values.
    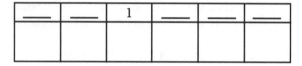

5. We can distinguish where the whole numbers end and the fractional parts begin by using a marker which we will call the **decimal point marker**. Place the decimal point marker on the place value chart above. This marker will separate the 1 and 1/10 columns. Fill in the place values in the drawings below:

    a.   b.   c.

    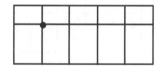   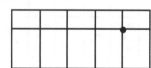   

6. Using chips and the chip abacus on Materials Card 7.1, represent the following and draw a picture of your results.

    a. 321.04   b. 3.2104   c. 32.104

    How are the representations of these three numbers alike? How are they different? How can you represent all three numbers without moving chips?

7. Write the expanded fractional form for the numbers above. For example,

    321.04 = 3(100) + 2(10) + 1+ 0(1/10) + 4(1/100)

    3.2104 =

    32.104 =

OBJECTIVE: **Write numerals and word names
                  for number representations**

You Will Need: Your base ten pieces and your
                     chip abacus

1. Let the flat represent the unit whole.
    a. Collect the following pieces: 12 tenths and 12 hundredths.
        By making exchanges, represent this number with the
        fewest number of base ten pieces. Record how many of
        each piece you have in the chart. Now write the
        corresponding numeral, placing the decimal point in the correct position.

B	F	L	U

    b. Next, exchange all the tenths for hundredths. Now, how many of each piece do you
        have? This is the name given to the decimal with the decimal point being read as "and".
        What is the name of this decimal number?

2. Let the block represent the unit whole.

B	F	L	U

    a. Represent the following on your chart:
        2 hundredths and 25 thousandths. After
        making appropriate exchanges, what pieces will you have? Write the numeral.

    b. Exchange all hundredths for thousandths. What is the name of this decimal number?

3. Write the numerals and the word names for the numbers illustrated below:

    a. 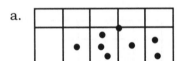   b. 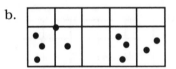   c.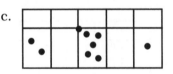

4. Move your decimal point markers in part 3 one column to the right and write the new
    numerals and word names.

5. Write the decimal numerals to represent the following numbers.
    a. Thirty two and thirteen hundredths

    b. Five hundred and twenty one thousandths

    c. $10\ 10/1000 =$

    d. $34\ 11/100 =$

    e. $5\ 15/1000 =$

6. a. To answer the question in part 5, one student wrote 32.013, 500.0021, 10.0010,
        34.011, 5.0015. What is this student doing wrong? How might you help the student?

    b. Another student answered part 5b as 0.521. What did this student forget? What is the
        name for 0.521?

OBJECTIVE: **Represent and compare decimals using decimal squares**

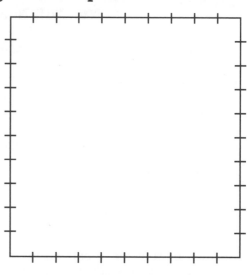

1. The large square represents a whole unit.
   a. Draw horizontal lines connecting the marks. How many strips are formed?

   What decimal part does each strip represent?

   b. Draw vertical lines connecting the marks. How many small squares are formed?

   What decimal part does each small square represent?

2. What part of each square is shaded? Write the decimal numeral.

   a. 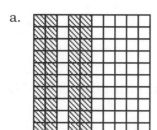   b. 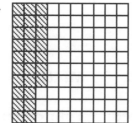   c.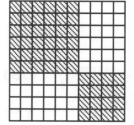

3. Shade each square to represent the number indicated.

   a. 0.3 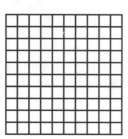   b. 0.18 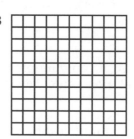   c. 0.76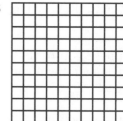

4. a. In which of 0.18 or 0.76 in part 3 is more area shaded? Complete with < or >, 0.18 _____ 0.76.

   b. In which of 0.3 or 0.18 is more area shaded? Complete: 0.3_____ 0.18

5. Compare the following pairs of decimals. Put < , >, or = in the space. Explain how you determined.

   a.   0.6 _____ 0.21   b.   0.3 _____0.37   c.   0.4 _____0.40

6. A student claims that 0.3 < 0.25 because 3 < 25. Is the student correct? Why or why not?

OBJECTIVE: **Compare addition and subtraction of whole numbers and decimals**

You Will Need: Your chip abacus

1. Compute these using your chip abacus:

    a. 31.12 + 4.6 = _____   b. 5.213 + 0.4 = _____

    c. 3.12 - 1.5 = _____   d. 13.213 - 7.508 = _____

2. Compute these using your chip abacus:

    a. 3112 + 460 = _____   b. 5213 + 400 = _____

    c. 312 - 150 = _____   d. 13,213 - 7,508 = _____

3. Relate the problems in part 1 with their counterparts in part 2 and explain how addition or subtraction of decimals is related to addition or subtraction of whole numbers.

OBJECTIVE: **Multiply and divide decimals by 10**

You Will Need: Your chip abacus

1. Recall the base ten pieces we have worked with. What happens when we have 10 small cubes (units), 10 longs, or 10 flats?

2. Suppose you have 2 small cubes. If you multiply by 10 by replacing each one with 10 copies, what will you have then? How could we express this using the fewest number of pieces?

3. Suppose you had 5 longs that are multiplied by 10 in the same way. What do you have as a result?

4. Represent 3.57 on this chart:

    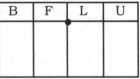

    If you multiply this by 10, what will become of the 7 small cubes (units)? What will become of the 5 longs? the 3 flats?

    Represent the result on this chart:

    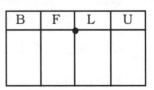

    How could you have obtained the second chart from the first chart?

5. Represent 1.72 on this chart:

B	F	L	U

   If you multiply this by 100, predict what will happen.

   What will the 2 small cubes (units) become?

   What will the 7 longs become?

   What will the flat become?

	B	F	L.	U

   Represent the result on this chart:

   How could you have obtained the second chart from the first?

   Describe a shortcut to use when multiplying by 10, by 100, by 1000.

   ---

6. a. What do you have if you divide a block by 10 by subdividing it into 10 equal-sized pieces?

   b. What do you have if you divide a flat by 10? a long?

7. Represent 6.13 on the chart:

B	F	L	U

   a. If you divide by 10, what will become of the 6 blocks? What will become of the 1 flat? the 3 longs?

   Represent the result on this chart:

B	F	L	U

   How could you have obtained the second chart from the first?

   b. If you were to divide the original 6.13 by 100, how could you obtain the result?

   Describe a shortcut to use when dividing by 10, by 100, by 1000.

   ---

8. Think about what you have done in this activity. What is the effect on a number when the decimal point marker is moved one column to the right?

What about moving it two columns to the right?

One column to the left?

Two columns to the left?

9. Describe the decimal point marker moves that are equivalent to the following procedures:

a. multiplying by 10

b. dividing by 1000

c. dividing by 10

d. multiplying by 10,000

OBJECTIVE: **Multiply decimals**

You Will Need: Your base ten pieces from Materials Card 4.7

Recall that the product of two numbers can be represented as the area of the rectangle with the factors being the dimensions of the rectangle.

1. The large square is the unit whole and the length of its side is 1 unit.

   What is the length of each subdivision of the sides?

   What amount does the area of each small square represent?

2. What are the lengths of the sides of rectangle A?

   _____ by _____

   What is the area of rectangle A? _____

3. Record the dimensions of each rectangle as well as its area.

Rectangle B   ____ × ____ = ____   Rectangle C   ____ × ____ = ____

Rectangle D   ____ × ____ = ____   Rectangle E   ____ × ____ = ____

Rectangle F   ____ × ____ = ____   Rectangle G   ____ × ____ = ____

Rectangle H   ____ × ____ = ____   Rectangle I   ____ × ____ = ____

4. Summarize how to multiply tenths by tenths.

5. Using base ten pieces we can model the product 1.2×2.3.

We will let the flat represent our unit whole. The length of its edge is 1.

To model this product we need to build a rectangle 2.3 units long and 1.2 units wide as illustrated.

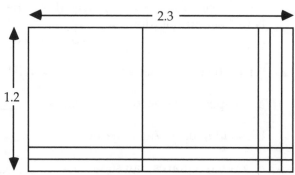

We see that the resulting area is covered by 2 flats, 7 longs, and 6 small cubes. Since the flat represents 1, each long represents 1/10 and each small cube represents 1/100, so the final product is 2.76.

Build rectangles to represent each of the following products and find the result.

a. 1.1×2.5 b. 2.4×3.2 c. 0.8×1.3

Draw your rectangles here.

6. Notice that the arrangement of pieces in part 5 is the same as we could use to model 12×23 when the small cube represents the unit. How could you estimate where to place the decimal point in the following problems?

a. 1.2×2.3 b. 1.2×23 c. 0.12×0.23

The next activities are devoted to the ideas of ratio and proportion. When you are able to use ratios and know how to set up proportions you will be able to solve problems more easily. First, let's look at the meaning of ratio.

OBJECTIVE: Discover the meaning of ratios

You Will Need: Materials Card 7.7

1. Place the following pieces in a group in front of you:

    2 striped squares   3 dotted squares   4 solid squares

    A **ratio** is an ordered pair of numbers indicating relative amounts. For example, the ratio 2:9 represents the ratio of striped squares to all squares. Another way to show this ratio is in fraction notation:

    2/9 = striped squares/all squares

2. Write the ratios that represent these relationships:

    a. striped squares/dotted squares = _____

    b. solid squares/all squares = _____

    c. dotted squares : all squares = ____:____

    d. solid : not solid = ____:____

3. A ratio can show the relationship of a *part to a part* or of a *part to the whole*. For example, striped squares : all squares shows the relationship of a part to the whole.

    Look at the examples in part 2. Which examples represent the relationship of a part to the whole?_____   Which examples represent the relationship of a part to a part?_____

4. Repeat part 2 using the following pieces:

    4 striped squares   1 dotted square   2 solid squares

    a._____   b._____   c._____   d._____

5. Now place the following pieces in front of you:

    3 striped squares   4 dotted squares   4 solid squares

    Write 4 ratios that relate a part to a part and one ratio that relates a part to the whole.

It is often useful to compare ratios to see if they are equivalent. If you wish to enlarge or reduce a recipe for example, the ratio of each ingredient to the whole amount must stay the same if the results are to be satisfactory. The next activity will give you practice in determining when ratios are equivalent.

OBJECTIVE: **Find equivalent ratios**

You Will Need: Materials Card 7.8

1. Cover a rhombus with triangles. How many triangles exactly cover the rhombus?_____

    We can say there are _____ triangles per rhombus or that the ratio of triangles : rhombuses is _____ : _____ .

    Cover a trapezoid with triangles. How many triangles exactly cover the trapezoid?_____

    We can say there are _____triangles per trapezoid or that the ratio of triangles : trapezoids is _____ : _____ .

    Cover a hexagon with triangles. How many triangles exactly cover the hexagon?_____

    What is the ratio of triangles : hexagons?   _____ : _____

2. Using only the rhombuses, trapezoids, and hexagons, find pieces that have a ratio equivalent to triangles : rhombuses. What are these pieces called?

    _____ and _____

    So we can say that the ratio of _____ : _____ is 2:1.

    Can you find pieces that have the same ratio as triangles : trapezoids? What are these

    pieces called? _____ and _____ .

    So we can say the ratio of _____ : _____ is 3:1.

    Can you find pieces that have the same ratio as triangles : hexagons?_____ Why or why not?

3. Can you design a shape that has a ratio of 4:1 with the rhombus and of 6:1 with the trapezoid?_____ Draw your shape within the outlines below:

a. 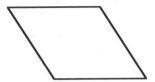   b.

   Hint: Use the triangle to find the new shape. What is your new shape called?_____
   Draw it here:

4. How many rhombuses does it take to cover a trapezoid?____
   It may be easier to look at this problem in a different way. First form a hexagon from 2 trapezoids. Now cover the trapezoids with rhombuses. There are ____rhombuses and 2 trapezoids, so the ratio of rhombuses to trapezoids is ____: 2. Now let's answer the first question in a different way:

   rhombuses : trapezoids = ____: 1

   You have written two ratios that are equivalent to each other. Write two more ratios that are also equivalent to these. Hint: Build 2 hexagons from trapezoids then cover with rhombuses, etc.

   _____

   When you know how to set up ratios you can solve a variety of problems.
   A **proportion** is a statement that two ratios are equal. Proportions are
   especially useful in solving percent problems or problems involving
   other ratios. For example, suppose that 2 out of 5 students in
   elementary education are male. Then, if we know the total
   number of students in elementary education, we can
   determine the number of male students in
   elementary education.

   _____

OBJECTIVE: **Use proportions to solve problems**

You Will Need: Materials Card 7.9 and a clock or watch with a second hand

1. Compute your number of heart beats in one minute as follows: Find your pulse. Count the number of heart beats in 6 seconds. Write that number in the blank numerator below:

$$\frac{\rule{2cm}{0.4pt}}{6 \text{ sec.}} = \frac{n}{60 \text{ sec.}}$$

Now use cross multiplication to find the number of heart beats (n) in one minute. For example, if a heart beats 10 times in 6 seconds the proportion is:

$$\frac{10}{6} = \frac{n}{60} \quad \text{or} \quad 10 \times 60 = 6n \quad \text{or} \quad n = \frac{10 \times 60}{6}$$

In this case the heart beats 100 times in 1 minute.

How many times did *your* heart beat in 1 minute? $n =$ _____

2. Use the information about your own heart rate to determine the following: How many times does your heart beat in one hour?

Hint: $\dfrac{\text{heart beats}}{\text{minute}} = \dfrac{x}{60 \text{ minutes}}$

At this rate, how many times will your heart beat in one day?_____

one week?_____ one year?_____ 80 years?_____

3. Repeat parts 1 and 2, but first do 25 jumping jacks and then quickly take your pulse. Try resting, running in place, or some other physical activity and then repeat parts 1 and 2.

4. Construct the metric tape on Materials Card 7.9. Measure your height in centimeters. _____

Measure the height of your head in centimeters. _____

To be a professional model, one asset is to have a ratio of height to head height of 8 to 1. Most people have a height : head height ratio of 7:1.

Use a proportion to determine your ratio, e.g.

$$\frac{\text{height}}{\text{head height}} = \frac{n}{1}$$

What is your height : head height ratio? _____ : 1

If a girl is 182 cm tall, what head height should she have in order to be of average height?

$$\frac{182}{n} = \frac{7}{1} \qquad n = \text{_____}$$

What head height should she have in order to qualify as a model?

$$\frac{\text{\_\_\_\_\_}}{n} = \text{\_\_\_\_\_} \qquad n = \text{_____}$$

The next activity will help you understand the meaning of percent.

OBJECTIVE: **Use the chip abacus to understand percent**

You Will Need: Your chip abacus

1. The notation $n\%$ means $n \cdot (1/100)$, or $n/100$. For example, $20\% = 20 \cdot (1/100) = 20/100 = 0.20$. Both the original whole number part of the percent and the decimal can be represented on the chip abacus.

EXAMPLE:

20   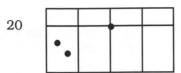   20% or 0.2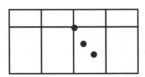

For each percent given, represent the whole number part of the percent on your chip abacus. Then represent these percents as decimals on your chip abacus. Record your results in the drawings below:

a. 10%   b. 27%   c. 1%   d. 300%

Whole number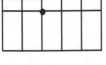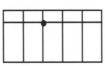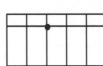

Decimal (or %)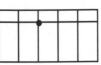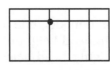

2. Look at the results in part 1. If you are given the decimal, could you find the equivalent percent by simply moving your decimal point marker?_____
    Explain:

    If you were given the percent, could you find the equivalent decimal by moving your decimal point marker?_____
    Explain:

What is the relationship between the decimal and its equivalent percent?

3. Represent the following numbers on your abacus. Then change each percent to its equivalent decimal and vice versa by moving only your decimal point marker.

    a. 42%   b. 0.03   c. 7.5   d. 0.1%

MENTAL MATH

Use proportions to solve these mental math problems. Which item is the better buy?

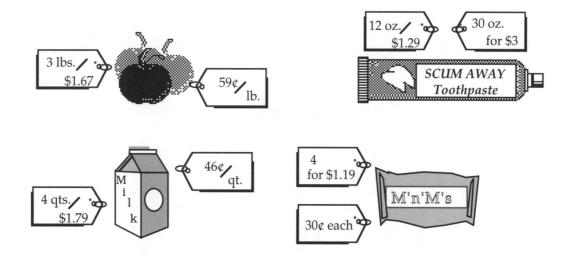

EXERCISES

What did the decimal point say to the dollar sign?

The numbers in the columns below are to be used to complete the problems involving that operation. For example, the numbers in the addition column are to be used to complete the addition problems. An extra number is contained in each column. Determine the number that would replace each numbered circle. Take the letter of the replacement number and place it in the blank that has the same number as the circle. Do as much mentally as you can.

ADDITION		SUBTRACTION		MULTIPLICATION		DIVISION	
N	74.59	W	10.9	S	3.2	E	3.92
A	72.9	N	8.39	H	2.7	I	1.9
H	7.8	O	5.93	E	8.06	I	0.7
E	15.4	A	12.7	M	12.42	T	5
K	17.87	T	6.4	N	10.58	C	6.21
Y	87.9	H	13.13	S	6.08	E	9.69
A	98.6	M	9.28	O	5	B	14.6

smaller
① + ② = 106.4   ⑨ + 57.5 = ⑩   17.3 - ⑰ = ⑱ smaller

③ - ④ = 7.2   ⑪ ÷ 5.6 = ⑫   4.6 × ⑲ = ⑳

smaller
⑤ × ⑥ = 40.3   ⑬ - 0.89 = ⑭   56.72 + ㉑ = ㉒

⑦ ÷ ⑧ = 5.1   ⑮ × 1.9 = ⑯   31.05 ÷ ㉓ = ㉔ smaller

$23.56

___ ___ , ___ ___ ___ ___ ___ ___ ___ ___ ___
 1   12   8   2   13   18 3   9   4   14   7

___ ___ ___   ___ ___ ___ ___ ___   ___ ___ ___ ___ ___!
17 19   5   20 10 21 6   15   23 11 22 24 16

☆ ☆ ☆ MAGIC STAR ☆ ☆ ☆

Solve the proportions and ratio problems below. Each problem is designated by a letter and that letter appears in one of the circles in the star. When you find the answer to each problem, put it in the corresponding circle.

A. $10/6 = n/12$

B. $35/n = 21/9$

C. $13/n = 65/95$

D. $4/9 = 16/n$

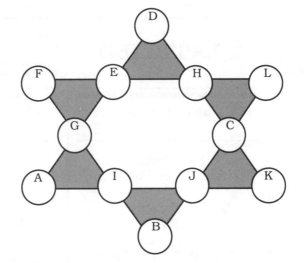

E. A photo that is 3.5 cm by 6 cm is enlarged. Its new dimensions are n cm by 24 cm. What is n?

F. The scale on a map is given as 6 inches = 75 miles. If you take a 475 mile trip, what would it be on the map (in inches)?

G. The ratio of the weight of an object on Jupiter to its weight on Earth is 8 to 3. How much would an 11.25-pound rock on Earth weigh on Jupiter?

H. If 3.7 grams of salt will dissolve in 10 grams of water, how many grams of salt will dissolve in 100 grams of water?

I. The ratio of boys to girls in a class is 1 : 2. If there are 51 students in the class, how many boys are there?

J. If you can buy 24 pencils for 88 cents, how much will you pay for 15 pencils?

K. If 192 meters of pipe weighs 48 kg, how much pipe would weigh 2 kg?

L. Your car has traveled 93.5 km on 8.5 liters of gas. How many km/liter did your car average?

WHAT IS THE MAGIC OF THE STAR?

A DREAM COME TRUE !

You have just received a check as a winner in the USA lottery. The check you receive is for $98,000. After paying 21% of that amount in taxes, you go on a shopping spree. Will you be able to buy all the items listed below?

CLASSIFIED

118   Home Entertainment

CANON 600 HiFi VCR, 27" Zenith Color TV and Nikko Stereo, Total Value $1595. Will sell for 60% off.

120   Household Goods

WASHER/DRYER pair.
Washer: 2 speed, 3 cycle
Dryer: 5 cycle,
3 temperature
Pair Price $899. Will sell for 9% cash discount.

140   Resort Rentals

YACHATS Resort Home, beach access, river view, sleeps 8. Spa/pool, tennis/etc. $55/night. One month (30 day) contract + 1% cleaning fee.

160   Automotive Display

The Dodge
"Caravan of Values"

DRIVE ONE HOME

* 1990 Dodge Colt

* 1989 4 x 4 DL Wagon

* 1989 Dodge Daytona

$9599 + 8% license
and dealer's costs

BRONCOS &

BLAZERS

1989 Chevy S-Blazer 4 x 4

Sporty, 4.3 liter, pep!
Power steering-windows-locks
air, AM/FM. Like new!

Was $14,995

Will discount 15%

165   Boats & Equipment

SAIL BOAT, well maintained. Ericson 25, Galley, sleeps 4, 10 hp outboard, depth sounder, compass, CB, dinghy, custom trailer, $18,500 + 6% sales tax.

172   Motor Homes

1989 19' FALCON
motor home, fully equipped,
3,800 miles, $29,000,
Will discount 3% for
cash payment.

185   Motorcycles

1987 Hurricane
Like new. Only 1500 miles.
Must see to appreciate.
$2750
+ 2% for licensing, etc.

SELF-TEST

1. If the expanded form of a number is $3(10^2) + 7 + 4(1/10) + 5(1/10^3)$, then the numeral representing that number has how many digits?

   a. 4　　　　　　b. 5　　　　　　c. 6　　　　　　d. None of a, b, or c.

2. Which of the following numbers is the greatest?

   a. 0.51　　　　b. 0.5101　　　c. 0.5　　　　　d. 0.5097

3. Express $0.\overline{36}$ as a fraction in simplest form. The sum of the numerator and denominator of this fraction is

   a. 136　　　　b. 15　　　　　c. 34　　　　　d. 135

4. If 0.000004205 is divided by 0.0006001, the answer is approximately

   a. 0.7　　　　b. 0.07　　　　c. 0.007　　　　d. 0.0007

5. Which is the best buy?

   a. 13 oz. for 70 cents　　　　b. 27 oz. for $1.68
   c. 24 oz. for $1.36　　　　　d. 32 oz. for $2.00

6. Which of the following proportions have the same solution?

   (i) $12/22 = 30/n$　　　(ii) $15/9 = n/33$　　　(iii) $n/66 = 135/162$

   a. i and ii only　　　　　　　　b. i and iii only
   c. ii and iii only　　　　　　　 d. i, ii, and iii

7. Miss Kelley and Mr. Peabody have 25 and 36 children in their classrooms, respectively. The ratio of boys to girls in Miss Kelley's classroom is $3 : 2$ and the ratio of girls to all the children in Mr. Peabody's classroom is $1 : 3$. If the two classes are combined, the ratio of girls to boys is

   a. $3 : 5$　　　　b. $2 : 7$　　　　c. $22 : 39$　　　　d. $19 : 42$

8. Which of these are equal?　(i) 0.52　　(ii) 5.2%　　(iii) 13/25

   a. i and ii　　　b. i and iii　　　c. ii and iii　　　d. None of a, b, or c.

9. If a $15.00 shirt is reduced 35% and a $24.00 pair of pants is reduced 15%, what is the total sale price of the two items?

   a. $8.85　　　　b. $19.50　　　　c. $30.15　　　　d. None of a, b, or c.

10. An item was marked up 25% and then this price was marked down 20%. The *net effect* of these two markings is a

   a. 0% markup
   c. 5% markup

   b. 2.5% markup
   d. Not enough information to work the problem.

SOLUTIONS

Warm-up

Use a chart to help you organize your information:

Chuck

	Chuck	Mark	Paul
Chicago	✗	😊	✗
Montreal	✗	✗	😊
Philadelphia	😊	✗	✗

Ann

	Ann	Amy	Alice	Angie
Apples	✗	✗	😊	✗
Apricots	✗	😊	✗	✗
Asparagus	✗	✗	✗	😊
Anchovies	😊	✗	✗	✗

Hands-on Activities

Activity 1

1. 10, 100, 1000; The long represented 10 since 10 units were equivalent to a long. Likewise 100 units made up a flat and 1000 units made up a block. 1000, 100, 10.
2. 10, 1/10, 1/100; Since 10 longs make up a flat, one long is one of ten equal pieces making up the whole, or 1/10. Similarly, one small cube is one of a hundred making up the whole, or 1/100. 10, 1/10, 1/100.
3. 1,100, 1/1000, 1/10; One long is one of a hundred needed to make a block so a long is 1/100, etc. 1/10, 1/100, 1/1000.
4. a. 10 times larger
    b. 1/10 as large
    c. Dividing by 10
    d. 100, 10, 1/10, 1/100, 1/1000
5. a. 1, 1/10, 1/100, 1/1000, 1/10000   b. 1000, 100, 10, 1, 1/10
    c. 10, 1, 1/10, 1/100, 1/1000
6. a. Decimal point after 1
    b. Decimal point after 3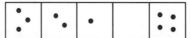
    c. Decimal point after 2
    These representations all have the same arrangement of chips. The decimal point is in a different position for each one. They can be represented by moving the decimal point.
7. 3 + 2(1/10) + 1(1/100) + 4(1/10000);   3(10) + 2 + 1(1/10) + 4(1/1000)

Activity 2

1. a. 1F, 3L, 2U; 1.32
   b. 1F, 32U; one and thirty two hundredths
2. a. 4L, 5U; 0.045
   b. Forty five thousandths
3. a. 13.12   thirteen and twelve hundredths
   b. 3.1032   three and one thousand thirty two ten thousandths
   c. 20.501   twenty and five hundred one thousandths
4. a. 131.2   one hundred thirty one and two tenths
   b. 31.032   thirty one and thirty two thousandths
   c. 205.01   two hundred five and one hundredth
5. a. 32.13   b. 500.021   c. 10.010 or 10.01   d. 34.11   e. 5.015
6. a. To write 13/100 the student is moving to the hundredths place and then writing 13. To
      help the student, it might be useful to review values of the places and do more
      representing and exchanging as in this activity.
   b. The student forgot "and" represented the decimal point. Five hundred twenty one
      thousandths.

Activity 3

1. a. 10, 0.1   b. 100, 0.01
2. a. 0.4   b. 0.27   c.   0.54
3. a. 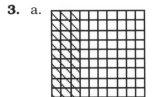   b. 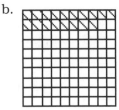   c.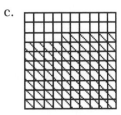

4. a. 0.76, <   b. 0.3, >
5. a. >   b. <   c. =
   It may be helpful to shade in decimal squares to compare. Also, since the tenths column
   represents how many strips are shaded, one could check that column first. In part (a),
   since 6 strips are clearly more than 2 strips, 0.6 > 0.21. In part (b), since the same number
   of strips are shaded, it is necessary to compare hundredths. In yet another approach, one
   could compare how many small squares each number represents; for example, 60 as
   compared to 21 in part (a). This converts both decimals to hundredths and then,
   essentially, the numerators are compared.
6. No; We cannot compare 3 to 25 since the 3 represents tenths and the 25 represents
   hundredths. They would have to have the same denominator before comparing in this way.

Activity 4

1. a. 35.72   b. 5.613   c. 1.62   d. 5.705
2. a. 3572   b. 5613   c. 162   d. 5705
3. Each of the addends in part 1 is multiplied by a power of ten to give the problems in part 2.
   The sum is also multiplied by the same power of 10. The same is true for the subtraction
   problems.

Activity 5

1. The 10 small cubes became a long, the 10 longs a flat, and the 10 flats a block.
2. 20 small cubes or 2 longs
3. 50 longs or 5 flats

4. 7 longs, 5 flats, 3 blocks; The second could be obtained from the first by moving the decimal point one place to the right (and also the B, F, L, U labels).

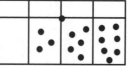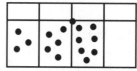

5. 2 flats, 7 blocks, a "long block"; by moving the decimal point 2 places to the right (and also the B, F, L, U labels)
   Move the decimal one place to the right when multiplying by 10, two places to the right when multiplying by 100, three places to the right when multiplying by 1000.

6. a. a flat   b. a long, a small cube

7. a. 6 flats, 1 long, 3 small cubes; by moving the decimal point (and labels) one place to the left.
   b. By moving the decimal point 2 places to the left.
   Move the decimal one place to the left when dividing by 10, two places when dividing by 100, and three places when dividing by 1000.

8. It is multiplied by 10. It is multiplied by 100. It is divided by 10. It is divided by 100.

9. a. Move 1 place to the right   b. Move 3 places to the left
   c. Move 1 place to the left   d. Move 4 places to the right
   Move the decimal point marker to the right or left as many spaces as the power of 10 used, e.g. 10^3 yields 3 spaces right when multiplying and left when dividing.

Activity 6

1. 1/10, 1/100
2. 0.6, 0.2, 0.12
3. B   0.4, 0.5, 0.20 or 0.2   C   0.5, 0.3, 0.15   D   0.1, 0.7, 0.07
   E   0.3, 0.3, 0.09   F   0.4, 0.3, 0.12   G   0.2, 0.3, 0.06
   H   0.9, 0.2, 0.18   I   0.1, 0.1, 0.01
4. Tenths multiplied by tenths yields hundredths
5. a. 2.75   b. 7.68   c. 1.04

6. a. 1 times 2 should be about 2
   b. 1 times 23 should be about 23
   c. 0.1 times 0.2 should be about 0.02

Activity 7

2. a. 2/3   b. 4/9   c. 3:9   d. 4:5
3. b & c; a & d
4. a. 4/1   b. 2/7   c. 1:7   d. 2:5
5. Answers may vary: 3/4 = striped/dotted; 4/4 = dotted/solid; 4/3 = solid/striped;
   4/7 = dotted/not dotted;   3:11 = striped:all

Activity 8

1. 2, 2, 2 : 1;   3, 3, 3 : 1;   6, 6 : 1
2. Trapezoids & hexagons; trapezoids : hexagons
   Yes, rhombuses & hexagons; rhombuses : hexagons
   No. You would need a shape smaller than the triangle.

3. Yes, a triangle equivalent to half the given triangle.
4. 1 1/2, 3, 3, 1 1/2 , 6:4, 9:6

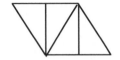 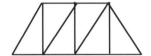

Activity 9
1. Answers will vary.
2. 60 *n*; 1440 *n*; 10,080 *n*; 525,600 *n*; 42,048,000 *n*
3. Answers will vary.
4. Answers will vary.
    n = 26 cm head height   182/*n* = 8/1   *n* = 22.75 cm

Activity 10
2. Yes. The percent name is found by multiplying the decimal equivalent by 100.
    Yes. Remove the percent sign and move the decimal 2 places to the left.
    The % sign simply means "hundredths". These are two ways to name the same number.
3. a. 42% = 0.42   b. 0.03 = 3%   c. 7.5 = 750%   d. 0.1% = 0.001

Mental Math
3 lbs. for $1.67   30 oz. for $3.00   4 qts. for $1.79   4 for $1.19

Exercises

What Did the Decimal Point Say to the Dollar Sign?

1 - 7.8	9 - 15.4	17 - 10.9
2 - 98.6	10 - 72.9	18 - 6.4
3 - 13.13	11 - 3.92	19 - 2.7
4 - 5.93	12 - 0.7	20 - 12.42
5 - 5	13 - 9.28	21 - 17.87
6 - 8.06	14 - 8.39	22 - 74.59
7 - 9.69	15 - 3.2	23 - 6.21
8 - 1.9	16 - 6.08	24 - 5

Hi, I am the one who makes cents!

MAGIC STAR
A. 20 **B.** 15 **C.** 19 **D.** 36 **E.** 14 **F.** 38 **G.** 30 **H.** 37
I. 17 **J.** 55 **K.** 8 **L.** 11   Each straight line of four circles totals 100.

A DREAM COME TRUE!
    Yes. You pay $20,580 in taxes, leaving you with $77,420.

Home Entertainment:	$638.00	Sailboat:	$19,610.00
Washer/Dryer:	$818.09	Motor home:	$28,130.00
Resort home:	$1,666.50	Suzuki:	$2,805.00
Dodge:	$10,366.92		
Blazer:	$12,745.75	Total:	$76,780.26

Self-Test
1. c **2.** b **3.** b **4.** c **5.** a **6.** d **7.** c **8.** b **9.** c **10.** a

RESOURCE ARTICLES

Boling, Bruce A. "A Different Method for Solving Percentage Problems." *Mathematics Teacher* 78 (October 1985): 523-524. *A unique method presented.*

Coburn, Terrence G. "Percentage and the Hand Calculator." *Mathematics Teacher* 79 (May 1986): 361-367. *Activities using and estimating percentages.*

Cramer, Kathleen, Nadine Bezuk, and Merlyn Behr. "Proportional Relationships and Unit Rates." *Mathematics Teacher* 82 (October 1989): 537-544. *Activities for grades 6-8 interpreting relationships using a unit-rate approach.*

Cramer, Kathleen A., Thomas R. Post, and Merlyn J. Behr. "Interpreting Proportional Relationships." *Mathematics Teacher* 82 (September 1989): 445-452. *Activities for grades 6-8 involving proportional and nonproportional reasoning.*

Dewar, Jacqueline M. "Another Look at the Teaching of Percent." *Arithmetic Teacher* 31 (March 1984): 48-49. *Concrete version of a proportional approach to percent problems.*

Glatzer, David J. "Teaching Percentage: Ideas and Suggestions." *Arithmetic Teacher* 31 (February 1984): 24-26. *Teaching the concept of percentage and ways of finding it.*

Grossman, Anne S. "Decimal Notation: An Important Research Finding." *Arithmetic Teacher* 30 (May 1983): 32-33. *Understanding of decimal notation.*

Hampel, Paul J. "Computer Corner." *Arithmetic Teacher* 32 (September 1984): 46. *Program changing fractions into decimals.*

Hiebert, James. "Research Report: Decimal Fractions." *Arithmetic Teacher* 34 (March 1987): 22-23. *Summarizes research findings and suggests instructional strategies.*

Payne, Joseph N., and Ann E. Towsley. "Ideas." *Arithmetic Teacher* 34 (March 1987): 26-32. *Activities with decimals.*

Payne, Joseph N., and Ann E. Towsley. "Implementing the Standards for Teaching Fractions and Decimals." *Arithmetic Teacher* 37 (April 1990): 23-26. *Building conceptual foundation and meaningful computational procedures.*

Quintero, Ana Helvia. "Helping Children Understand Ratios." *Arithmetic Teacher* 34 (May 1987): 17-21. *Describes different levels of difficulties and activities with ratios.*

Wiebe, James H. "Manipulating Percentages." *Mathematics Teacher* 79 (January 1986): 23-26, 21. *Discusses two concrete models.*

DIRECTIONS IN EDUCATION

Matching Strategies to Outcomes — The Teacher As Decision Maker

Learner outcomes may vary from lesson to lesson. Some lessons have as their goal the mastery of basic skills or the recall of factual information. Other lessons are designed to assist students in the development of conceptual understanding. Still other lessons may provide opportunities for students to apply learning in new or diverse ways. Some lessons may even have as their underlying objective social skills which enhance the learning environment of the classroom. Academic goals in such lessons may be of secondary importance. Teachers must make key decisions about the type of learner outcome expected for each lesson. In conjunction with the consideration of these outcomes, the teacher must select appropriate instructional delivery models with which outcomes may be achieved. While instructional models exist in great variety, each model is better matched to certain types of learner outcomes than to others. It is the ability to appropriately match teaching models to expected learner outcomes which distinguishes the professional teacher.

Teaching models which support various learner outcomes:

- **Mastery strategies.** Direct instruction, mastery learning, programmed instruction, and teacher-directed instruction are some of the terms used to describe models of teaching in which the desired outcome of the lesson is skill acquisition or factual recall. These models are designed to be structured and directed by the teacher or by a carefully sequenced set of instructional materials to lead every student in the class to the same destination, but perhaps at different rates.

- **Conceptual strategies.** Concept attainment, concept formation, inquiry and discovery learning are some of the models which may be used when the desired outcome of the lesson is conceptual processing or the formation of links with prior knowledge to expand conceptual understanding. While the lesson may be structured in advance by the teacher, the learner assumes greater responsibility for the learning with the teacher serving in the role of mediator or facilitator.

- **Divergence strategies.** Problem solving, inventive strategies, synectics (or metaphorical thinking), and open-ended discussions are instructional models which may be used when the goal of the lesson is application of knowledge in divergent, self-directive ways. In these lessons, the teacher provides the catalyst for the learning by posing interesting problems or questions — providing the "cognitive itch". The learner, once engaged in the activity, has sole responsibility for the outcome of the process. The role of the teacher is to serve as a resource when called upon and to pose additional problems or questions to keep the process in motion once begun.

- **Involvement strategies.** Some strategies have as their primary objective the involvement of students in the learning process. Cooperative learning, team games or tournaments, quality circles, and peer partnerships are some of the strategies which increase student participation in the lesson. These strategies can be used to teach the social skills necessary for the classroom as well as to facilitate the acquisition of skills and concepts or the application of prior learning. These strategies may also be used in conjunction with the previous strategies to enrich the classroom environment.

Thinking skills are enhanced by the use of varied teaching strategies.

- Students can be helped to understand that they move through various levels of knowledge acquisition and use by being told the desired outcome of each lesson. They can learn to match what they are doing to a taxonomy of knowledge levels such as that of Benjamin Bloom. In this way, they can be taught to engage in metacognition — thinking about their own thinking processes.

- By engaging in divergent and involvement strategies, students can begin to see themselves as being in charge of their own learning and as being able to serve as a resource for their fellow students. In this way, students begin to sense the power of learning and to see themselves as lifelong learners.

- Teachers who can move comfortably from the directive role to the mediative role to the supportive role and back again are able to provide for learning at all levels of the taxonomy.

- Teachers who are able to engage in divergent thinking and decision making project this open-minded, flexible attitude in their classrooms. Students are given a clear message that thinking is valued.

- A classroom environment rich in varied teaching and learning models is interesting to students and promotes active participation in the learning. While some routine is desirable for the handling of everyday tasks such as role taking and paper collection, daily repetition of a single lesson model over time can create detachment of learner interest and limitation of learner outcomes.

As you think about matching strategies to outcomes, ask yourself:

- Which of the teaching models have I observed in classrooms?

- How comfortable do I feel about the directive role? mediative role? supportive role?

To learn more:

Bloom, Benjamin S. *Taxonomy of Educational Objectives*. New York: David McKay, 1956.

Costa, Art. *Developing Minds, Part VII*. Virginia: Association for Supervision and Curriculum Development, 1985.

Hanson, J. Robert, Harvey F. Silver, and R.W. Strong. *Teaching Styles and Strategies*. New Jersey: Hanson, Silver & Strong Associates, 1986.

Joyce, Bruce, and Marsha Weil. *Models of Teaching*. New Jersey: Prentice-Hall, 1986.

8 Integers

THEME: Understanding Integers and their Operations

**Strategy Review:
Draw a Diagram.**
You can refer to
this strategy in
Chapter 2 of the text.

A survey was taken in a school cafeteria. Of the 125 students surveyed, 47 liked hamburgers, 30 liked pizza, and 12 liked both pizza and hamburgers. How many students did not like pizza or hamburgers? Hint: Use a Venn Diagram.

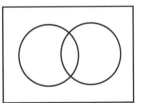

HANDS-ON ACTIVITIES

The first three activities in this chapter are designed to give you practice in representing positive and negative integers using black and red chips to build models of the integers.

OBJECTIVE: **Build models of integers**

You Will Need: Materials Card 8.1

1. These sets are models of 5 and -6.

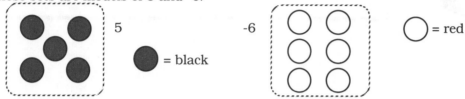

2. Using the chips from Materials Card 8.1, make models of these integers.
   Record how each was made:

8   -7   4   -3   -5

OBJECTIVE: **Use opposites to represent 0**

You Will Need: Materials from Activity 1

1. These black and red chips can be matched in a 1-to-1 correspondence.

We say that the red chips "cancel" the black chips (and vice versa) and that the entire set represents the number 0.

Because of this, -3 is called the **opposite** of 3. Also, 3 is called the opposite of -3.

2. Using the black and red chips, show four different ways to represent 0. Record. Name the pairs of opposites as illustrated:

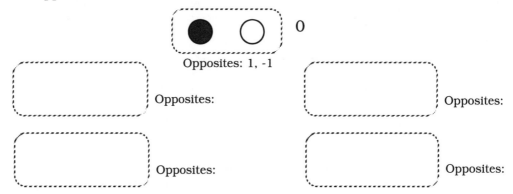

Opposites: 1, -1

Opposites:

Opposites:

Opposites:

Opposites:

OBJECTIVE: **Represent integers in alternate ways**

You Will Need: Materials from Activity 1

1. Chips can be used to represent -6 in many different ways. Two ways are shown below:

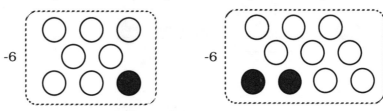

Circle pairs of chips that cancel each other.

2. Use chips to show two ways to represent -3. Record. Circle pairs of chips that cancel each other.

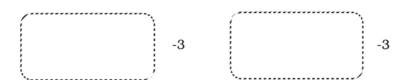

-3

-3

3. Find four ways to represent 5. Record. Circle pairs of chips that cancel each other.

5

5

5

5

Now that you know how to represent integers using the black and red chips, you are ready to look at models for addition and subtraction of integers.

OBJECTIVE: **Represent addition of integers using black and red chips**

You Will Need: Materials from Activity 1

1. This model shows how to add 3 and 4 using black chips:

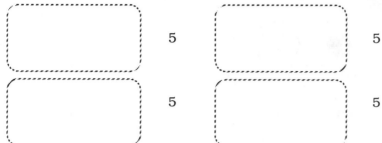

7

3 + 4 = 7

2. Use red chips and black chips to find the sum of -5 and 2. Record by picture. Circle the chips that cancel each other. Record the sum.

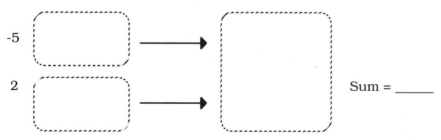

-5

2

Sum = _____

3. Use your chips to compute and record the following sums:

   a. 7 + (-3) =   b. -4 + (-3) =   c. -8 + 2 =

State a rule for adding integers.

4. Use your rule to compute the following sums without chips:

   a. 5 + (-4) =   b. -6 + (-8) =   c. -6 + 4 =

OBJECTIVE: **Subtract integers using the take-away model**

You Will Need: Materials from Activity 1

1. These models show "take-away" subtractions. Try them with your chips.

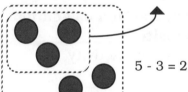

5 - 3 = 2

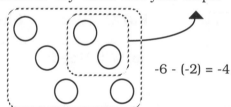

-6 - (-2) = -4

2. Use chips to find these differences. Record by picture.

   -5 - (-3) = _____   6 - 1 = _____

   -4 - (-2) = _____

3. The take-away model can also be used to find 5 - 8.
   Think of a plan to get enough black chips to be able to take 8 of them away.

   Hint: Find another representation of 5.

   Record: 5 - 8 = _____

Use your method to find these differences. Record your pictures.

a. 4 - 6 =   b. 2 - 6 =   c. 3 - 9 =

4. You can also use the take-away model to find -3 - 5.
   First : Count out 3 red chips.

   Then : Put 5 black chips and 5 red chips with the 3 red chips.

   What integer is represented here?_____

   (You now have enough black chips to
      take away 5 black chips.)

   Finally : Find the difference by taking away the 5 black chips.   -3 - 5 =_____

5. Use chips to find these differences. Record your pictures.

   a. 5 - (-2) =   b. -3 - 2 =   c. -3 - (-4) =

OBJECTIVE: **Show subtraction as adding the opposite**

You Will Need: Materials from Activity 1

1. Use red and black chips to find -3 - 4 = _____ . With pictures, record the sequence of steps you used to find the result.

   At some point, did you add 4 black chips and 4 red chips? What happened to the 4 black chips after that?

   What happened to the 4 red chips?

   Explain a shortcut you could use to find -3 - 4.

2. Verify these equations using chips:

   a. -5 - 4 = -5 + (-4)   b. 3 - (-2) = 3 + 2

Summary: In order to subtract two integers, you can rewrite the difference as the first integer plus the _____ of the second integer and follow the rules for addition.

OBJECTIVE: **Show subtraction with missing-addend addition**

You Will Need: Materials from Activity 1

1. Use some black chips and 3 red chips to represent 5. Record by picture.

   How many black chips did you use?

   What number can be added to -3 to get 5?

2. Use some red chips and 4 black chips to represent -3. Record by picture.

   How many red chips did you use?

   What number can be added to 4 to get -3?

3. Compute 5 - (-2) by using chips to find the missing addend in the equation
   _____ + (-2) = 5. Record.

4. Compute -6 - 3 by using the missing-addend method.

   Hint: Ask yourself, "What can I add to 3 to get -6?"

   $$-6 - 3 = _____$$

5. Compute these differences by using the missing-addend model.
   Record your results:

   a. -7 - 3 =   b. 4 - (-1) =   c. -7 - 8 =

The last two activities in this chapter will present models for multiplication
and division of integers.

OBJECTIVE: **Use representations of 0 to multiply integers**

You Will Need: Materials from Activity 1

1. The equation $2 \times 3 = 6$ means $3 + 3 = 6$. If we start with a representation of 0 like this

   and then add 3 black chips two times we get  = 6.

   The problem 2×3 tells us we must *put in* 3 black chips 2 times.

2. Use red or black chips to compute these products:

   a. $3 \times 4 =$ ⬚ ____   b. $4 \times 2 =$ ⬚ ____

   c. $2 \times (-2) =$ ⬚ ____   d. $3 \times (-5) =$ ⬚ ____

   The problem $2 \times (-2)$ tells us we must _____2 red chips 2 times.

3. We can also find products for problems of this type -2×3.

   To do this, we must use a different representation of 0.

   This problem tells us we must *take out* 2 groups of 3 black chips.
   Therefore, we begin with this representation of 0.

      0

   Now *take out* 2 groups of 3 black chips. What chips remain?____
   What integer is represented by the remaining chips?_____

   Thus, $-2 \times 3 =$ ____

4. Use your chips to find these products. Start with an appropriate representation of zero; in part (a) this has been done for you.

a. $-4 \times 2 =$

b. $-1 \times 3 =$

c. $-2 \times (-2) =$

d. $-3 \times (-2) =$

The problem $-2 \times (-2)$ tells us we must _____ 2 red chips 2 times.

5. Use your answers to parts 2 and 4 to record these products:

a. $3 \times 4 =$ _____

b. $4 \times 2 =$ _____

c. $2 \times (-2) =$ _____

d. $3 \times (-5) =$ _____

e. $-4 \times 2 =$ _____

f. $-1 \times 3 =$ _____

g. $-2 \times (-2) =$ _____

h. $-3 \times (-2) =$ _____

State a shortcut for multiplying integers.

6. Use your pattern to compute these products without using chips:

a. $3 \times 6 =$ _____

b. $-4 \times 5 =$ _____

c. $7 \times (-2) =$ _____

d. $-3 \times (-6) =$ _____

ACTIVITY
9

OBJECTIVE: **Divide integers**

You Will Need: Materials from Activity 1

1. To find the quotient -8 ÷ 2 we must find n such that -8 = 2 × n , i.e. n = -4.

    Use the chips and the multiplication model from Activity 8 to check your solution.

2. Compute these quotients by finding a value for n that makes each statement true.

    a. 6 ÷ 3 = _____   b. -10 ÷ 5 = _____
        6 = n × 3 n = _____   -10 = n × 5 n = _____

    c. 8 ÷ (-4) = _____   d. -6 ÷ 6 = _____
        8 = n × (-4) n = _____   -6 = n × 6 n = _____

    Use chips to check your answers.

    ┌───┐
    │   │
    │   Look at the problems above. State a pattern for division of integers.   │
    │   │
    │   │
    │   │
    └───┘

3. Find these quotients using your pattern:

    a. 15 ÷ (-3) = _____   b. -12 ÷ 6 = _____   c. -7 ÷ (-7) = _____   d. 153 ÷ 3 = _____

MENTAL MATH ═══════════════════════════════

Determine today's temperature at 5:00 P.M.

At 1:00 A.M. the temperature was 30°. By 5:00 A.M. it had dropped 13°. It then began to rise at the rate of 2° per hour. This rate continued until noon when the rate of increase changed to 3° per hour.   At 4:00 P.M. it reached its peak and began dropping 2° per hour. What was the temperature at 5:00 P.M.?_____

EXERCISES

Why did the bike racer go to the psychiatrist?

Solve each problem. Place the letter preceding the problem above the solution at the bottom of the page. Be sure to put the letter above the solution each time it appears.

U 27 - (-8) = _____
T -18 - 5 = _____
H 18 + (-12) = _____
A -45 + (-30) = _____
F 60 + (-40) = _____
E -11 - 6 = _____
V -15 + 41 = _____
L -3 + 15 = _____
S -47 - (-77) = _____

W 4 + (-22) = _____
D 7 + (-20) = _____
O 15 - 45 = _____
I -1 - (-20) = _____
G -8 + 4 - (-9) = _____
C -78 + (-37) = _____
N 22 + (-9) = _____
Y 1 - 12 = _____

6 -17   -18 -75 30   6 -75 26 19 13 5

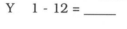

-115 -11 -115 12 -17   12 -30 5 19 -115 -75 12

-13 19 20 20 19 -115 35 12 -23 19 -17 30 !

Designing with Integers

Connect each problem number (BIG NUMERALS on the inside circle) to its solution (small numerals on the outside circle) in the circle following. Use a straightedge to draw the lines. Item number 7 has been done as an example. Your finished work will make a lovely design.

1. $2 \times (-4) =$ ____
2. $-90 \div 9 =$ ____
3. $-36 + 76 =$ ____
4. $8 - 26 =$ ____
5. $-10 \times (-13) =$ ____
6. $65 - (-20) =$ ____
7. $75 \div (-5) =$ __-15__
8. $60 \div (-6) =$ ____
9. $34 + (-56) =$ ____
10. $90 \div (-5) =$ ____
11. $-15 - (-84) =$ ____
12. $6 \times (-6) =$ ____
13. $2 \times (-45) =$ ____
14. $-3 \times (-15) =$ ____
15. $-42 - (-7) =$ ____
16. $-4 \times (-18) =$ ____
17. $-11 + (-3) =$ ____
18. $-63 \div 9 =$ ____
19. $-11 + 3 =$ ____
20. $-225 \div (-5) =$ ____
21. $-20 \times (-2) =$ ____
22. $-24 - (-96) =$ ____
23. $-20 + 150 =$ ____
24. $105 \div (-3) =$ ____
25. $21 + (-36) =$ ____
26. $-13 \times (-3) =$ ____
27. $-3 - 19 =$ ____
28. $-53 - (-53) =$ ____
29. $-23 \times (-3) =$ ____
30. $-200 \div (-4) =$ ____
31. $-56 + (-34) =$ ____
32. $-23 - (-62) =$ ____
33. $26 + (-26) =$ ____
34. $56 \div (-4) =$ ____

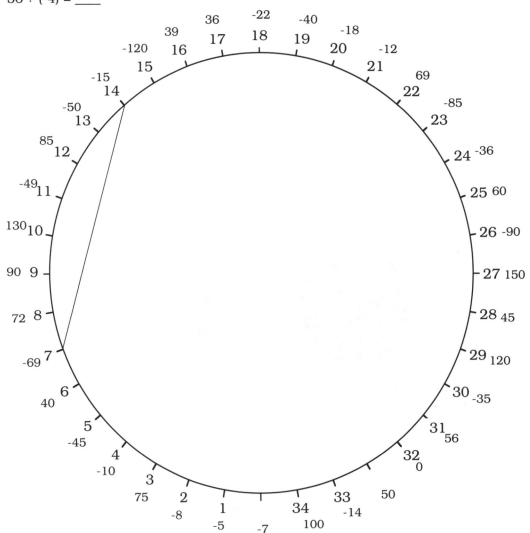

SELF-TEST

1. Which of the following is *false*?

   a. The opposite of an integer is always negative.
   b. Every negative integer is the opposite of an integer.
   c. The opposite of a negative integer is always positive.
   d. None of a, b, or c.

2. B's are positive, R's are negative, and B + R is zero. What problem is illustrated here?

   R̸ R̸ R̸ R̸ R̸   a. 5 + (-9) = -4   b. 9 - 5 = 4
   B̸ B̸ B̸ B̸ B̸ B B B B   c. -5 + 9 = 4   d. None of a, b, or c.

3. Which of the following is the *adding-the-opposite* equivalent of -8 - 6 = _____?

   a. 8 + (-6) = _____   b. -8 + (-(-6)) = _____   c. 8 + (-(-6)) = _____   d. -8 + (-6) = _____

4. Which of the following is the *missing-addend* equivalent of (-9) - (-4) = _____?

   a. -9 + _____ = -4   b. -4 + _____ = -9   c. -(-4) + _____ = -9   d. -(-4) + _____ = 9

5. B's are positive, R's are negative, and B + R is zero. What problem is shown here?

   B̸ B̸ B̸ B̸ R R R R R R   a. 4 - 10 = -6   b. 10 - 4 = 6
   B̸ B̸ B̸ B̸ B̸ B̸   c. -6 - (-4) = 10   d. -6 - 4 = 10

6. Which of these is true?

   a. $((a - b) - c)d = ((a - c) - b)(- d)$ b. $(a - b)(- c) = (b - a)(- c)$

   c. $(- a - b)c = (- b - a)c$ d. None of a, b, or c.

7. What can be concluded from the following "proof"?

   $$\mathbf{0} = -6(7 + (- 7)) = (-6)7 + (-6)(-7) = \mathbf{-42 + (-6)(-7)}$$

   a. 7 - 7 = 0   b. (-6)7 = -42   c. (-6)(-7) = 42   d. (-6)0 = 0

8. Which of the following is *not* a property of integers?

   a. distributivity   b. additive inverse

   c. multiplicative inverse   d. multiplicative identity

9. For integers a and b, $a < b$ if there is a positive integer c such that:

    a. $a - c = b$ b. $c = a + b$ c. $a - b = c$ d. $a + c = b$

10. If a, b, c are integers, which of the following is *false*?

    a. If $a < b$ and $b < c$, then $a + b < b + c$.   b. If $a < b$, then $a + c < b + c$.

    c. If $a < b$ and $c \geq 0$, then $ac \leq bc$.   d. If $a < b$ and $c < 0$, then $ac < bc$.

SOLUTIONS

Warm-up
60 students

Hands-on Activities

Activity 1
2. 8 black chips, 7 red chips, 4 black chips, 3 red chips, 5 red chips

Activity 2
Answers can vary.

Activity 3
Each black chip cancels one red chip.

Activity 4
2. -3
3. a. 4   b. -7   c. -6
    Rule: The sum of 2 negatives or 2 positives is the sum of the whole numbers, the sign does not change; the sum of a positive and a negative is the whole number difference, the sign will be that of the greater whole number.
4. a. 1   b. -14   c. -2

Activity 5
2. -2, 5, -2
3. -3 (represent 5 as 8 black chips and 3 red chips);   a. -2   b. -4   c. -6
4. -3, -8
5. a. 7   b. -5   c. 1

Activity 6
1. -7. Yes. They were taken away. These were the chips that were combined with the 3 red chips to find the result. All you need to do is add the opposite of what is being subtracted.
2. Opposite

Activity 7
1. 8 black chips; 8
2. 7 red chips; -7
3. 7
4. -9
5. a. -10   b. 5   c. -15

Activity 8
2. a. 12   b. 8   c. -4   d. -15; put in
3. 6 red chips, -6, -6
4. a. -8   b. -3   c. 4   d. 6; take out
5. a. 12   b. 8   c. -4   d. -15   e. -8   f. -3   g. 4   h. 6
A negative times a negative is a positive, a positive times a positive is a positive, a positive times a negative is a negative.
6. a. 18   b. -20   c. -14   d. 18

Activity 9
2. a. 2   b. -2   c. -2   d. -1
Division with 2 negatives or with 2 positives gives a positive quotient, division with a positive and a negative gives a negative quotient.
3. a. -5   b. -2   c. 1   d. 51

Mental Math
41 degrees

Exercises

Why did the bike racer go to the psychiatrist?
U 35   W -18   T -23   D -13   H 6   O -30   A -75
I 19   F 20   G 5   E -17   C -115   V 26   N 13
L 12   Y -11   S 30
HE WAS HAVING CYCLE-LOGICAL DIFFICULTIES !

Designing with Integers
1. -8   2. -10   3. 40   4. -18   5. 130   6. 85
7. -15   8. -10   9. -22   10. -18   11. 69   12. -36
13. -90   14. 45   15. -35   16. 72   17. -14   18. -7
19. -8   20. 45   21. 40   22. 72   23. 130   24. -35
25. -15   26. 39   27. -22   28. 0   29. 69   30. 50
31. -90   32. 39   33. 0   34. -14
You should find a cardioid (heart-shaped) design.

Self-Test
1. a   **2.** c   **3.** d   **4.** b   **5.** a   **6.** c   **7.** c   **8.** c   **9.** d   **10.** d

RESOURCE ARTICLES

Battista, Michael T. "A Complete Model for Operations on Integers." *Arithmetic Teacher* 30 (May 1983): 26-31. *A concrete model for teaching the four basic operations on the set of integers.*

Chang, Lisa. "Multiple Methods of Teaching the Addition and Subtraction of Integers." *Arithmetic Teacher* 33 (December 1985): 14-19. *Relating operations with integers to real-world situations.*

Crowley, Mary L., and Kenneth A. Dunn. "On Multiplying Negative Numbers." *Mathematics Teacher* 78 (April 1985): 252-256. *The ideas involved in the multiplication of negative numbers.*

Dirks, Michael K. "The Integer Abacus." *Arithmetic Teacher* 31 (March 1984): 50-54. *Help in understanding the algebraic rule of signs.*

Sarver, Vernon Thomas, Jr. "Why Does a Negative Times a Negative Produce a Positive?" *Mathematics Teacher* 79 (March 1986): 178-180. *Provides an interesting concrete interpretation.*

Willy, W. Edward. "Addition of Antinumbers." *Mathematics Teacher* 78 (November 1985): 606-608. *A motivational technique for introducing addition of integers.*

DIRECTIONS IN EDUCATION

Forming Mathematical Connections - Getting It All Together

Being mathematically literate means that students not only possess the ability to use their math skills and understanding in the context of the mathematics classroom, but also that they think to use their math skills and knowledge in contexts which occur outside of the mathematics classroom. In addition, being mathematically literate means that students call upon prior math learning to assist and enrich new learning in mathematics. Connecting these previously attained skills and knowledge to new contexts is the focus of curriculum integration.

Curriculum integration may be viewed from the perspective of a single content area such as mathematics. When integration is examined from this point of view, the teacher is looking for ways to form connections among concepts and over time. In mathematics, integration is the means by which students are helped to see that math is not a series of discrete skills, but rather a whole with many interconnected parts.

In the classroom, curriculum integration may also be viewed from the perspective of the total instructional program. The teacher who practices this type of curriculum integration looks for goals from different content areas which overlap or which complement each other. A science activity in which data is collected may incorporate some graphing and statistical manipulation of that data. An art lesson about mosaic art might incorporate the study of tessellations. A health lesson about target heart rates might include calculation of personal heart rates and comparison of classroom average rates. In fact, a single lesson may meet instructional objectives from many individual content areas. This holistic approach to instruction provides the means by which children can form connections between the classroom and the real world.

Benefits of forming connections within the mathematics curriculum include:

- The opportunity to link conceptual and procedural knowledge.

- The ability to relate various representations of concepts or procedures to one another.

- The ability to recognize relationships among different topics in mathematics.

- The opportunity to see mathematics as an integrated whole.

- The opportunity to explore problems and describe results using graphic, numerical, physical, algebraic, and verbal mathematical models or representations.

- The ability to use a mathematical idea to further understanding of other mathematical ideas.

- The opportunity to reinforce and expand prior learning in a meaningful context.

Benefits of forming connections between mathematics and other curriculum content areas include:

- The opportunity to see mathematical skills and knowledge as useful in other content areas.

- The ability to use mathematics in daily life.

- The ability to apply mathematical thinking and modeling to solve problems that arise in other disciplines, such as art, music, psychology, science, and business.

- Acceptance of the value of mathematics in our culture and society.

As you think about forming mathematical connections, ask yourself:

- Must students have mastered every aspect of a skill before they are able to deal with it in an integrated context? Can the integrated lesson provide further motivation for skill attainment or refinement?

- How does the teacher determine when direct skill or concept instruction is required and when students are ready to encounter the mathematical idea in an integrated setting?

- How does the teacher provide meaningful instruction in various content areas without giving only superficial treatment to other areas in an integrated lesson?

- Do I understand and appreciate connections within mathematics in such a way that I can communicate those connections to my students?

- Do I know how to plan lessons which form connections between mathematics and the real world?

To learn more:

Silverman, Helene. "Ideas." *Arithmetic Teacher* 36 (September 1989, November 1989, January 1990).

Spence, Carolyn, and Carol S. Martin. "Mathematics + Social Studies = Learning Connections." *Arithmetic Teacher* 36 (December 1988): 2-5.

9

Rational Numbers and Real Numbers, with an Introduction to Algebra

THEME: Extending Number Systems

WARM-UP

Strategy Review:
Use Properties of Numbers.
This strategy, introduced in Chapter 5, will help you solve this problem.

I'm thinking of a number. It is a prime number less than 100. The sum of its digits is 16. If you reverse the digits, the resulting number is also prime. What's the number?

HANDS-ON ACTIVITIES

The activities in this chapter will use the Pythagorean theorem to help you gain an understanding of irrational numbers. The geoboard, a useful classroom manipulative, will be utilized for these activities.

OBJECTIVE: **Find areas on the geoboard**

You Will Need: A geoboard (optional)

1. The geoboard is a 5 by 5 array of pegs. Rubber bands are used to form the shapes as illustrated:

This square will be our unit of area measure.

⬜ = 1 square unit.

Construct this square on your geoboard.

Construct each of these shapes on your geoboard. What is the area of each shape?
Hint: How many ⬜ are in each shape?

a.

area = _____

b.

area = _____

c.

area = _____

2. Now find the area of each of the square regions below:

Area of R_1 = _____
Area of R_2 = _____
Area of R_3 = _____
Sum of R_1 & R_2 = _____

What do you notice about the area of R_3 and the sum of the areas of R_1 and R_2?_____

3. Now find the areas of these square regions given on a square lattice:

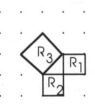

Area of R_4 = _____
Area of R_5 = _____

Their sum = _____

One way to find the area of R_6 is by finding the areas of the regions determined by the dashed lines as illustrated:

Area of R_6 = _____

Describe another way for finding the area of R_6.

OBJECTIVE: **Investigate the Pythagorean theorem**

You Will Need: Materials Card 9.2 and scissors

1. Cut out the figure on Materials Card 9.2.

2. Cut away the square on side x, the square on side y, and the square on side z.

3. Now cut the square with side y into 4 pieces as indicated by the dashed lines.

4. Arrange square x and the pieces of square y to fit exactly into square z. (It can be done!)

> What have you shown about the areas of the three squares?
> Interpret this in terms of the original right triangle given.

OBJECTIVE: **Develop the Pythagorean theorem algebraically**

You Will Need: Materials Card 9.3 and scissors

1. Cut out the four copies of the right triangle with sides x, y and z from Materials Card 9.3. Arrange them to form a square "donut" with a square hole as shown:

   Now answer these questions:

2. The length of any side of the donut is side _____ of the triangle plus side _____ of the triangle, or _____+_____ (in terms of x, y, and z).

   What is the area of the larger square?_____
   We will call this area A_1.

3. What is the length of any side of the donut hole?_____
   What is the area of the hole?_____ We will call this area A_2.

4. What is the area of each right triangle?_____
    (Remember that the area of a triangle is 1/2 the base times the height. This is easy to see here since two of the triangles can be fitted together to make a rectangle with dimensions x and y.)

5. What is the sum of the areas of the four right triangles?_____
    We will call this area S.

6. Write an equation involving A_1, A_2, and S. _____
    Now substitute the x, y, and z values for A_1, A_2, and S.
    Simplify your equation.

7. Explain your simplified equation in geometric terms that apply to the right triangle.

8. Using this equation, we know that 3, 4, and 5 could be the sides and hypotenuse of a right triangle because $3^2 + 4^2 = 5^2$. Which of the following triples could be the lengths of the sides and hypotenuse of a right triangle?

    a. 6, 8, 10   b. 5, 12, 13   c. 15, 112, 113   d. 7, 25, 26

We can now use our knowledge of right triangles and the lengths of their sides and hypotenuse to explore real numbers. Again, we will use the geoboard.

ACTIVITY 4

OBJECTIVE: **Construct real number lengths on the geoboard**

You Will Need: A geoboard (optional)

DEFINITION: If r is any nonnegative number, then $\sqrt{r}$, called the **square root** of r, is the nonnegative number whose square is r. In symbols, $\sqrt{r}$ satisfies the two properties:

$$\text{(i)} \quad \sqrt{r} \geq 0 \qquad \text{and} \qquad \text{(ii)} \quad (\sqrt{r})^2 = r$$

For example, $\sqrt{4} = 2,$ $\sqrt{9} = 3,$ $\sqrt{144} = 12$

1. In the given isosceles right triangle, the sides have length 1 and the hypotenuse has length c.

   We can say $1^2 + 1^2 = c^2$, or $2 = c^2$.

   Therefore, the length of the hypotenuse $c = \sqrt{2}$.

   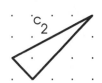

2. Find the length of each hypotenuse below:

   a.

   b.

   $(c_1)^2 = \underline{\quad}^2 + \underline{\quad}^2$

   $c_1 = \underline{\qquad\qquad}$

   $(c_2)^2 = \underline{\quad}^2 + \underline{\quad}^2$

   $c_2 = \underline{\qquad\qquad}$

3. Determine which of the following can be represented on a 5 by 5 geoboard. Give your rationale by describing the right triangle whose hypotenuse has that length. Draw your triangles on the 5 by 5 arrays given below. For example, the right triangle with sides

   3 and 1 can be used to represent the length $\sqrt{10}$, because $3^2 + 1^2 = (\sqrt{10})^2$.

   a. $\sqrt{17}$ $\underline{\quad}^2 + \underline{\quad}^2 = (\sqrt{17})^2$ b. $\sqrt{32}$ $\underline{\quad} + \underline{\quad} = \underline{\qquad}$

   c. $\sqrt{18}$ $\underline{\quad} + \underline{\quad} = \underline{\qquad}$ d. 5 $\underline{\quad} + \underline{\quad} = \underline{\qquad}$

   e. $\sqrt{28}$ $\underline{\quad} + \underline{\quad} = \underline{\qquad}$ f. $\sqrt{22}$ $\underline{\quad} + \underline{\quad} = \underline{\qquad}$

MENTAL MATH

If  is balanced by , and if ● is balanced by   ,

How many 𝖖 will balance ● ?

EXERCISES

Just FOUR You!

Express each whole number from 1 to 10 using a number sentence that involves the number **four** exactly **four** times and at least one square root.

For example, $4 \times \sqrt{4} + 4 \times \sqrt{4} = 16$

_____ = 1   _____ = 6

_____ = 2   _____ = 7

_____ = 3   _____ = 8

_____ = 4   _____ = 9

_____ = 5   _____ = 10

What happens to frogs who double park?

Decide whether each number is rational or irrational. Circle the letter in the appropriate column at the right. When you are finished, print the circled letters above the appropriate blanks at the bottom of the page to solve the riddle.

		Rational	Irrational
1.	22/7	E	I
2.	π	W	T
3.	6.125	G	A
4.	0.571428571428 . . .	W	A
5.	$\sqrt{225}$	Y	S
6.	$\sqrt{49}$	Y	S
7.	$\sqrt{2}$	B	T
8.	-4/3	A	R
9.	3.1415925385 . . .	C	A
10.	0.060060006 . . .	A	H
11.	0.135135135 . . .	T	E
12.	-0.999199911999 . . .	R	A
13.	3.40764076 . . .	D	T
14.	-9.7071212212221 . . .	A	O
15.	$\sqrt{13}$	R	E

Letter Answer   _ _ _ _   _ _ _   _ _ _ _   _ _ _ _ !

Question Number   7 10 1 5   3 15 11   2 14 8 13   9 4 12 6

SELF-TEST

1. If W, F, I, and Q represent the whole numbers, fractional numbers, integers, and rational numbers, respectively, which of the following is false?

    a. $F \cup I = Q$ b. $W \subseteq I \subseteq Q$ c. $W \subseteq F \subseteq Q$ d. None of a, b, or c.

2. Which of the following properties, among others, make this computation easy?

    $$(-5/3 + 4/7 + 5/3) \times 7/4$$

    (i) additive inverse   (ii) distributive property   (iii) multiplicative inverse

    a. i only   b. i and ii only   c. i and iii only   d. i, ii, and iii

3. Which of the following quotients is not equal to -4/7?

    a. $8/(-15) \div 14/15$ b. $12/35 \div (-3)/5$

    c. $-42/18 \div 12/9$ d. $(-10)/(-21) \div 5/(-6)$

4. Which of the following orderings is correct?

    a. $-3/8 < 2/-5 < 1/3 < 1/2$ b. $-2/7 < -3/11 < 2/5 < 3/8$

    c. $3/-10 < -2/9 < 5/7 < 7/9$ d. None of a, b, or c.

5. The number 0.121221222. . . is

    a. rational and real.   b. irrational and real.

    c. rational but not real.   d. irrational but not real.

6. Which set contains only rational numbers?

    a. $\{\ \sqrt{1},\ \sqrt{2},\ \sqrt{3}\ \}$ b. $\{\ \sqrt{4},\ \sqrt{9},\ \sqrt{16}\ \}$

    c. $\{\ \sqrt{4},\ \sqrt{5},\ \sqrt{9}\ \}$ d. None of a, b, or c.

7. What is the length of the diagonal on the geoboard shown?

    a. 5   b. 6

    c. 3 1/2   d. None of a, b, or c.

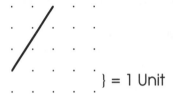

$\}$ = 1 Unit

8. Which of the following is equal to $(-125)^{(2/3)}$?

    (i) $\sqrt[3]{(-125)^2}$ (ii) 1/25   (iii) -25

    a. i and ii only   b. i and iii only   c. ii only   d. i only

9. Solve the following equation, and write your answer in simplest form.

$$(3/4)x - 4/5 = (2/3)x + 1/2$$

What is the denominator?

    a. 4   b. 5   c. 3   d. 2

10. Solve the inequality: $5 - 3x \geq 20$

    a. $x \leq -5$ b. $x < -5$ c. $x \geq -5$ d. $x \geq 25/3$

SOLUTIONS

Warm-up
79 or 97

Hands-on Activities

Activity 1
1. a. 2   b. 3   c. 2
2. 1, 1, 2, 2; equal
3. 4, 1, 5, 5, Find the sum of the areas of R_4 and R_5.

Activity 2
The sum of the areas of the squares on the sides of a right triangle is equal to the area of the square on the hypotenuse.

Activity 3
2. $x, y, x + y, (x+y)^2$
3. z, z^2
4. $xy/2$
5. $2xy$
6. $A_1 - A_2 = S$ $(x+y)^2 - z^2 = 2xy;$ $x^2 + 2xy + y^2 - z^2 = 2xy$ or $x^2 + y^2 = z^2$
7. See Activity 2 solution.
8. a, b, c

Activity 4
2. $2^2 + 3^2$, $\sqrt{13}$, $(\sqrt{2})^2 + (\sqrt{18})^2$, $\sqrt{20}$
3. a. $4^2 + 1^2$ b. $4^2 + 4^2 = (\sqrt{32})^2$ c. $3^2 + 3^2 = (\sqrt{18})^2$
   d. $3^2 + 4^2 = 5^2$ e. and f.   cannot be done

Mental Math
Three tacks will balance one marble.

Exercises
  Just FOUR You !   What happens to frogs who double park?
  - - answers will vary.   THEY GET TOAD AWAY !

Self-Test
1. a   **2.** c   **3.** c   **4.** c   **5.** b   **6.** b   **7.** d   **8.** d   **9.** b   **10.** a

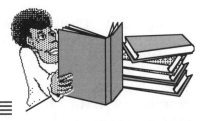

RESOURCE ARTICLES

Barson, Alan, and Lois Barson. "Ideas." *Arithmetic Teacher* 35 (January 1988): 19-24. *Activities with rational numbers in the form of fractions, decimals, and percent.*

Berman, Barbara, and Fredda Friederwitzer. "Algebra Can Be Elementary... When It's Concrete." *Arithmetic Teacher* 36 (April 1989): 21-24. *Describes a model for teaching early algebraic concepts using manipulative materials.*

DiDomenico, Angelo S. "Pythagorean Triples from the Addition Table." *Mathematics Teacher* 78 (May 1985): 346-348. *An investigation using the addition table.*

Drysdale, Ron. "An Act of Creation in First-Year Algebra." *Mathematics Teacher* 78 (April 1985): 266-268. *A motivational technique for first-year algebra students.*

Giambrone, Tom M. "Challenges for Enriching the Curriculum: Algebra." *Mathematics Teacher* 76 (April 1983): 262-263. *Problems that require students to use techniques other than the known algorithms.*

Harder, Ken. "Algebra Tic-tac-toe." *Mathematics Teacher* 76 (January 1983): 34-36. *A game format for practice with factoring.*

Hawkins, Vincent J. "The Pythagorean Theorem Revisited: Weighing the Results." *Arithmetic Teacher* 32 (December 1984): 36-37. *Using Cuisenaire rods to investigate the Pythagorean theorem.*

Hollis, L. Y. "Teaching Rational Numbers — Primary Grades." *Arithmetic Teacher* 31 (February 1984): 36-39. *What can and should be taught in the primary grades.*

Jacobson, Marilyn Hall. "Teaching Rational Numbers — Intermediate Grades." *Arithmetic Teacher* 31 (February 1984): 40-42. *A model for the introduction of decimals.*

Kieren, Thomas E. "Helping Children Understand Rational Numbers." *Arithmetic Teacher* 31 (February 1984): 3. *A discussion of the mechanisms, images, and language needed for the development of rational-number ideas.*

Lester, Frank K., Jr. "Preparing Teachers to Teach Rational Numbers." *Arithmetic Teacher* 31 (February 1984): 54-56. *Suggestions for instruction in rational numbers for pre-service teachers.*

Levine, Deborah R. "Proof by Analogy: The Case of the Pythagorean Theorem." *Mathematics Teacher* 76 (January 1983): 44-46. *A special case involving the Pythagorean theorem.*

Marche, M. M. "A Pythagorean Curiosity." *Mathematics Teacher* 77 (November 1984): 611-613. *A method for finding integral values for the three sides of a right triangle.*

Ockenga, Earl. "Chalk Up Some Calculator Activities for Rational Numbers." *Arithmetic Teacher* 31 (February 1984): 51-53. *Create interest in the study of fractions by using the calculator.*

Payne, Joseph N. "Curricular Issues: Teaching Rational Numbers." *Arithmetic Teacher* 31 (February 1984): 14-17. *A discussion of the debate on relative emphasis to be given fractions and decimals.*

Prevost, Fernand J. "Teaching Rational Numbers - Junior High School." *Arithmetic Teacher* 31 (February 1984): 43-46. *Extending whole number operations to rational numbers.*

Ryden, Robert. "Nearly Isosceles Pythagorean Triples." *Mathematics Teacher* 76 (January 1983): 52-56. *The beauty of patterns in the Pythagorean triples.*

Skypek, Dora Helen B. "Special Characteristics of Rational Numbers." *Arithmetic Teacher* 31 (February 1984): 10-12. *Interpretations and coding conventions of rational numbers.*

Trafton, Paul R., and Judith S. Zawojewski. "Teaching Rational Number Division: A Special Problem." *Arithmetic Teacher* 31 (February 1984): 20-22. *Division of fractions and decimals.*

Usiskin, Zalman, and Max S. Bell. "Ten Often Ignored Applications of Rational-Number Concepts." *Arithmetic Teacher* 31 (February 1984): 48-50. *A look at the variety of contexts in which numbers appear in today's world.*

Wagner, Sigrid. "What Are These Things Called Variables?" *Mathematics Teacher* 76 (October 1983): 474-479. *Suggestions for overcoming difficulties related to variables for beginning algebra students.*

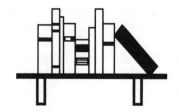

DIRECTIONS IN EDUCATION

Assessment Techniques - Inspect What You Expect

Testing can have a major impact on the content of classroom instruction. Results of testing may be used to evaluate the performance of individual schools or of individual classroom teachers. For that reason, it is imperative that assessment techniques used in the classroom examine student progress in the full range of skill acquisition, conceptual understanding, problem solving, and applications of knowledge expected in that classroom. Tests which do not match classroom instruction give feedback which is of extremely limited use for evaluation of individual student progress or for prescribing further instructional needs.

Standardized tests, which may be useful in comparing schools or school districts, have limited value in the individual classroom because the results are not received for several weeks after the testing session. In addition, the goals are drawn from popular national textbooks and are designed to be general enough to meet the needs of a full array of classrooms across the nation. Individual test items may match only a limited portion of the curriculum in an individual classroom and may test that portion of the curriculum in a format different from the one used for instruction.

If we are to prepare students to function in an information-based society, we must move away from assessment instruments which give product-oriented feedback on skill acquisition alone. We must seek assessment techniques which also give feedback on a process-oriented curriculum.

What is objective assessment?

- Tests such as nationally standardized tests are designed to have a single correct answer to each test item. Administration and scoring of the tests is controlled to maintain uniformity of experience for all students.

- Most testing programs designed by textbook publishers to support the use of that single textbook program are objective in nature. They are frequently limited to multiple choice, true-false, matching, and fill-in-the-blank formats.

- Teacher-made tests have traditionally been objective in nature because they provide for uniform grading in a timely manner.

- Individual test items are designed to assess student ability on a single instructional objective.

- Student answers indicate only that the student gave a correct or an incorrect response to the question.

- Most objective testing is done in a paper-and-pencil format with some exception in tests designed for use with primary grade children.

What is subjective assessment?

- Assessment which involves the application of some criteria by a teacher or other evaluator is known as subjective assessment. Criteria may include, but are not limited to such things as a scoring guide which gives partial credit for success with individual steps in a multi-step problem, evidence of application of steps within a process, or comparison of student work against established models.

- Types of subjective assessment which are designed for application of pre-determined criteria include:

  - direct observation of student performance on a specific task that identifies points during the application of a process where the student is particularly skilled or where the student needs additional process instruction.
  - direct observation of student behavior that can assist in designing instruction to meet individual learning styles.
  - portfolios of student work collected over time that show individual student growth and provide diagnostic information for future instruction.
  - student journals or logs that give feedback on changing student attitudes and insights.
  - long-term projects that can be evaluated not only for product, but for design and implementation of project plans.
  - interviews of individual students that can help teachers identify student misconceptions and design instruction which addresses individual strengths and interests.
  - essay or open-ended questions which provide for diverse student responses.

- It is essential that teachers work with their peers to develop and refine the criteria by which these subjective assessments are made. In that way, students will receive consistent feedback over time. In addition, teachers will improve their skill with subjective assessment when they see their own judgments in comparison with those of their peers.

As you think about classroom assessment, ask yourself:

- What are the advantages/disadvantages of objective assessment? of subjective assessment?

- How might students benefit from a wide range of classroom assessment techniques?

To learn more:

Charles, Randall, Frank Lester and Phares O'Daffer. *How to Evaluate Progress in Problem Solving.* Reston, Virginia: National Council of Teachers of Mathematics, 1987.

Association for Supervision and Curriculum Development. "Focus issue: Redirecting Assessment." *Educational Leadership* 46 (April 1989).

10

Statistics

THEME: Organizing, Picturing, and Analyzing Data

Strategy Review:
Solve an Equation.
This strategy was
presented in
Chapter 9 of the text.

Each row, column, and diagonal has
the same sum.

-7	x	-8
$2y$	-5	-4
$x-2$	-10	y

What is that sum ?_____

$x =$ _____ $y =$ _____

HANDS-ON ACTIVITIES

The activities in this chapter will help you organize, represent, and analyze
data using a variety of picturing techniques. Depending on the data, it may be
appropriate to use a bar graph, line graph, pictograph, or circle graph. These
are explored in the following activities.

OBJECTIVE: **Represent data with a bar graph**

Data can be represented in a variety of ways that are appropriate for the age and developmental level of the audience or students.

1. Across the chalkboard or on the floor in front of the classroom, write the months of the year. Have each person in the class line up beside the month in which they were born.

    a. How many were born in September?   in December?

    b. How many were born in the same month you were?

    This is an example of a **real graph** because real objects, in this case people, are used to build the graph. This kind of graph is a good beginning point, particularly with younger children.

2. Next, on a sheet of paper, draw a portrait of yourself. Using the same categories as in part 1, build a graph by lining up the pictures under the appropriate month on a chalkboard or bulletin board.

    a. Were more people born in July than in May?

    b. How many were born in January and February?

    This kind of graph is a **representational graph** because pictures of real objects are used for making the graph.

3. On a small card or sheet of paper, write your name, Make a graph of birth months by placing these name cards under the appropriate month.

    a. Are any columns the same?

    b. Are there any months in which no one has a birthday?

    This is an example of an **abstract graph** because symbols, in this case names, are used for graphing instead of real objects or pictures.

4. Another abstract version of this graph can be drawn on the following grid. Color in a space for each person in the class to make bars for each month showing the number of people who were born in that month.

Birth Months of Class

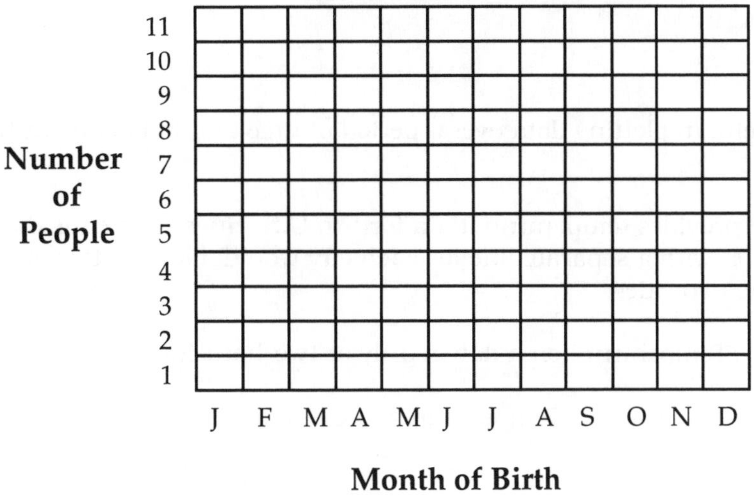

Number
of
People

11
10
9
8
7
6
5
4
3
2
1

J F M A M J J A S O N D

Month of Birth

A **bar graph** can be used when you want to make comparisons between several quantities or make comparisons over a period of time.

5. You can now use your graph to answer these questions:

   a. During which month did the greatest number of births occur?_____

      the fewest births?_____

   b. During which quarter of the year did the greatest number of births occur?_____

      the fewest?_____

   c. What was the total number of births in 31-day months?_____

      in months with fewer than 31 days?_____

6. Think of 3 more questions that could be answered by your graph.

OBJECTIVE: **Represent data with a line graph**

A **line graph** is useful in plotting data over a period of time and in looking at trends.

The following table provides temperature data for two U.S. cities (M means data is missing). Drawing a line graph with a separate line for each city would allow us to compare the temperatures in the two cities.

Temperature on a day in July at two-hour intervals

Temperatures in Celsius

	12 Midnight	2	4	6 A.M.	8	10	12 Noon	2	4	6 P.M.	8	10	12 Midnight
Denver, CO	20	18	19	22	24	28	32	35	34	30	27	M	M
Washington, DC	25	24	23	25	28	30	32	33	32	30	28	M	M

1. In order to draw a line graph, we first need to determine the horizontal and vertical scales. The horizontal scale for time has already been drawn on the graph shown. What would be an appropriate scale for the vertical temperature axis? Hint: Remember it should start at zero.

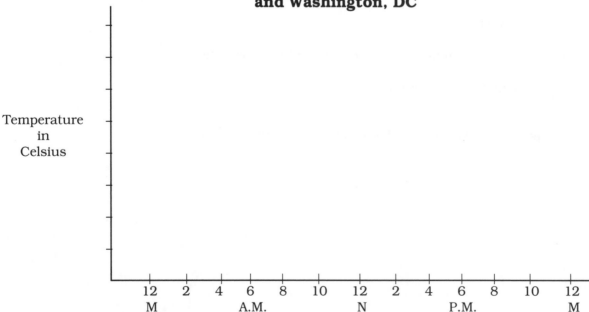

July Temperatures in Denver, CO and Washington, DC

Time of Day in Two-Hour Intervals

2. Now mark dots corresponding to the numbers for each city. Connect the dots for Denver with solid line segments and the dots for Washington with dashed line segments.

3. Use your graph to answer the following questions.

   a. Which city reached the warmest temperature during the day? the coolest temperature?

   b. Which city was warmer at 10 a.m.? at 2 p.m.? at 8 p.m.?

   c. During which hours was Washington warmer than Denver?

   d. During which hours was Denver warmer than Washington?

   e. When were the temperatures in Denver and Washington the same?

   f. What was the approximate temperature at 9 a.m. in Washington? in Denver?

   g. At approximately what time was the temperature in Denver equal to 25° C?

   h. Assuming the trend of the temperatures since 6 p.m. continues, what would you estimate the temperatures to be at 12 midnight at the end of the day in Denver? in Washington?

OBJECTIVE: **Represent data with a pictograph**

A **pictograph** uses a small drawing to symbolize the quantities being represented. A pictograph can be used to make comparisons between similar situations or across time.

The following table provides data for the sales of a textbook in six selected states.

State	Number of books sold
New York	670,643
Massachusetts	231,506
Kentucky	163,114
Michigan	355,860
California	810,520
Montana	98,478

1. In order to draw a pictograph, you will need to decide how to label your axis. You will also need to choose a symbol and decide how many books it will represent.

   a. What symbol will you use?

   b. If you let each symbol represent 10,000 books, how many symbols would be needed to represent the smallest amount? the largest amount? Is this a reasonable choice?

   c. If you let each symbol represent 200,000 books, how many symbols would be needed to represent the smallest amount? the largest amount? Is this a reasonable choice?

   d. What might be a more reasonable choice to let each symbol represent?

   e. You also need to decide whether you want to round your data to use a whole number of symbols or to represent a fraction of your symbol. What will you do here?

2. On the axes provided, draw a pictograph using the given data.

3. Using your pictograph, answer the following questions.

   a. Which state had the largest sales? the smallest sales?

   b. In which states were fewer books sold than in Massachusetts?

   c. In which states were approximately twice as many books sold as in Kentucky?

   d. In which states were approximately one-third as many books sold as in New York?

OBJECTIVE: **Represent data with a circle graph**

You Will Need: Materials Card 10.4 and a calculator

A **circle graph** can be used when you want to show the fractional parts into which a whole has been divided and to compare their relative sizes.

1. Fill in this chart based on how you spent your time yesterday and compute the percent of time spent in each activity. Remember, you can use a proportion to compute percent. For example, if you spent 8 hours sleeping, your proportion would be:

$$8/24 = n/100 \qquad n = \underline{\hspace{1cm}}$$

Time in Hours

Sleep	Eat	Travel	School	Work	Study	Exercise	Chores	TV	Other
___	__	___	___	__	__	___	___	__	__
___ %	__ %	___ %	___%	___ %	___ %	___ %	___ %	___ %	___%

Now construct a circle graph that represents your data. Remember to multiply each percent by 360° to find the measure of the central angle for each sector.

How I Spend My Time

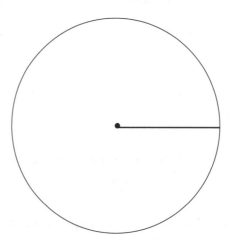

Label each sector of your graph with % and category (written horizontally).

2. Find the percent of time spent in recreational activities. _____%

   Find the percent of time in work-related activities, including school. _____%

3. How might your graph be different if you kept track of your time for an entire week?

   What factors might cause this graph to be a poor representation of how you usually spend your time?

OBJECTIVE: **Organize data with a stem and leaf plot.**

1. Find the armspans of 20 people; that is, measure the distance in centimeters from fingertip to fingertip with arms outspread. Identify whether each measurement is for a male or female.

2. a. To make a stem and leaf plot, find the smallest and largest measurement. Using the tens and hundreds digits as the stem, record the stems vertically from the smallest value to the largest. For example, if values range from 75 to 118, you would record stems of 7, 8, 9, 10, and 11.

Stems	Leaves

   b. For each item of data, record a leaf by placing the ones digit to the right of the corresponding stem. For example, for 96, place a 6 to the right of the stem 9.

   c. After all leaves have been recorded, rearrange the leaves in increasing order.

3. a. Are there any intervals in which no items of data occur?

   b. Are there any groups of data that cluster close together?

   c. Are there any items of data that differ significantly from the rest?

4. Stem and leaf plots can also be used to compare two sets of data. On the grid given below construct a stem and leaf plot of the armspans of the males on the left and of the females on the right. The stems for both go in the middle column.

Males			Females

   Describe the comparison and contrast between the two sets of data.

Numbers that provide information about the overall "average" of a group are called **measures of central tendency.** The following activity explores three of these measures and a measure of the overall spread of the data.

OBJECTIVE: **Analyze data**

1. Find the heights of 20 people (in centimeters). List the heights here in order from shortest to tallest:

2. a. The heights range from the shortest of _____ to the tallest of _____. The **range** of heights is the tallest minus the shortest or _____.

   b. The height shared by the most people is called the **mode**. What height is that?_____

   c. The height that is in the middle of the list is called the **median**. There are the same number of heights above and below this height. Since there is an even number of heights in this case, take the value midway between the two middle scores (add the two middle scores and divide by 2). What is the median height?_____

   d. The **mean** is determined by adding all of the heights together and then dividing by the number of people measured.   What is the mean height for your group of 20 people?_____

3. Using the graph paper on the next page, construct a bar graph that represents your data. What will be an appropriate scale for the horizontal axis? the vertical axis?

4. Draw a dashed line (-----) vertically through your graph to represent the mean height. Are there an equal number of people represented on your graph to the left and to the right of the mean?

   Draw a dotted line (. . . . .) vertically to represent the mode. Do you have an equal number of people to the left and to the right of the line?

   Draw a dot/dash line (._.._._.) vertically to represent the median. Do you have an equal number of people to the left and to the right of the line?

Height of People

Number
of
People

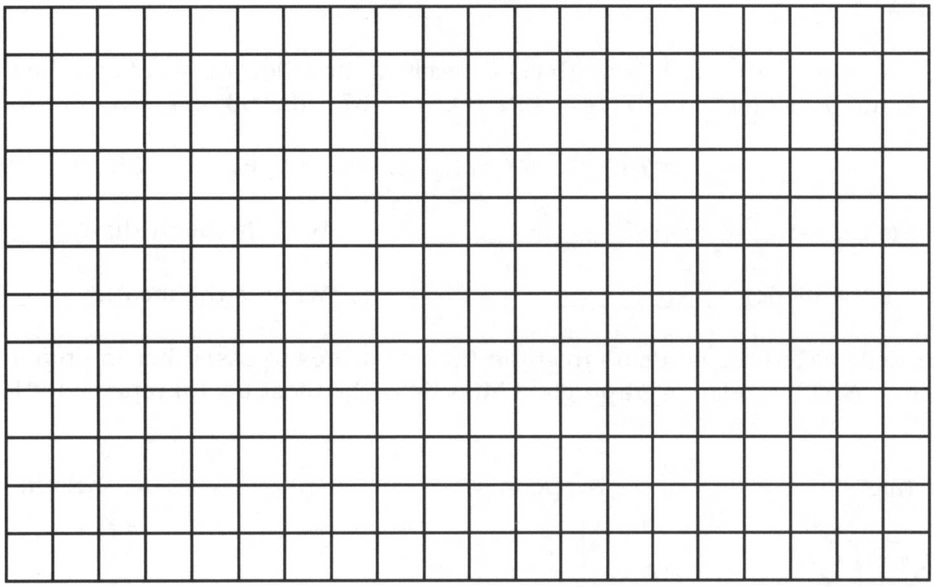

Height in Centimeters

5. a. Which of the three, mean, mode, or median, is most likely to divide your graph
        so that the same number of people are to the left and to the right of the line?

    b. What factors might cause the mode to be off-center?

    c. What factors might cause the mean to be off-center?

    d. Why will the median be most likely to divide your graph evenly?

In the last activity, you will use what you have learned in the first activities
to help you determine the best way to represent given data in graphical form.

OBJECTIVE: **Select appropriate graph for representation of data**

1. The students in Miss Kelly's math class received the following scores on their semester test: (85 points possible)   67, 42, 59, 80, 71, 67, 48, 53, 64, 73, 56, 77, 40, 35,

   78, 67, 59, 44, 76, 75, 42, 67, 65, 58, 31, 79, 56, 67

2. What is the range of scores?_____   What is the median?_____

   What is the mode?_____   What is the mean?_____

3. Miss Kelly asked the students to graph the test scores to assist her in preparing final grades. Which student's graph gives Miss Kelly the most useful representation of the data?

a. Craig

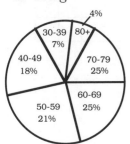

b. Dennis

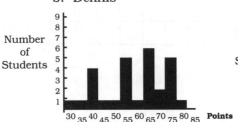

NOTE: Data rounded down to multiple of 5

c. Kristin

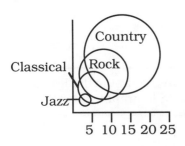

MENTAL MATH

In a recent survey of 50 music lovers, 15 preferred rock music, 7 preferred classical music, 25 preferred country music, and 3 preferred jazz. Which graph most accurately represents this data?

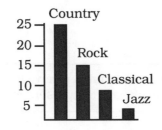

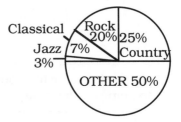

EXERCISES

What do you put on a sick pig?

Put the letter of the correct answer on the appropriate line at the bottom of the page.

1. What is the range of the recorded temperatures?
   - **A. 10°F**
   - **O. 12°F**

2. What was the temperature at 4 AM?
   - **I. -2°F**
   - **B. 4°F**

3. When was the temperature 10°F?
   - **R. 2 PM**
   - **N. Noon**

4. What is the median of temperatures recorded from 4 AM through noon?
   - **S. 3.5°F**
   - **K. 4°F**

5. What is the mean of the temperatures recorded from noon through 6 PM?
   - **M. 6.7°F**
   - **T. 10.3°F**

6. For how long was the temperature below 0°F?
   - **E. 5.5 hr.**
   - **F. 7 hr.**

7. What was the temperature at 3 PM?
   - **G. -5°F**
   - **N. 7°F**

8. What is the mean of the temperatures recorded from 1 AM through 6 PM?
   - **H. -1.3°F**
   - **T. 4.2°F**

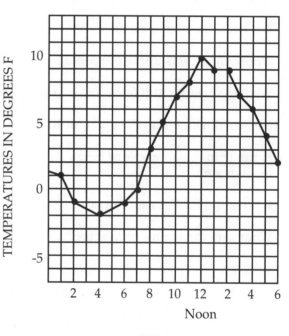

**HOURLY TEMPERATURES
JANUARY 1**

TEMPERATURES IN DEGREES F

TIME

— — — — — — — — !
1   2   3   4   5   6   7   8

How is a sick bird like robbing a bank?

Put the letter of the correct answer on the appropriately-numbered line below.

The Pin Busters Bowling Team bowled 3 games.   Use their scores to answer these questions:

1. Who had the greatest range of scores?

S. Wally   O. Molly

2. Who had the lowest mean score?

R. Holly   H. Dolly

3. What was the mean score for the team (for all 15 games)?

L. 166   P. 171

4. Who bowled the median game score (for all 15 games)?

J. Pauly   R. Holly

5. What was the team mean for game 1?

Y.   171   G. 181

6. Who had the higher mean score?

C. Molly   B. Pauly

7. Whose mean was above the overall team mean?

I. Wally   K. Dolly

8. Who was nearest the team mean in game 3?

V. Pauly   S. Wally

9. For which game was the team mean lowest?

A. #2   U. #1

10. Is the team mean above or below the median game?

E. Below   F. Above

11. Who had the least range of scores?

L. Holly   G. Pauly

12. What was the team's total score?

T. 2491   W. 2563

	GAME 1	GAME 2	GAME 3	TOTAL PINS
Dolly	142	136	157	
Molly	173	131	209	
Pauly	169	171	180	
Wally	216	154	172	
Holly	153	167	161	
TEAM SCORES				

$\overline{}$ $\overline{}$ $\overline{}$ $\overline{}$ $\overline{}$ $\overline{}$ $\overline{}$ $\overline{}$ $\overline{}$ $\overline{}$ $\overline{}$ $\overline{}$ $\overline{}$ $\overline{}$ $\overline{}$ $\overline{}$ $\overline{}$ $\overline{}$!

12 2 10 5   9 4 10 6 1 12 2 7 3 3 10 9 11 3 10 8

SELF-TEST

1. Which bar graph best represents the frequency table?

	Frequency
x	卌 IIII
y	III
z	卌

   a.   b.   c.   d.

2. The third letter of the name of the graph that best illustrates relative amounts of chemicals in a substance is

   a. c   b. r   c. n   d. s

3. Which of the following is most affected by one extremely low score?

   a. mean   b. median   c. mode   d. All are equally affected.

4. Which is false for the data 2, 2, 5, 4, 2 ?

   a. The mode equals the median.   b. The mean is greater than the median.

   c. The median is 3.   d. The mode is less than the mean.

5. Find the median, standard deviation, mean and variance for the following data: 2, 8, 10, 14, 26. Add your answers together to obtain an answer below.

   a. 84   b. 124   c. 94   d. None of a, b, or c.

6. What is the sum of the mean and standard deviation of the following data: 0, 24, 32, 48, 96 ?

   a. 78   b. 40   c. 72   d. 32

7. The following test scores have been recorded by Ms. Burton. What is the z-score (to the nearest hundredth) for the second to the highest score?
Scores: 24, 72, 79, 83, 83, 86, 90, 123.

   a. 0.14   b. 10   c. 2.55   d. 0.39

8. Which is true when comparing two sets of scores?

   (i) The larger standard deviation comes from the set with the larger mean.

   (ii) If the means are equal, so are the variances.

   a. i only   b. ii only   c. i and ii   d. Neither is true.

9. Given 12, 14, 14, 20, which number has a z-score of -1 ?

   a. 12   b. 14   c. 20   d. None of a, b, or c.

10. Which of the following is false about a normal distribution?

   (i)   Mean = median

   (ii) The higher the standard deviation, the higher the "peak".

   (iii) The interval from 2 standard deviations below the mean to 2 standard deviations
         above the mean contains about 68% of the measurements.

   a. i and ii only   b. i and iii only   c. ii and iii only   d. None of a, b, or c.

SOLUTIONS

Warm-up
Sum -15, $x = 0$, $y = -3$

Hands-on Activities

Activity 1
Answers will vary.

Activity 2
1. Let each mark represent 5° C.
3. a. Denver;   Denver   b. Washington;   Denver;   Washington
   c. 12 midnight to 12 noon and after 6 pm   d. 12 noon to 6 pm
   e. 12 noon and 6 pm   f. 29° C; 26° C   g. 8:30 am   h. 21° C; 24° C

Activity 3
1. a. A drawing of a book would be one possibility   b. About 10, about 81, probably not
   c. Less than 1/2 a symbol, about 4, probably not
   d. Probably something between 50,000 and 100,000
   e. For example, if you let each symbol represent 100,000 you could round to the nearest
       25,000 and draw quarters of the symbol.
3. a. California, Montana   b. Kentucky, Montana   c. Michigan
   d. Massachusetts

Activity 4
Answers will vary.
3. More representative; may have been a week-end, a day with no classes, you might have
   been ill or worked overtime, etc.

Activity 5
Answer will vary.

Activity 6
Answers will vary.

5. a. Median   b. A small group of tall or short people in the sample

     c. A few very tall or very short people   d. It is the middle height.

Activity 7
2. Range = 49 points; mode = 67; median = 64.5; mean = 60.57

3. Dennis' graph is the most accurate even though he grouped the data. The sectors in Craig's graph are the wrong size and Kristin's graph suggests scores that do not exist (between 35 and 40 for example).

Mental Math
The bar graph is most accurate. The area of the circles in the pictograph is misleading. The percentages in the circle graph are inaccurate.

Exercises

What do you put on a sick pig?   OINKMENT!

How is a sick bird like robbing a bank?   THEY ARE BOTH ILL-EAGLES!

Self-Test
1. d   **2.** b   **3.** a   **4.** c   **5.** c   **6.** c   **7.** d   **8.** d   **9.** a   **10.** c

RESOURCE ARTICLES

Barson, Alan, and Lois Barson. "Ideas." *Arithmetic Teacher* 35 (March 1988): 19-24. *Activities involving gathering and interpreting data.*

Bruni, James V., and Helene J. Silverman. "Developing Concepts in Probability and Statistics - and Much More." *Arithmetic Teacher* 33 (February 1986): 34-37. *A four-step approach using manipulatives to develop statistics concepts.*

Bryan, Elizabeth H. "Exploring Data with Box Plots." *Mathematics Teacher* 81 (November 1988): 658-663. *Activities for organizing, displaying, and comparing data with box-and-whiskers graphs.*

Collis, Betty. "Teaching Descriptive and Inferential Statistics Using a Classroom Microcomputer." *Mathematics Teacher* 76 (May 1983): 318-322. *A framework for integrating a microcomputer into a statistics unit.*

Dickinson, J. Craig. "Gather, Organize, Display: Mathematics for the Information Society." *Arithmetic Teacher* 34 (December 1986): 12-15. *Activities for organizing and displaying data.*

Goldman, Phyllis H. "Teaching Arithmetic Averaging: An Activity Approach." *Arithmetic Teacher* 37 (March 1990): 38-43. *Sequence of tasks developing concept of mean.*

Hinders, Duane C. "Examples of the Use of Statistics in Society." *Mathematics Teacher* 83 (February 1990): 136-141. *Examples include opinion polling, sports, draft lottery, and the law.*

Kelly, Margaret. "Elementary School Activity: Graphing the Stock Market." *Arithmetic Teacher* 33 (March 1986): 17-20. *Graphing activities based on the stock market.*

Kimberling, Clark. "Mean, Standard Deviation, and Stopping the Stars." *Mathematics Teacher* 77 (November 1984): 633-636. *Generating data on the spot with computers for early experiences with the study of statistics.*

Kissane, Barry V. "'Easy' Statistical Exercises." *Mathematics Teacher* 76 (February 1983): 101-104. *Exercises with "nice" numbers for initial experience with statistical computations.*

Klitz, Ralph H., Jr., and Joseph F. Hofmeister. "Statistics in the Middle School." *Arithmetic Teacher* 26 (February 1979): 35-36, 59. *Getting students involved with data sets that are of genuine interest and concern to the students.*

Landwehr, James M., and Ann E. Watkins. "Stem-and-Leaf Plots." *Mathematics Teacher* 78 (October 1985): 528-532, 537-538. *A method for displaying data.*

McNeil, Vanessa. "From the File: Change Partners." *Arithmetic Teacher* 37 (December 1989): 21. *Activity builds on work with coins and leads to constructing a human graph and then a chalkboard graph.*

Pagni, David L. "A Television Programming Challenge: A Cooperative Group Activity That Uses Mathematics." *Arithmetic Teacher* 36 (January 1989): 7-9. *An interdisciplinary activity to gather and interpret data, draw conclusions and make suggestions based on their findings.*

Ryoti, Don E. "Computer Corner." *Arithmetic Teacher* 34 (April 1987): 42-44. *Use of computer to process data.*

Shaw, Jean. "Let's Do It: Making Graphs." *Arithmetic Teacher* 31 (January 1984): 7-11. *Organizing data and interpreting results by gathering data from classmates.*

Shaw, Jean. "Let's Do It: Dealing with Data." *Arithmetic Teacher* 31 (May 1984): 9-15. *Experiences with collecting and handling data.*

Shulte, Albert P. "A Case for Statistics." *Arithmetic Teacher* 26 (February 1979): 24. *A rationale for teaching statistics in the elementary and middle school.*

Zawojewski, Judith S. "Teaching Statistics: Mean, Median, and Mode." *Arithmetic Teacher* 35 (March 1988): 25-26. *Applications of research to understanding of statistics.*

DIRECTIONS IN EDUCATION

Questioning Strategies - The Answer Is...But What Was The Question?

Questions posed by the classroom teacher allow the teacher to probe and extend student understanding, to promote divergent thinking, and to allow students to hear divergent responses, as well as to provide the teacher with immediate feedback on student progress which determines the appropriate course for the lesson. Both the quality of the teacher's questions and the teacher's behavior set the stage for thoughtful responses by students. By explaining, modelling, and encouraging appropriate responses, the teacher can establish a classroom climate in which students are actively involved in the questioning process. Students can learn to consider answers to questions posed by the teacher or by others. When this thoughtful climate for questioning is established, the quality of student responses is enhanced, thus providing the teacher with rich and meaningful glimpses of student thinking.

What kinds of questions may be posed by the teacher?

- Questions may ask for simple recall of factual information —"What is 4 times 5?" or "What are the factors of 12?"

- Conceptual understanding can be checked with questions such as —"How is multiplication like addition?" or "Describe the relationship between fractions and decimals."

- Questions can be posed in such a way that divergent responses are encouraged as well —"If the answer is 7, what is the question?" or "How would our use of mathematics be different if we did not have multiplication or division?"

- Student responses can provide the starting point for further questions —"Craig says that decimals are fractions written in a different way. Do you agree or disagree? Why?" or "What did you do to arrive at that answer?"

- Questions may be used to assess the group's readiness for instruction and to prescribe specific instructional needs —"Tell me all the ways I can make a mistake in working this problem." or "What strategies might be useful in solving this problem?"

- Students can be encouraged to think about their own responses through the use of questions which ask them to examine their thinking —"Why did you decide to multiply?" or "You drew a picture. How did that help you to solve this problem?"

Teacher behaviors can enhance the quality of student responses.

- Use wait time to encourage students to think about their responses. Wait time may vary according to the type of response desired. For example, simple recall may require wait time of 3 seconds or less. Questions that require divergent responses should be given wait time of 15 to 20 seconds depending on the age of the students and the complexity of the question. Older students may learn to accept even longer wait time. **It is essential that teachers avoid calling on or recognizing any student until after the wait time has been given. This encourages all students to engage in thinking about an appropriate response to the question.**

- Value student responses by accepting them, clarifying them when necessary, probing for further information when appropriate, and using the response as the basis for further questions when possible. The teacher's use of student responses will be determined by factors such as the level of thinking required by the question, the needs of the individual student for certain types of feedback, and the overall goals of the questioning. **Do not treat the response as the end point of the question/answer process, but rather as an integral part of an on-going discussion.**

- Model careful consideration of student questions by avoiding impulsive responses on your part. Create a classroom climate in which students are encouraged to pose questions for the teacher or for other students. Value student questions by answering them thoughtfully and by extending the questions to other students in the classroom. **Help students to see that questioning is a two-way activity and not something reserved for teachers.**

- Teach and reinforce student behaviors which enrich the questioning process in the classroom. Students can learn to clarify their own responses and to ask for clarification from others. They can learn to probe for more information and they can learn to encourage the questions of others. **Create a climate which encourages comments such as, "That's an interesting question. Let me think about it." or "When you say... do you mean...?"**

When you think about questioning strategies, ask yourself:

- What kinds of questions are used most often in my lessons?

- Can I develop a series of questions which range from recall to divergent thinking on a single topic?

- How much time elapses between my question and the acceptance of a response?

- Can I list factors such as teacher behaviors or student behaviors which enhance/inhibit questioning in the classroom?

To learn more:

Costa, Art, editor. *Developing Minds, Part VI*. Virginia: Association for Supervision and Curriculum Development, 1985.

Hanson, J. Robert, Harvey F. Silver and R.W. Strong. *The Questioning Styles and Strategies*. New Jersey: Hanson, Silver & Strong Associates, 1986.

11 | Probability

THEME: Using Mathematics to Predict

Strategy Review:
Use Direct Reasoning.
This strategy was
presented in
Chapter 3.

Guess how this grid is colored.
Row 1 has a yellow, a blue, and a red.
Column 2 has 2 yellows and a red.
Row 2 has 2 greens and a red.
Column 3 has a red, a green, and a blue.
One of the diagonals has 2 reds and a yellow.

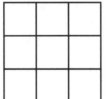

HANDS-ON ACTIVITIES

Probability has useful applications in the sciences, in business, and in sports because it indicates the likelihood of uncertain events. The first few activities introduce you to the concept of probability.

OBJECTIVE: **Compute experimental and theoretical probability**

You Will Need: Materials Card 11.1

1. One kind of probability is called **experimental probability**. The experimental probability of an event is found by actually performing the experiment several times and then comparing the number of outcomes favorable to the event to the total number of outcomes. In other words, the experimental probability (denoted Pr) of an event E is

$$Pr(E) = \frac{\text{number of outcomes favorable to E}}{\text{total number of outcomes}}$$

For example, cut out one block each of those labeled blue, red, and yellow from Materials Card 11.1. Place them face down on the table and mix them up. Draw one, record its color, and return it to the table face down. Draw a block from the table 10 times, tallying your results below.

■ BLUE   **▯ RED**   **▯ YELLOW**

The experimental probability of drawing a blue block is

$$Pr(blue) = \frac{\text{number of times blue was drawn}}{\text{total number of draws}} = \frac{}{10}$$

Determine the following.

a. Pr(red) = _____   b. Pr(yellow) = _____

2. Repeat part 1 and compute the experimental probabilities again.

a. Pr(blue) = _____   b. Pr(red) = _____   c. Pr(yellow) = _____

Do you get the same experimental probabilities?

3. The **theoretical probability** of an event, if all outcomes are equally likely, is found by considering an ideal experiment and comparing the total possible outcomes of an event to the total number of outcomes in the sample space. Consider the blue, red, and yellow blocks again. To determine the theoretical probability (denoted P) of drawing a blue block, we consider how many blocks satisfy the condition "blue" out of the total number of blocks. Since there is one blue block and three blocks altogether, P(blue) = 1/3. Determine the following.

a. P(red) = _____   b. P(yellow) = _____

4. Using all the cubes from Materials Card 11.1, perform the experiment of selecting a cube. Repeat 10 times and compute the following probabilities.

   a. Pr(blue) = _____   b. Pr(red) = _____   c. Pr(yellow) = _____

   d. P(blue) = _____   e. P(red) = _____   f. P(yellow) = _____

 **OBJECTIVE:** **Compare experimental and theoretical probability**

You Will Need: Materials Card 11.2

1. Look at the circle below. Compute the theoretical probability of landing in each area.

   a. P(plain) = _____

   b. P(striped) = _____

   c. P(dotted) = _____

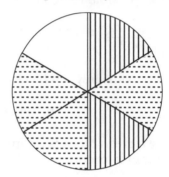

2. Now, using the spinner as directed on Materials Card 11.2, spin 10 times and record your spins here.

Plain	
Striped	
Dotted	

Compute your experimental probability after 10 spins.

   a. Pr(plain) = _____   b. Pr(striped) = _____   c. Pr(dotted) = _____

Continue spinning and recording 40 more times, then compute the experimental probability again, based on 50 spins.

   d. Pr(plain) = _____   e. Pr(striped) = _____   f. Pr(dotted) = _____

Which experimental probability most closely resembles the theoretical probability?

OBJECTIVE: **Explore properties of probability**

1. Suppose that a box contains blue, red, and yellow blocks. An experiment consists of drawing a block from the box and recording its color. Suppose that the experiment is repeated 10 times.

   a. What is the fewest number of times that the blue block could have been chosen? _____

      What is the smallest possible value for Pr(blue)? _____

   b. What is the greatest number of times that the blue block could have been chosen? _____

      What is the largest possible value for Pr(blue)? _____

   c. Fill in the blanks.   _____ ≤ Pr(blue) ≤ _____

2. Suppose that a box contains only red blocks. Compute the following.

   a. Pr(green) = _____   b. Pr(red) = _____

   The event of selecting a green block is an **impossible** event. The event of drawing a red block is an event **certain** to occur.

3. Suppose that a box contains 2 blue blocks, 4 red blocks, and 6 yellow blocks. Compute the following.

   a. P(blue) = _____   b. P(red) = _____   c. P(yellow) = _____

   d. P(blue) + P(red) + P(yellow) = _____

4. Suppose that a box contains 3 blue blocks, 5 green blocks, and 2 red blocks. In how many ways can you select a blue block or a green block? _____

   a. What is P(blue or green)? _____

   Compute the following.

   b. P(blue) = _____   c. P(green) = _____   d. P(blue or green) = _____

   e. In this case, the event of drawing a blue block is disjoint from the event of drawing a green block. Is the following true? _____

            P(blue or green) = P(blue) + P(green)

5. Suppose that a box contains 2 blue blocks, 3 yellow blocks, and 4 red blocks. The event of "not selecting a blue block" is called the **complement** of the event of "selecting a blue block." Compute the following.

a. P(blue) = _____

b. P(not blue) = _____

c. P(yellow) = _____

d. P(not yellow) = _____

e. P(red) = _____

f. P(not red) = _____

g. How is the probability of the complement of an event related to the probability of the event?

Summarize the properties of probability.

a. For any event E, _____ ≤ P(E) ≤ _____

b. P(impossible event) = _____

c. P(event certain to occur) = _____

d. If A and B are disjoint events, then P(A or B) = _____

e. If $\overline{A}$ denotes the complement of event A, then P($\overline{A}$) = _____

Now that you have computed probabilities for some simple experiments, let's consider some more complicated situations. The next few activities introduce some useful tools for computing probabilities.

OBJECTIVE: **Compute probabilities when tossing dice**

You Will Need: Your die from Materials Card 2.2 or a pair of dice

1. Toss your pair of dice 20 times (or the single die twice each time), and tally the sum each time in the table below.

2	3	4	5	6	7	8	9	10	11	12

Compute the probabilities of getting the following sums.

a. Pr(7) = _____

b. Pr(3) = _____

c. Pr(12) = _____

d. Pr(less than 5) = _____

e. Pr(more than 6) = _____

2. Now let's analyze all the outcomes in another way. Fill in the sums in the chart.

Die #1

+	1	2	3	4	5	6
1						
2						
3						
4						
5						
6						

Die #2

Summarize the number of ways of getting each possible outcome in the table.

Sum	2	3	4	5	6	7	8	9	10	11	12
Number of ways											

This table will come in handy in dice-tossing experiments.

3. Compute the following probabilities.

a. P(7) = _____

b. P(3) = _____

c. P(12) = _____

d. P(less than 5) = _____

e. P(more than 6) = _____

OBJECTIVE: Compute probabilities when tossing coins

You Will Need: 2 coins

1. Two coins are tossed 10 times. If there is a match (two heads or two tails), Player 1 gets a point. If there is no match (one head and one tail), player 2 gets 2 points.

   Toss both coins 10 times and record each toss below:

Toss #	1	2	3	4	5	6	7	8	9	10	
Match											Total Matches _____
No Match											Total No Matches _____

   Who won the game?_____

   Based on your experiment, compute the following.

   a. Pr(match) = _____   b. Pr(no match) = _____

2. Now let's compute the theoretical probability of "match" or "no match." First, we must count the possible outcomes. A **tree diagram** can be used to represent all possible outcomes when tossing coins.

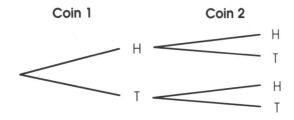

   By following the branches of our tree we see that there are four possible outcomes: { (H,H), (H,T), (T,H), (T,T) } .

   Now compute the theoretical probabilities:

   a. P(match) = _____   b. P(no match) = _____

3. Is this a fair game?_____ How can we make it fair?

OBJECTIVE: **Use Pascal's triangle to compute probabilities**

You Will Need: 1 coin

1. Toss your coin three times and record how it landed (HTH for example). Perform 9 more sets of three tosses until you have recorded ten outcomes. Compute the following probabilities.

    a. Pr(exactly 1 head) = ____   b. Pr(at least one head) = ____

    c. Pr(all tails) = ____   d. Pr(less than two tails) = ____

2. Again, a tree diagram is useful in representing all possible outcomes.

First toss

Second toss

Third toss

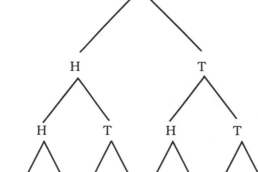

List all possible outcomes. (For example, the leftmost branch is represented by HHH.)

Compute the following probabilities.

    a. P(exactly 1 head) = ____   b. P(at least one head) = ____

    c. P(all tails) = ____   d. P(less than 2 tails) = ____

3. Extend the tree from part 2 to illustrate all the outcomes for tossing the coin 4 times. Complete the following tables.

Toss a coin	1 time		2 times			3 times				4 times				
Number of H's	0	1	0	1	2	0	1	2	3	0	1	2	3	4
Number of ways	1	1	1	2	1									

4. The lower rows of the tables in part 3 can be arranged to show an array called **Pascal's triangle**. See if you can discover the pattern that yields each row from the entries in the previous row. Hint: Consider the lines drawn.

Pascal's Triangle

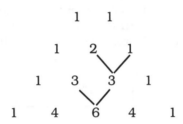

Extend the triangle to the row that begins 1 8 . . . and ends . . . 8 1.

Give an interpretation of that row in terms of a coin-tossing experiment. Hint: Consider what the top row of the table for tossing a coin 8 times would look like in part 3.

5. Using Pascal's triangle, compute the following probabilities.

a. P(4 heads when tossing 6 coins) = _____

b. P(at least 5 heads when tossing 8 coins) = _____

c. P(at least 1 head when tossing 5 coins) = _____
    Hint: Consider the complement.

OBJECTIVE: **Compute probability geometrically**

You Will Need: Materials Card 11.7, thumbtacks

1. An airplane drops a box of relief supplies onto a drought-stricken savannah. Because of wind currents and variations in release elevation and location, it is expected that the box will land in a random location on the field. If the field is divided as pictured, estimate the probability that it drops in section A.

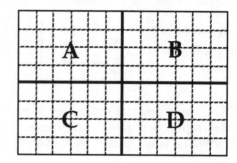

2. On Materials Card 11.7, divide the grid into regions as indicated above. Model the situation by randomly dropping thumbtacks from a cup onto the grid. The region in which the point lands determines the outcome. If the thumbtack bounces off the grid, do not record the toss. Tally results until at least 50 drops have been recorded (dropping several tacks at the same time will speed the process).

Plot A	Plot B	Plot C	Plot D	Total

3. a.   What is the experimental probability of landing in region A?

   b.   What is the theoretical probability of landing in region A?

   c.   Does the box have an equal chance to land on all parts of the field? Why or why not?

4. If the field were divided as shown, estimate the probability that the box lands in region E? in region F?

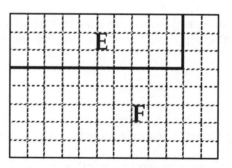

5. Shade the grid on Materials Card 11.7 and repeat the experiment in part 2 with these regions.
   What is the experimental probability that the box lands in region E? in region F?

6. How many squares are in region E? in region F? in the two plots combined?

   What is the theoretical probability of landing in region E? in region F?

OBJECTIVE: **Compute probability geometrically**

You Will Need: Pennies, toothpicks or pins, paper

1. Draw parallel lines 1 inch apart on a sheet of paper. If a penny were dropped randomly on this sheet of paper, what do you think the probability would be that the penny will not land on a line?

2. Perform the following experiment.

    a.   Toss 10 pennies on the paper 10 times, or similarly obtain 100 tosses. Coins that land off the paper do not count and should be retossed.

    b.   Count the number of pennies that do not fall on a line.

    c.   What is the experimental probability that a coin will not land on a line?

3. The diameter of a penny is 3/4 inch. In what regions must the center of the penny fall for the penny not to be touching a line?

    How does the area of these regions compare with the total area?

    What is the theoretical probability that a coin will not land on a line?

4. If lines were drawn both directions to form a 1-inch grid on the paper, then what would the probability be that a coin will not land on a line?

5. The following famous problem was first presented by Count Buffon, a French naturalist, in the 1700's. Buffon's Needle Problem is a way of approximating π using probability methods.

    a.   As the "needles", use short needles, pins or toothpicks. Cutting toothpicks to 1-inch lengths would work. Find the length, l, of the objects you are using.

    b.   Choose a distance, d, which is twice as long as l, and draw parallel lines d units apart on a sheet of paper.

    c.   The "needles" are randomly and repeatedly dropped from a reasonable height onto the sheet of paper. Count the number landing on a line and the total number dropped. What is the probability, P, that the "needle" touches one of the lines?

    d.   Compute 1/P. By calculus this can be shown theoretically to equal the value of π. How close was your experimental value?

OBJECTIVE: **Analyze a game using probabilities**

You Will Need: Your die from Activity 4 and a coin

1. Dennis the delivery boy delivers sandwiches for the local Deli. His boss tells Dennis that he can keep all of the tips from businesses A, B, D and W, Y, Z. He must give his boss all of the tips from businesses C and X. Is the boss making Dennis a fair offer?

A	B	C	D	DELI	W	X	Y	Z

Place your coin on the square marked DELI. The destination of each delivery is determined by rolling a die 4 times. If the roll is odd, move the coin one space to the left. If the roll is even, move the coin one space to the right. Repeat this procedure for four rolls of the die. Record where Dennis made the delivery at the end of 4 rolls (or if he returned to the deli for directions and no tip). This constitutes one turn. Take 10 turns.

NOTE: Always place the coin back on the square marked DELI after a turn of 4 rolls is completed.

	TOTAL
A	
B	
C	
D	
Deli	
W	
X	
Y	
Z	

Number of tips
Dennis keeps =_____

Number of tips
boss keeps = _____

Number of times for
no tip = _____

Is this a fair deal for Dennis? _____ Why or why not?

2. Let's list all the possible outcomes of 4 rolls of the dice:

No Evens	1 Even	2 Evens	3 Evens	4 Evens
OOOO	EOOO	EEOO	EEEO	EEEE
	OEOO	EOEO	EEOE	
	OOEO	EOOE	EOEE	
	OOOE	OEEO	OEEE	
		OEOE		
		OOEE		

To compute the theoretical probability of landing on each business, follow each possible turn and place a tally mark where the delivery was made (i.e. the square you land on at the end of 4 rolls). Compute the following probabilities.

a. P(keeping tip) =_____   b. P(giving tip to boss) =_____   c. P(no tip) = _____

Is Dennis' boss fair? ____ Explain.

OBJECTIVE: **Compute expected value**

You Will Need: Your die from Activity 4

1. In a certain gambling casino, a player rolls two dice or one die twice. He wins $5 if he rolls a sum of 7 or 11 and loses $1 if he throws anything else. Play the game for 36 throws to see who has the advantage, the player or the casino.   Record your throws here:

a.   The total number of 7's and 11's
_____ × $5 = Player's winnings

_____

b.   The total number of all other throws = Casino's winnings

_____

```
2   3   4   5   6   7   8   9   10  11  12
```

Based on your experiment, who will come out ahead?_____

2. Using the chart you made in Activity 4, compute the following probabilities.

a. P(7) = _____   b. P(11) = _____   c. P(7 or 11) = _____

3. Complete the following table.

	Win (7 or 11)	Lose
Outcome	$5.00	-$1.00
Probability		

Compute: (Amount won) × P(win) + (Amount lost) × P(lose) = _____

This is called the **expected value** of the payoff. Do you, the player, come out ahead, or does the casino? How is this related to the expected value of the payoff?

4. Repeat part 3, assuming that a loss costs $2.00. Who comes out ahead now?

OBJECTIVE: **Do a simulation**

You Will Need: A coin and a die

1. Frank and Hazel are lost in the University Library. Frank likes history and Hazel likes poetry. They must stay together since only Hazel has a library card. The library is set up like a maze because Franny, the librarian loves to play tricks on people. Frank and Hazel are now at Point A. At points A, B, C, and D, all choices are equally likely.

   Where do you predict Frank and Hazel will end up - in the history section or the poetry section?

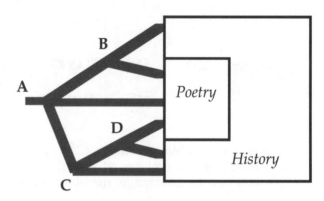

2. To simulate this experiment, roll the die at point A. If it lands with 1 or 2, go up; if it lands 3 or 4, go straight; if 5 or 6, go down. At points B, C, and D, flip the coin. Go up if head, down if tail. Perform this simulation 10 times. Record the destination each time.

Repetition

	1	2	3	4	5	6	7	8	9	10	
Poetry											Pr(Poetry) = _____
History											Pr(History) = _____

3. We can use a tree diagram to determine the theoretical probability of ending in the poetry or history section.

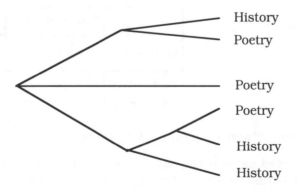

Place the appropriate probabilities along each branch of the tree. To find the probability of following any particular path, multiply the probabilities of the branches covered.

a. How many of the paths end in the history section? _____

   What is the sum of the probabilities for those paths? _____

b. How many of the paths end in the poetry section? _____

   What is the sum of the probabilities for those paths? _____

c. Which destination is more likely?

MENTAL MATH

Fern, the school cook, surveyed 20 students to determine their favorite lunch. The results of her survey were:

HAMBURGERS	10
HOT DOGS	5
PIZZA	3
FISHWICH	2

She wants to please everyone once in a while. What is the probability that a student will be smiling when he comes through the lunch line on Hot Dog Day? _____

on Hamburger Day? _____   on Fishwich Day? _____

What is the probability he will *not* be smiling on Pizza Day? _____

EXERCISES

What do you get when you cross an owl with an oyster?

For each problem below, find the correct answer. Write the letter of that answer on the line above the problem number it matches at the bottom of the page.
Use the answers below to complete problems 1 - 4.

B 1/2   **V** 1/4   **A** 1/3   **C** 7/12   **L** 2/3   **J** 3/4   **F** 1/6   **U** 5/12

Look at this spinner. If the arrow is spun, what is the probability that it will stop on a number that is

1. a multiple of 2?
2. a multiple of 3?
3. a multiple of 2 *and* a multiple of 3?
4. a multiple of 2 *or* a multiple of 3?

Use the answers below to complete problems 5 - 18.

H 7/15   **O** 1/3   **I** 2/5   **W** 1/15

T 2/15   **P** 3/5   **S** 4/15   **K** 11/15

R 2/3   **M** 8/15   **E** 1/5   **D** 4/5

G 1   **Y** 1/2   **N** 0   **Q** 1/4

If a card is picked at random from the group of cards above, what is the probability that the card

5. is hexagonal (six-sided)?
6. is dotted?
7. has more than 4 sides *and* is not white?
8. is striped?
9. is triangular?
10. is a multiple of 3 *or* square?
11. is not dotted?

12. is even *or* dotted?
13. is odd?
14. is dotted *and* pentagonal (five-sided)?
15. is not circular?
16. is not triangular?
17. is dotted *or* striped *or* white?
18. is odd *and* a multiple of 2?

$$\overline{}_2 \quad \overline{}_1 \; \overline{}_8 \; \overline{}_{11} \; \overline{}_{15} \quad \overline{}_5 \; \overline{}_{10} \; \overline{}_2 \; \overline{}_5$$

$$\overline{}_{16} \; \overline{}_7 \; \overline{}_7 \; \overline{}_{12} \; \overline{}_9 \quad \overline{}_{15} \; \overline{}_{11} \; \overline{}_6 \; \overline{}_{12} \; \overline{}_{12} \; \overline{}_8 \; \overline{}_{18} \; \overline{}_{17} \quad \overline{}_{12} \; \overline{}_7 \; \overline{}_2 \; \overline{}_{11} \; \overline{}_4 \; \overline{}_9$$

$$\overline{}_6 \; \overline{}_3 \quad \overline{}_{14} \; \overline{}_8 \; \overline{}_9 \; \overline{}_{15} \; \overline{}_6 \; \overline{}_{13} \, !$$

SELF-TEST

1. If you have 3 sweaters, 4 skirts, and 5 pairs of shoes, how many different sweater/skirt/ (pairs of) shoes combinations can you wear?

   a. 60   b. 12   c. $(3^4)^5$ d. None of a, b, or c.

2. The sample space of the experiment "tossing 3 coins" consists of how many elements?

   a. 6   b. 27   c. 8   d. 9

3. Which of the following is the tree diagram for the experiment "toss 4 coins"?

   a.    b.    c.

   d. None of a, b, or c.

4. Which of the sample spaces for the following experiments consists of an odd number of elements?

   a. Tossing 3 dice   b. Tossing 7 coins
   c. Drawing a card from a 52-card deck   d. None of a, b, or c.

5. The probability of tossing at least two heads if six coins are tossed is:

   a. 27/32   b. 15/16   c. 57/64   d. None of a, b, or c.

6. Find the probability of getting exactly 2 heads and a number greater than 8 when tossing 3 coins and 2 dice.

   a. 13/44   b. 5/12   c. 5/48   d. 13/36

7. What is the probability of getting 100% on a multiple choice (a,b,c,d) math quiz? There are 12 questions and you guess on all 12 of them.

   a. $\dfrac{1}{12^4}$ b. $\dfrac{1}{4^{12}}$ c. $\dfrac{1}{4}$ d. $\dfrac{1}{48}$

8. There are 26 names in a hat, 13 girls' names, and 13 guys' names. What is the probability that 2 girls' names will be drawn?

   a. 4/25   b. 1/4   c. 6/25   d. 1/3

9. If two cubes have the numbers 1, 2, 3, and 4 on each of four sides
    leaving the other two sides with 0, what is the probability of getting
    an even number as a sum on the two cubes?

    a. 1   b. 5/9   c.   1/3   d. None of a, b, or c.

10. The odds that the horse Apollo 1000 wins Race 1 are 4 : 5, and the odds that he wins
    Race 6 are 11 : 3. What is the probability that he wins Race 1 and comes back to win
    Race 6 also?

    a. $\dfrac{4}{5} + \dfrac{3}{11}$ b. $\dfrac{4}{5} \times \dfrac{3}{11}$ c. $\dfrac{4}{9} \times \dfrac{11}{14}$ d. $\dfrac{4}{9} + \dfrac{3}{14}$

SOLUTIONS

Warm-up   B Y R
                 G R G
                 Y Y B

Hands-on Activities

Activity 1
1. Answers will vary.   2. Answers will vary and may differ from results in part 1.
3. a. 1/3   b. 1/3
4. Experimental probabilities will vary.   d. 1/2   e. 3/8   f. 1/8

Activity 2
1. a. 1/6   b. 1/3   c. 1/2
2. Answers will vary.   Generally, experimental probability will be closer to theoretical
    probability after more repetitions.

Activity 3
1. a. Zero times, 0   b. 10 times, 1   c. 0, 1
2. a. 0   b. 1
3. a. 1/6   b. 1/3   c. 1/2   d. 1
4. 8 ways   a. 4/5   b. 3/10   c. 1/2   d. 4/5   e. yes
5. a. 2/9   b. 7/9   c. 1/3   d. 2/3   e. 4/9   f. 5/9
    g. P(complement of event E) = 1 - P(event E)
    Summarize: a. 0, 1   b. 0   c. 1   d. P(A) + P(B)   e. 1 - P(A)

Activity 4
1. Answers will vary.
2. Usual addition table   1 2 3 4 5 6 5 4 3 2 1
3. a. 6/36 = 1/6   b. 1/18   c. 1/36   d. 1/6   e. 7/12

Activity 5
1. Answers will vary.   **2.** a. 1/2   b. 1/2
3. No. Give an equal number of points for match and no match.

Activity 6
1. Answers will vary.
2. HHH, HHT, HTH, HTT, THH, THT, TTH, TTT   a. 3/8   b. 7/8   c. 1/8   d. 1/2
3. 1, 3, 3, 1; 1, 4, 6, 4, 1
4. Add the two elements of the row above.
   Next rows: 1, 5, 10, 10, 5, 1;   1, 6, 15, 20, 15,   6, 1;
   1, 7, 21, 35, 35, 21, 7, 1; 1, 8, 28, 56, 70, 56, 28, 8, 1;
   There is 1 way of getting no heads, 8 ways of getting 1 head and 7 tails, 28 ways of getting
   2 heads and 6 tails, etc. when tossing 8 coins (or tossing a coin 8 times).
5. a. 15/64   b. 93/256   c. 31/32

Activity 7
3. b. 1/4   c. Yes, because all 4 regions have the same area.
6. 30, 66, 96, 30/96 = 5/16, 66/96 = 11/16

Activity 8
3. The center must land in the 1/4-inch strip down the middle between lines. This has an
   area 1/4 of the total area. 1/4
4. 1/16. The center would have to land in a square 1/4 inch by 1/4 inch in the center of
   each 1 inch by 1 inch square.
5. Answers will vary.

Activity 9
1. Answers will vary.   **2.** a. 1/8   b. 1/2   c. 3/8
   No. Dennis will only keep the tip for 2 out of 16 deliveries.

Activity 10
1. Answers will vary.   **2.** a. 1/6   b. 1/18   c. 2/9
3. 2/9, 7/9, (2/9) × (5) + (7/9) × (-1) = 1/3 = $0.33
   The player comes out ahead by an average of $0.33 per game.
4. (2/9) × (5) + (7/9) × (-2) = -4/9 = - $0.44; The casino gains an average of $0.44 per game.

Activity 11
1. Answers will vary.   **2.** Answers will vary.
3. a. 3 paths, 5/12   b. 3 paths, 7/12   c. Poetry

Mental Math
Hot Dog = 1/4; Hamburger = 1/2; Fishwich = 1/10; Not smiling on Pizza = 17/20

Exercises
What do you get when you cross an owl with an oyster?
   A bird that keeps dropping pearls of wisdom!

Self-Test
1. a   **2.** c   **3.** a   **4.** d   **5.** c   **6.** c   **7.** b   **8.** c   **9.** b   **10.** c

RESOURCE ARTICLES

Bright, George. "Teaching Mathematics with Technology: Probability Simulations." *Arithmetic Teacher* 36 (May 1989): 16-18. *Short program in BASIC or Logo to generate data for probability activities.*

Bruni, James V., and Helene J. Silverman. "Developing Concepts in Probability and Statistics - and Much More." *Arithmetic Teacher* 33 (February 1986): 34-37. *A four-step approach using manipulatives to develop probability concepts.*

Ernest, Paul. "Introducing the Concept of Probability." *Mathematics Teacher* 77 (October 1984): 524-525. *An intuitive approach to probability.*

Fennell, Francis (Skip). "Ya Gotta Play to Win: A Probability and Statistics Unit for the Middle Grades." *Arithmetic Teacher* 31 (March 1984): 26-30. *Relating probability, statistics, and particularly gaming to the curriculum in grades 5-8.*

Haigh, William E. "Using Microcomputers to Solve Probability Problems." *Mathematics Teacher* 78 (February 1985): 124-126. *Using the computer to simulate or imitate probability problems.*

Horak, Virginia M., and Willis J. Horak. "Let's Do It: Take a Chance." *Arithmetic Teacher* 30 (May 1983): 8-15. *Introducing children to the basic ideas of probability.*

Jones, Graham. "A Case for Probability." *Arithmetic Teacher* 26 (February 1979): 37, 57. *A rationale for inclusion of probability in the mathematics curriculum.*

Ott, Jack A. "Who's Going to Win the Playoff?" *Mathematics Teacher* 78 (October 1985): 559-563. *A real world probability activity.*

Santulli, Tom. "Playing with Probability." *Mathematics Teacher* 76 (October 1983): 494-496. *An introductory probability activity.*

Shulte, Albert P. "Research Report: Learning Probability Concepts in Elementary School Mathematics." *Arithmetic Teacher* 34 (January 1987): 32-33. *Research findings concerning elementary school students' understanding of probability.*

Swift, Jim. "Challenges for Enriching the Curriculum: Statistics and Probability." *Mathematics Teacher* 76 (April 1983): 268-269. *A series of challenge problems for junior high and high school.*

Vissa, Jeanne M. "Probability and Combinations for Third Graders." *Arithmetic Teacher* 36 (December 1988): 33-37. *Activities involving probability and combinations and incorporating concepts of multiplication, graphs, and fractions.*

DIRECTIONS IN EDUCATION

Incorporating Technology in the Math Classroom – What's New

Most of today's students have access to calculators and computers. The question is no longer, "Should students be allowed to use calculators and computers in the math classroom?", but "What are appropriate uses of calculators and computers in the classroom?" To insure that **every** student has access to such technology, mathematics instruction at all levels must incorporate the tools of current technology.

The National Council of Teachers of Mathematics, in their *Curriculum and Evaluation Standards for School Mathematics,* **have recommended that:**

- Appropriate calculators should be available to all students at all times.
- A computer should be available in every classroom for demonstration purposes.
- Every student should have access to a computer for individual and group work.
- Students should learn to use the computer as a tool for processing information and performing calculations to investigate and solve problems.

What are requirements of appropriate instruction in the use of calculators?

- An understanding of times when calculators are useful and when mental or paper-and-pencil algorithms are more appropriate.

- An understanding of the potential for error with calculators and skills for assessing the reasonableness of results obtained on the calculator.

- An awareness that facility with basic skills, particularly mental skills, enhances calculator use.

- The opportunity to view the calculator as one of many tools available to the student of mathematics.

- The opportunity for students to self-select times to use the calculator on an individual assignment or a group activity.

- The opportunity to solve real world problems with numbers that exceed the students' paper-and-pencil skills.

- The opportunity to use calculators in testing situations.

- An environment which encourages calculator usage.

What is appropriate instruction in the use of computers?

Classroom computer instruction may be of several distinct types: computer-assisted instruction, environments for forming and testing conjectures, exploration, drill and practice, and computer applications.

- Computer-assisted instruction (or programmed learning) may be interesting and motivational for some students on a limited basis. It is often of the drill and practice nature and is frequently limited to objective "right/wrong" responses. While this type of computer use may be appropriate for limited outcomes, it does little to enable students to see the richness of the potential for applications of computers in the world of mathematics.

- Applications of computers in the classroom may take on many distinctly different roles including:
  - The use of commercially (or teacher) prepared software such as spread sheets to collect and manage data which may be used in problem solving or in the study of statistical concepts.

  - The use of commercially prepared software such as LOGO or the Geometric Supposer to explore concepts, to form and test conjectures, and to solve problems.

  - Student-generated software which provides solutions to single problems or to categories of problems - some facility with programming language may be required.

- Classroom use of computers should serve to illustrate:
  - The power of the computer to perform repeated calculations in short periods of time, particularly in performing simulations.

  - The versatility of the computer as a mathematical tool.

  - The applications of mathematics on the computer in the real world.

  - The role of mathematics in enhancing the utility of computers in other fields such as science.

As you think about using technology in your classroom, ask yourself:

- How proficient am I in the use of calculators and computers?

- Am I familiar with software and/or instructional materials which facilitate the use of calculators and computers in my classroom?

- How can I keep my skills up-to-date as technology continues to advance?

- How can I keep informed of new developments in the use of technology?

To learn more:

Mathematical Sciences Education Board and National Research Council. *Everybody Counts: A Report to the Nation on the Future of Mathematics Education.* Washington, DC: National Academy Press, 1989.

12

Geometric Shapes

THEME: Analyzing Geometric Shapes

Strategy Review:
Use Direct Reasoning.
This strategy was
introduced in
Chapter 3 of the text.

Guess My Number!
$n > 25$
n is odd
n is not prime
$n < 75$
Sum of digits = 9
The tens digit is a multiple
of the ones digit.

What is the number?_____

HANDS-ON ACTIVITIES

The activities in this chapter will help you recognize, reason about, and analyze
geometric shapes. This first activity is a warm-up to sharpen your skills in
visual thinking.

OBJECTIVE: **Use visual cues to reason about shapes**

You Will Need: Blocks (optional)

1. Each set of dots below can be connected to form these two shapes:

For example,

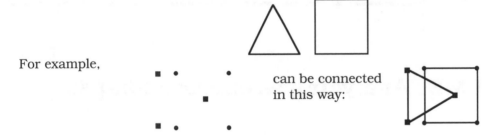

can be connected in this way:

Connect each set of dots to form these two shapes. (They must be the same size as the examples.)

a.

b.

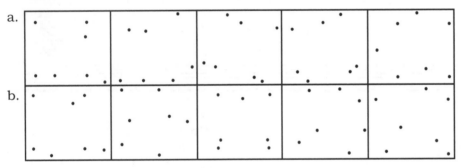

You should have found a square and a triangle in each box.

2. Each shape given below was built from two puzzle pieces.

For example:

Shade part of each shape to show how the pieces fit together.

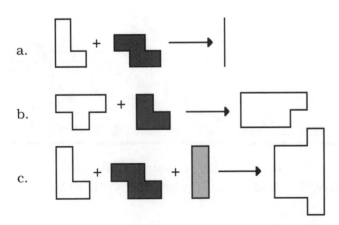

3. In each of these pictures a mirror line has been drawn. Everything on one side of the mirror will appear to be on the other side, too, but in reverse or mirror image. Put in everything exactly as it would appear in the mirror. For example:

a.   b.

c.   d.

4. a. A building of blocks will be built on the floorplan given. The number in each square indicates how many blocks will be placed on that square. Of the silhouettes given, which of the following will be the front view?

the right view?

the left view?

	2	1	3	
Left	1	2	1	Right

Front

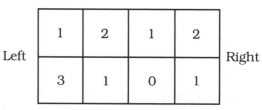

b. More floor plans are given. For each, draw the silhouette views from the front, right, and left. Hint: It may help to build them if you have blocks, e.g. sugar cubes.

	1	2	1	
Left	1	3	2	Right

Front

	1	2	1	2	
Left	3	1	0	1	Right

Front

The next activities explore the characteristics
of various geometric shapes

ACTIVITY 2

OBJECTIVE: **Construct shapes on a geoboard**

You Will Need: A geoboard (optional)

1. A triangle that has two or more sides the same length is called an
    isosceles triangle. The triangle shown is an isosceles triangle.

    Using your geoboard, make 5 different isosceles triangles.
    Record them here:

2. A triangle that has no two sides the same length is called a
    scalene triangle. The triangle shown is a scalene triange.

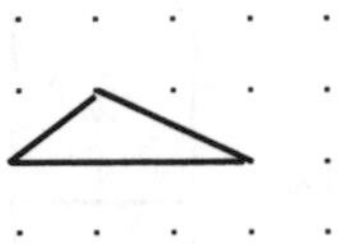

    Use your geoboard to construct 5 different scalene triangles.
    Record them here:

3. A triangle that has one right angle is a **right** triangle.
    A right triangle is shown.

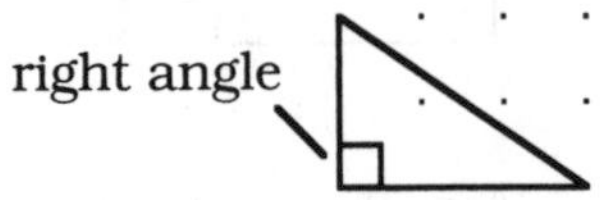

    right angle

    Construct 5 different right triangles. Record them here:

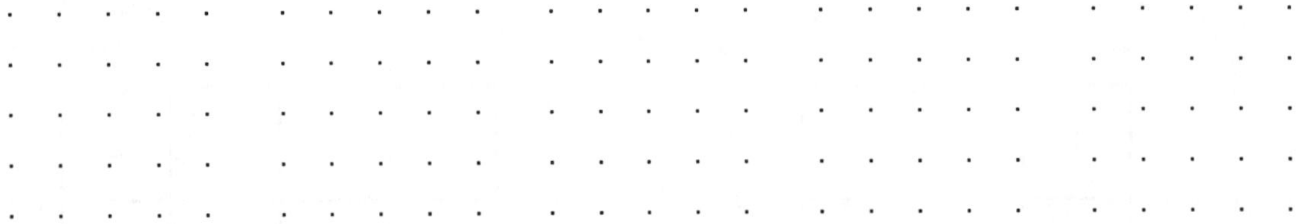

4. A **rhombus** is a quadrilateral with four sides the same length. One rhombus is shown.
    Construct 4 more on your geoboard. Record them here:

OBJECTIVE: **Explore geometric ideas with paper folding**

You Will Need: Materials Card 12.3, tracing paper

1. A figure that can be folded on a line so that one side of its outline exactly fits on the other side has **reflection symmetry**. The following figure is an example.

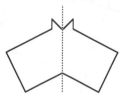

a. Trace each of the figures from Materials Card 12.3 and test them to see which ones have reflection symmetry. Draw them here and draw the line(s) of symmetry.

b. Which ones have more than one line of reflection symmetry?

c. Which figure has the most? Why?

2. A figure that can be turned about a fixed point, less than a full turn, so that the image matches the original figure perfectly has **rotation symmetry**.

a. Trace each of the figures from Materials Card 12.3 and test to see which ones have rotation symmetry. Draw them here and indicate how much to turn them.

b. Which ones have more than one turn of rotation symmetry?

c. Which figure has the most? Why?

3. Paper folding can be used to test if lines are parallel. Given two lines, *l* and *m*, fold on any fold line so that *l* folds onto itself. Does line *m* also fold onto itself? If so, lines *l* and *m* are parallel. Trace the lines given below and use this test to determine which pairs of lines are parallel.

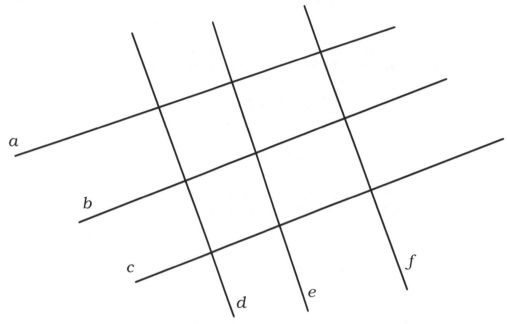

4. Lines can also be shown to be perpendicular by paper folding. Let point P be the intersection of lines *l* and *m*. Fold line *l* at point P so that line *l* folds across P onto itself. Does line *m* lie along the fold line? If so, lines *l* and *m* are perpendicular. Use this to determine which lines above are perpendicular.

OBJECTIVE: **Verify characteristics of quadrilaterals**

You Will Need: Materials from Activity 3, tracing paper

1. A **quadrilateral** is a closed figure composed of four line segments (sides). In this activity we will be exploring those shapes on Materials Card 12.3 which are quadrilaterals. Identify and trace them.

2. A quadrilateral with exactly one pair of parallel sides is a **trapezoid**. A quadrilateral with both pairs of opposite sides parallel is a **parallelogram**. Using the paper-folding test for parallel lines, determine which of the figures are trapezoids and which are parallelograms. On this part and following, it may be helpful to write the classification on corresponding shapes.

3. An **isosceles trapezoid** is a trapezoid in which the nonparallel sides have the same length. By paper folding, determine which of the figures are isosceles trapezoids.

4. Recall that a **rhombus** is a quadrilateral with four sides the same length. By folding one segment onto another to see if they have the same length, determine which of the figures are rhombuses.

5. A **rectangle** is a quadrilateral with four right angles. Using the paper-folding test for perpendicular lines (you will need to extend the sides), determine which of the figures are rectangles.

6. A **square** is a quadrilateral with four sides the same length and four right angles. From your results in parts 4 and 5, which of the figures are squares?

7. A **kite** is a quadrilateral with 2 nonoverlapping pairs of adjacent sides the same length. By paper folding, determine which of the figures satisfy that definition.

8. Construct a diagram showing the relationships among the quadrilaterals we have explored here. Begin with quadrilaterals. Use line segments to connect two figures if the set below is a subset of the set above.

Quadrilaterals

OBJECTIVE: **Discover properties of quadrilaterals**

You Will Need: Materials from Activity 3, tracing paper

In the previous activity you have classified quadrilaterals into various special categories. In this activity, you will discover some of the properties that these special quadrilaterals have. Use the means of paper folding or tracing and rotating to investigate each of the following properties. Indicate which figures have that property.

Two segments or sides are **congruent** if they have the same length. Likewise, two angles are congruent if they have the same measure.

	Parallelogram	Rhombus	Rectangle	Square	Kite	Isosceles Trapezoid
1. Opposite sides which are congruent						
2. Opposite angles which are congruent						
3. Pairs of adjacent angles which are congruent						
4. Diagonals which are congruent						
5. Diagonals which are perpendicular						
6. Diagonals which bisect each other						
7. Diagonals which divide the quadrilateral into 2 triangles of the same shape and size						

The tangram puzzle serves as the basis of the next activity
which asks you to explore a variety of shapes.

OBJECTIVE: **Use tangram pieces to form polygons**

You Will Need: Tangram pieces from Materials Card 6.4

Use the pieces of the tangram puzzle from Materials Card 6.4 to complete the chart below. For example, you can construct a square from 3 tangram pieces as illustrated in the chart already.

The pentagon (5-sided) and the hexagon (6-sided) constructed might not be regular (with congruent sides and congruent vertex angles).

Number of Tangram Pieces Used	Triangle	Square	Rectangle	Parallelogram	Trapezoid	Pentagon	Hexagon
1							
2					◻◹		
3		◻				⬠	
4							
5							
6							
7							

Are some boxes impossible to fill using the tangram pieces? You might check with other students and compare your findings.

The next activity will help you gain insight about the measure of the vertex
angles of regular polygons. A **regular polygon** has all sides and
all vertex angles congruent.

ACTIVITY 7

OBJECTIVE: **Determine the sum of the vertex angles of polygons**

You Will Need: Ruler, paper

1. Draw a triangle with a ruler. Tear off the 3 corners (vertex angles) of the triangle as indicated. Arrange them side by side as illustrated.

Notice that the sides of angles 1 and 3 form a straight line. What does this tell you about the sum of the angle measures?

2. Repeat part 1 with a different triangle. Describe the result.

3. Now draw any quadrilateral. Tear off the vertex angles and arrange as above. Draw your findings here.

What does this tell you about the sum of the angle measures?

4. You have found that the sum of the measures of the angles of a triangle is 180°. Notice that the diagonal from one vertex of a quadrilateral to the non-adjacent vertex divides the quadrilateral into two triangles. The sum of the angle measures of these two triangles is 360°, which is also the sum of the measures of the vertex angles of the quadrilateral.

We can use this technique to determine the sum of the measures of the vertex angles of any polygon. First draw all possible diagonals from the vertex marked by the arrow to all non-adjacent vertices.

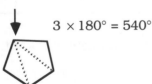
$3 \times 180° = 540°$

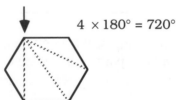
$4 \times 180° = 720°$

Then, find the number of triangles formed. Multiply the number of triangles by 180° to find the sum of the angle measures.

Find the sum of the angle measures for each of these polygons:

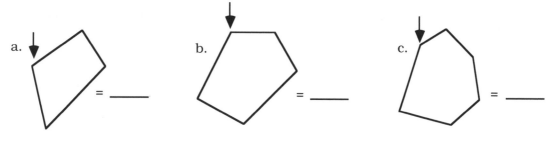

a. = _____   b. = _____   c. = _____

A **tessellation** is a covering of the plane with one or more shapes so that there are no gaps and no overlaps. In the next two activities, we will investigate tessellations with regular polygons of the same size.

OBJECTIVE: **Form tessellations with regular polygons**

You Will Need: Materials Card 12.8, scratch paper

1. The regular polygons from Materials Card 12.8 will serve as models for this activity. Take the triangle and try to tessellate a plain sheet of paper. Trace around the model, making sure the sides of the polygons meet exactly.

permitted   not permitted

Remember that the page must be covered completely with no gaps or overlappings (the borders do not matter). Can this be done with the triangle? _____

2. Try the same thing with the square, pentagon, hexagon, octagon, decagon, and dodecagon. Will all of the polygons tessellate? _____
Which ones will? Which will not?

You have discovered that certain regular polygons tessellate. Using that information in the next activity, we will investigate tessellations with other triangles and quadrilaterals.

OBJECTIVE: **Investigate other tessellations**

You Will Need: Materials Card 12.9, scratch paper

1. Will the isosceles triangle from Materials Card 12.9 tessellate?   Do the same with each of the other shapes.

2. Which of the shapes will tessellate?

Which will not?

> Write a statement that summarizes tessellating with triangles or quadrilaterals.

The last activity in this chapter deals with three-dimensional
shapes called polyhedra.

OBJECTIVE: **Build models of polyhedra**

You Will Need: Materials Card 12.10, plain paper,
scissors, and paper clips or tape

1. Remove the circle patterns from Materials Card 12.10. Find the pattern that has a square on it. Make 6 copies of this pattern. Fold each circle on the dotted lines as illustrated.

       Cube

Put the 6 squares together to form a cube. The flaps will be on the outside so that you can paper clip or tape the squares together. Notice that every face of the cube is a square.

2. A **regular polyhedron** (plural is polyhedra) is one in which all faces are identical regular polygonal regions and each vertex is surrounded by the same arrangement of polygons. Use the other polygon patterns to make the following regular polyhedra.

Make 2 polyhedra with triangular faces (one with 4 triangles and one with 8 triangles).

 Tetrahedron

 Octahedron

Make a polyhedron with 12 pentagonal faces.

 Dodecahedron

3. A **semiregular polyhedron** is one constructed from regular polygonal regions of more than one type such that each vertex is surrounded by the same arrangement of polygons.

   Make the following polyhedron with 8 triangles and 6 squares. Each vertex is surrounded by a triangle-square-triangle-square arrangement.

   Cube octahedron

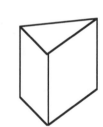

4. Make a triangular prism with 2 triangular bases and square faces.

   Also make a square pyramid from 4 triangles and one square.

5. An interesting relationship exists between the number of faces, vertices, and edges of a polyhedron. Using the models you have made, complete the following table.

	Faces (F)	Vertices (V)	Edges (E)
Cube			
Tetrahedron			
Octahedron			
Dodecahedron			
Cube octahedron			
Triangular prism			
Square pyramid			

What relationship do you observe? Hint: Add another column with F + V.

MENTAL MATH

It is possible to make one straight cut in each of these shapes so that the two pieces will form a square.

For example:

Draw a line on each figure to show where the cut should be made:

EXERCISES

Crossword Geometry

ACROSS

2. Consists of all points between A and B on line $\overleftrightarrow{AB}$, together with A and B.
5. A quadrilateral with four sides the same length.
7. Given two lines and a transversal, the angles on opposite sides of the transversal and interior to the lines are called _____ interior angles.
10. The set of points in three-dimensional space equidistant from a fixed point.
12. A quadrilateral with two pairs of parallel sides.
15. Formed by connecting each point of a circle to a fixed point in space.
16. A quadrilateral that is both a rectangle and a rhombus.
17. Given two points in the plane, there is a unique _____ that contains them.
19. Three or more points that lie on the same line are called_____.
20. Union of two line segments or rays with a common endpoint.
21. The angle $\angle POQ$ of a polygon where P and Q are consecutive vertices and O is the center is called a _____ _____ .

24. Polyhedron with two parallel opposite faces that are identical polygons and with rectangular lateral faces.
26. A polygon has _____ _____ if the polygon can be turned about a point less that 360° so that the turned image matches the original polygon perfectly.

DOWN

1. The sum of the measures of the vertex angles in a triangle is 180 _____.
3. A polygon with exactly 3 straight sides.
4. A pentagon has _____sides.
6. Set of all points in the plane that are a fixed, constant distance from a given point.
8. Angles formed by 2 intersecting lines that have only a vertex in common.
9. A triangle with 2 or 3 sides of the same length.
10. A triangle with 3 sides that are all different lengths.
11. The angle that forms a straight angle with the vertex angle of a polygon.
13. A quadrilateral with 4 right angles.
14. A tool, marked from 0° to 180°, that is useful in measuring angles.
18. Union of line segments forming a closed figure, where two segments intersect only at endpoints.
19. Analogous to prism, except has circular bases.
22. A location in the plane that has no size.
23. An angle measuring less than 90°.
25. Part of line $\overleftrightarrow{CD}$ that consists of point C and all points on the same side of C as point D.

Plane Slices

Each figure below is sawed in two by the plane indicated. Match the figure with the resulting cross section. Put the letter from the answer in the blank below that is numbered the same as the problem.

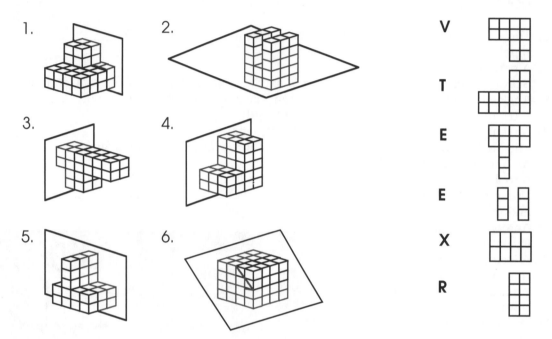

1.   2.

V

T

3.   4.

E

E

5.   6.

X

R

What the heroine said when the cowboy rescued her just as she was about to be sawed in two.

If it weren't $\underline{\ }\ \underline{\ }\ \underline{\ }\ \underline{\ }\ \underline{\ }\ \underline{\ }$ I would have been bisected!
$\quad\quad\quad\quad 1\ \ 2\ \ 3\ \ 4\ \ 5\ \ 6$

SELF-TEST

1. Lines l and m intersect and form

   (i) vertical angles
   (ii) complementary angles
   (iii) supplementary angles

   a. i only   b. i and iii only   c. ii and iii only   d. all of i, ii and iii

2. Add up the number of lines of reflection symmetry and the number of centers of rotation symmetry for this regular polygon.

    a. 5　　　　b. 6　　　　c. 10　　　　d. 11

3. A certain parallelogram has congruent diagonals (same length). Which of the following must it be?

    a. rectangle　　　　b. rhombus　　　　c. kite　　　d. None of a, b, or c.

4. Which of the following is (are) true?

    (i) If a figure is a rectangle, then it is also a parallelogram.
    (ii) If a figure is a rhombus, then it is also a square.
    (iii) If a figure is a square, then it is a rectangle and a rhombus.

    a. i and ii only　　　b. i and iii only　　　c. ii and iii only　　　d. i, ii, and iii

5. Which of the following regular polygons could *not* be used to tile a floor?

    a. 3-gon　　　　b. 4-gon　　　　c. 5-gon　　　　d. 6-gon

6. Which of these polygons always has rotation symmetry (through an angle less than 360°)?

    (i) parallelogram　　　　(ii) rectangle　　　　(iii) trapezoid

    a. i and ii only　　　b. i and iii only　　　c. ii and iii only　　　d. None of a, b, or c.

7. Which of the following is the largest?

    a.　Measure of a vertex angle of a regular 5-gon.
    b.　Measure of a vertex angle of a regular 10-gon.
    c.　Measure of a central angle of a regular 3-gon.
    d.　Measure of a central angle of a regular 6-gon.

8. Which regular polygon has a vertex angle sum of 900°?

    a. 5-gon　　　　b. 7-gon　　　　c. 9-gon　　　　d. None of a, b, or c.

9. How many faces in total does a hexagonal prism have?

    a. 6　　　　b. 7　　　　c. 8　　　　d. None of a, b, or c.

10. How many edges in total does a pentagonal pyramid have?

    a. 7　　　　b. 10　　　　c. 15　　　　d. None of a, b, or c.

SOLUTIONS

Warm-up

63

Hands-on Activities

Activity 1

1. a. [figures]

    b. [figures]

2. a. [figure]   b. [figure]   c. [figure]

3. a. [figures]   b. [figures]   c. [figures]   d. [figures]

4. a. B, D, G   b. [figures] and [figures]

Activity 2

Answers may vary.

Activity 3

1. a. C, E, F, H, I, J, K, R, S
    b. C, E, H, R, S
    c. A circle because any line through the center is a line of symmetry.
2. a. C, E, H, P, R, S
    b. C, E, S
    c. A circle because any turn about the center yields symmetry.
3. b and c, d and f
4. a and e, b and d, b and f, c and d, c and f

Activity 4

1. H, I, K, P, Q, R, S, T   2. Trapezoids: I, T   parallelograms: H, P, R, S

3. I **4.** H, S **5.** R, S **6.** S **7.** H, K

8.

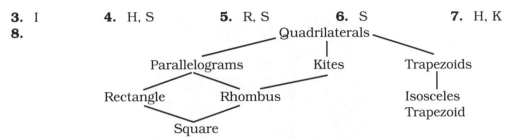

Activity 5
1. Parallelogram, Rhombus, Rectangle, Square; Isosceles trapezoid has one pair.
2. Parallelogram, Rhombus, Rectangle, Square; Kite has one pair.
3. Rectangle, Square; Isosceles trapezoid has 2 pairs of base angles.
4. Rectangle, Square, Isosceles trapezoid
5. Rhombus, Square, Kite
6. Parallelogram, Rhombus, Rectangle, Square; one diagonal of kite is bisected.
7. Parallelogram, Rhombus, Rectangle, Square; one diagonal of kite does.

Activity 6
Answers may vary.

Activity 7
1. Sum is 180°.   2. Sum is also 180°.   3. Sum is 360°.
4. a. 360°   b. 540°   c. 720°

Activity 8
1. Yes   2. No; square, hexagon will; the rest will not.

Activity 9
1. Yes
2. They all tessellate the plane.
   It is possible to tessellate the plane with any triangle or quadrilateral.

Activity 10

5.			
Cube	6	8	12
Tetrahedron	4	4	6
Octahedron	8	6	12
Dodecahedron	12	20	30
Cube octahedron	14	12	24
Triangular prism	5	6	9
Square pyramid	5	5	8

F + V = E + 2   This is called Euler's Formula (pronounced "oiler's")

Mental Math

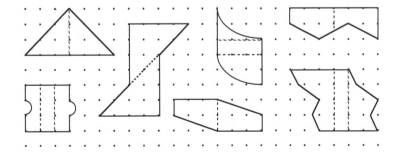

Exercises
Crossword Geometry

Plane Slices
  VERTEX

Self-Test

1. b   2. b   3. a   4. b

5. c   6. a   7. b   8. b

9. c   10. b

The crossword solution includes: SEGMENT, RHOMBUS, ALTERNATE, SPHERE, PARALLELOGRAM, CONE, SQUARE, LINE, COLLINEAR, ANGLE, CENTRAL ANGLE, PRISM, ROTATION SYMMETRY, and others (DEGREES, TRIANGLE, CIRCLES, FIVE, VERTICAL, EXTERIOR, PENTAGON, POLYGON, CYLINDER).

RESOURCE ARTICLES

Arithmetic Teacher 37 (February 1990). Focus issue on "Spatial Sense". *Entire issue devoted to developing spatial sense in students of all ages.*

Bledsoe, Gloria. "Guessing Geometric Shapes." *Mathematics Teacher* 80 (March 1987): 178-180. *Activity focusing on distinguishing features of geometric figures.*

Bright, George. "Teaching Mathematics with Technology: LOGO and Geometry." *Arithmetic Teacher* 36 (January 1989): 36. *Use of LOGO to explore angles, positions, and shapes.*

Bright, George W., and John G. Harvey. "Learning and Fun with Geometry Games." *Arithmetic Teacher* 35 (April 1988): 22-26. *Presents three games involving components of two- or three-dimensional objects.*

Brown, Susan A. "Drawing Altitudes of Triangles." *Mathematics Teacher* 78 (March 1985): 182-183. *Using graph paper to develop the concept of altitude of a triangle.*

Burger, William F. "Geometry." *Arithmetic Teacher* 32 (February 1985): 52-56. *How to develop geometric reasoning through the study of two-dimensional shapes.*

Butzow, John W. "Y is for Yacht Race: A Game of Angles." *Arithmetic Teacher* 33 (January 1986): 44-48. *Game approach for teaching concept of angle.*

Campbell, Patricia F. "Cardboard, Rubber Bands, and Polyhedron Models." *Arithmetic Teacher* 31 (October 1983): 48-52. *Constructing three-dimensional models.*

Carroll, William M. "Cross Sections of Clay Solids." *Arithmetic Teacher* 35 (March 1988): 6-11. *Exploring three-dimensional shapes and their cross sections.*

Clements, Douglas C., and Michael Battista. "Geometry and Geometric Measurement." *Arithmetic Teacher* 33 (February 1986): 29-32. *Illustrates use of manipulatives in geometry.*

Esbenshade, Donald H., Jr. "Adding Dimension to Flatland: A Novel Approach to Geometry." *Mathematics Teacher* 76 (February 1983): 120-123. *Expanding students' perceptions of geometry.*

Giganti, Paul, Jr., and Mary Jo Cittadino. "The Art of Tessellation." *Arithmetic Teacher* 37 (March 1990): 6-16. *Exploring figures and effects of changing figures through tessellation projects.*

Hollingsworth, Caroline. "Perplexed by Hexed." *Mathematics Teacher* 77 (October 1984): 560-562. *An exploration with pentominoes.*

Hollingsworth, Caroline. "Polyominoes: An Unsolved Problem." *Mathematics Teacher* 78 (May 1985): 364-365. *Looking for patterns using polyominoes.*

Horak, Virginia M., and Willis J. Horak. "Let's Do It: Using Geometry Tiles As a Manipulative for Developing Basic Concepts." *Arithmetic Teacher* 30 (April 1983): 8-15. *Developing and extending beginning geometric concepts.*

Juraschek, William. "Getting in Touch with Shape." *Arithmetic Teacher* 37 (April 1990): 14-16. *Kinesthetic activities to develop students' sense of shape and space.*

Kaiser, Barbara. "Explorations with Tessellating Polygons." *Arithmetic Teacher* 36 (December 1988): 19-24. *Activities involving tessellations with two-dimensional shapes, letters of the alphabet, and Escher-type shapes.*

Kennedy, Leonard M. "Geometry — More Than a Holiday Prelude." *Arithmetic Teacher* 33 (September 1985): 2. *Expanding elementary teachers' notions of geometry instruction.*

Kerr, Donald R., Jr. "A Case for Geometry: Geometry is Important, It is There, Teach It." *Arithmetic Teacher* 26 (February 1979): 14. *A rationale for the teaching of geometry.*

Kolnowski, Linda W., and Joann King Okey. "Ideas: See Shapes Book, What's Your Shape? and Puzzling Polygons." *Arithmetic Teacher* 34 (April 1987): 26-31. *Activities exploring shapes.*

Lappan, Glenda, Elizabeth A. Phillips, and Mary Jean Winter. "Spatial Visualization." *Mathematics Teacher* 77 (November 1984): 618-625. *Activities improving students' ability to visualize by building, drawing, and evaluating three-dimensional shapes.*

Larke, Patricia J. "Geometric Extravaganza: Spicing Up Geometry." *Arithmetic Teacher* 36 (September 1988): 12-16. *Describes how to organize a geometry fair at an elementary school.*

Maletsky, Evan M. "Generating Solids." *Mathematics Teacher* 76 (October 1983): 499-500, 505-507. *Activities for visualizing, identifying, and describing the solids generated by rotating polygons about axes.*

Mansfield, Helen. "Projective Geometry in the Elementary School." *Arithmetic Teacher* 32 (March 1985): 15-19. *Developing spatial skills and understanding.*

Mathematics Teacher 78 (September 1985). Focus issue on "Geometry". *Entire issue is devoted to sharing ideas about teaching geometry formally and informally.*

Moser, James M. "How Many Triangles?" *Mathematics Teacher* 78 (November 1985): 598-604. *A geoboard exploration.*

Ockenga, Earl, and Joan Duea. "Ideas." *Arithmetic Teacher* 31 (January 1984): 28-32. *Activities with shapes.*

Olson, Melfried, and Judith Olson. "Triangles, Rectangles, and Parallelograms." *Mathematics Teacher* 76 (February 1983): 112-117. *Activities for observing relationships between triangles and quadrilaterals.*

Prentice, Gerard. "Flexible Straws." *Arithmetic Teacher* 37 (November 1989): 4-5. *Building two- and three-dimensional figures for the study of shape and properties.*

Renshaw, Barbara S. "Symmetry the Trademark Way." *Arithmetic Teacher* 34 (September 1986): 6-12. *Teaching line and rotational symmetry using familiar trademarks.*

Rowan, Thomas E. "Implementing the Standards: The Geometry Standards in K-8 Mathematics." *Arithmetic Teacher* 37 (February 1990): 24-28. *Discussing implications of the Standards in developing geometric understanding.*

Silverman, Helene. "Geometry in the Primary Grades: Exploring Geometric Ideas in the Primary Grades." *Arithmetic Teacher* 26 (February 1979): 15-16. *Introducing geometric concepts in the primary grades.*

Souza, Ronald. "Golfing with a Protractor." *Arithmetic Teacher* 35 (April 1988): 52-56. *Game involving estimating and measuring angle measures and lengths.*

Troccolo, Joseph A. "The Rhombus Construction Company." *Mathematics Teacher* 76 (January 1983): 37-42. *Activities exploring properties of symmetry of geometric figures.*

Turner, Sandra. "Windowpane Patterns." *Mathematics Teacher* 76 (September 1983): 411-413, 428. *A computerized challenge in finding rectangles.*

Usiskin, Zalman. "Enrichment Activities for Geometry." *Mathematics Teacher* 76 (April 1983): 264-266. *Activities which instruct about mathematics as they instruct in mathematics.*

Van de Walle, John, and Charles S. Thompson. "Let's Do It: Cut and Paste for Geometric Thinking." *Arithmetic Teacher* 32 (September 1984): 8-13. *Use of simple materials to present geometric activities.*

Willcutt, Bob. "Triangles on a Grid." *Mathematics Teacher* 78 (November 1985): 608, 611-614. *Searching for right triangles on a grid.*

Zurstadt, Betty K. "Tessellations and the Art of M. C. Escher." *Arithmetic Teacher* 31 (January 1984): 54-55. *Introducing the art of tessellating to children.*

DIRECTIONS IN EDUCATION

Teacher Beliefs/Student Beliefs — Would You Believe?

The beliefs about mathematics that are held by students and teachers can have a profound effect upon the outcome of learning activities. Some of these beliefs are only myths and to guard against transmission of these myths to their students, teachers must examine their own beliefs and become aware of the myths. Teachers who understand the common myths about mathematics learning can be more effective in changing student beliefs.

What are some of the common math myths which negatively impact mathematics instruction?

- **MYTH: Students who are good in mathematics have a good memory.** Teachers who hold this belief tend to see math instruction as a series of rules and facts to be memorized. Students who are not good at memorization may begin to see themselves as unable to learn math.

- **MYTH: There is one best way to do an individual math problem.** Teachers reinforce this belief by requiring students to show their work and by counting the entire problem wrong if any step is omitted or done incompletely. During instruction the teacher demonstrates only one way to do the problems assigned and does not encourage discussion of alternative approaches. Students learn not to tune in on their own insights or to value those insights.

- **MYTH: Counting on the fingers is unacceptable.** Teachers who do not value the use of concrete representations of math concepts view the use of fingers as a form of "cheating." Such teachers tend to view math only as an abstract thinking activity and present instruction symbolically. Students who need concrete examples to assist them in working with abstract concepts begin to see themselves as inferior to fellow students who can simply do the work in their heads or on paper.

- Other myths about math which can impact classroom instruction include:
    - Math requires the use of logic, not intuition.
    - You must always know how you got the answer.
    - Math is done by working intensely until the problem is solved.
    - Men are better in math than women.
    - Mathematicians do problems quickly, in their heads.
    - Math is not creative.
    - There is a magic key to doing math.
    - The math I learned in school is good enough for today's students.
    - Increased reliance on standardized tests will improve student performance in mathematics.

What are some common math beliefs that can block progress?

- **Mathematics is computation.** Students tend to view math as the four basic operations. While study of other mathematical ideas such as geometry or statistical concepts may be interesting to students, they view their mathematical ability only in terms of facility with computation.

- **Math problems are quickly solvable in just a few steps.** Students who cannot quickly arrive at solutions to math problems tend to question their ability to solve the problem or to think that there is something wrong with the problem itself.

- **The purpose of doing math is to obtain the "right answer."** Students tend to view math in terms of absolutely right or absolutely wrong. They are unable to appreciate progress in the use of a difficult process if they do not obtain the right answer.

- **The role of the math student is to receive new mathematical knowledge and to be able to demonstrate it.** Students generally view math as something to be passively received and then duplicated on homework assignments and tests.

- **The role of the math teacher is to impart mathematical knowledge and to check student answers for correctness.** Students view the math teacher as the "Sage on the Stage" rather than the "Guide on the Side." As a result of this view, students limit their attempts to interact with the teacher in any discussion of mathematical ideas.

- **Math ability is related to innate ability more than to effort.** Students who see themselves as unable to learn math are seldom motivated to put much effort into the learning task. Since ability is not something within the student's control, math is also seen as outside the control of the student.

As you think about mathematical beliefs of yourself and your students, ask yourself:

- Does my teaching reflect my acceptance of any math myths?

- What can I do in my classroom to foster positive beliefs and attitudes about mathematics?

- As a student of mathematics, do I maintain a positive attitude about my own learning?

To learn more:

Frank, Martha L. "Problem Solving and Mathematical Beliefs." *Arithmetic Teacher* 35 (January 1988): 32-34.

Mitchell, Charlie. *Math Anxiety: What It Is and What to Do about It.* Tempe, AZ: Action Press, 1984.

13

Measurement

THEME: Using Real Numbers to Analyze Geometric Shapes

WARM-UP

Strategy Review:
Guess & Test.
You can review this strategy in Chapter 1 of the text.

These math problems appeared on a worksheet on the comet Computo. Can you describe the mathematical operation they call *cometication*?

4   5 = 29

2   12 = 38

3   6 = 27

How do you perform cometication?
Hint: Two of our operations are necessary to cometicate.

HANDS-ON ACTIVITIES

The first activities in this chapter will help you describe the measurement process and create your own system of measurement to determine measures of length.

OBJECTIVE: **Use body parts to measure length**

1. Early measurements were often reported in terms of body parts such as thumbs, hands, and feet. For this activity, you will use your thumbs, spans, and hands.

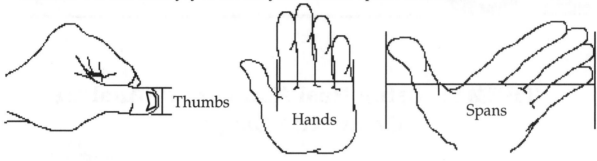

Thumbs

Hands

Spans

2. Measure the width of this page in thumbs.   Record: _____thumbs

   Measure the length of your leg in spans.   Record: _____spans

   Measure the width of your table in hands.   Record: _____hands

3. Now find these lengths. First, estimate each distance and then measure.

		ESTIMATE	MEASUREMENT
a.	the width of a window in spans	_____	_____
b.	the height of a door in hands	_____	_____
c.	the length of this page in hands	_____	_____
d.	the length of your pencil in thumbs	_____	_____
e.	the length of a table in thumbs	_____	_____

4. Can you think of a more appropriate unit to use in (e) above?

   Why might spans or hands be a better unit for measuring the length of a table?

   Why might a unit such as foot or pace be better for measuring distances like the width of a room?

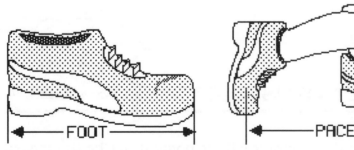

FOOT   PACE

When might you choose to use a smaller unit?

OBJECTIVE: **Develop a non-standard measurement system**

1. Often, you must use fractional parts of a unit to report the measurement of an object. For example, measure the length of this page from top to bottom in spans.
   Record: _____spans

   What special problems do we encounter with this measurement?

2. It is helpful to have smaller units to use in reporting measurements of this type. Let's use your pencil to create a system for measuring the length of this page.

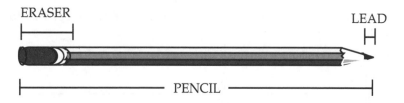

   Record the length of the page: _____pencils_____erasers_____leads

   Compare your measurement of the length of this page with another person's. What factors might cause your measurements to be different?

3. Find another object such as a shoe or book that can be used to create a measurement system similar to the "pencil system". Measure the following objects:

   a. height of your table   _____(whole) _____(part) _____(part)

   b. width of your chair seat   _____   _____   _____

   c. your height   _____   _____   _____

4. Now measure the same objects using the "pencil system".

   a. _____pencils_____erasers_____leads

   b. _____pencils_____erasers_____leads

   c. _____pencils_____erasers_____leads

5. Compare your measurements in part 3 and part 4. Why might it be difficult for you to communicate these lengths to someone who has not seen your measuring device?

The next two activities will help you use the metric system for linear measures by developing mental images of the units.

OBJECTIVE: **Use body parts to estimate metric measures**

You Will Need: Centimeter ruler from Materials Card 7.9

1. Certain body measurements correspond very closely to metric units of measure. For example, the width of the little finger is approximately one **centimeter**.
Check your little finger.

1 cm   ┝━━┥

Your hand (including your thumb) may be close to one **decimeter** in width. Check with your hand as illustrated:

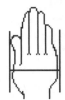

1 Decimeter

A **meter** is approximately the distance from your navel to the floor or the distance from your nose to the end of the hand when the head is turned to the opposite direction (see illustration).

Meter   ─── Meter ───

2. This information is very useful when no metric measuring device is available or when an estimate of the metric length is all that is needed.

Use your "personal" metric references to estimate these measurements. When you have completed your estimates, use the metric tape from Materials Card 7.9 and measure the metric length.

	ESTIMATE	MEASUREMENT
Height of the door	_____	_____
Height of the chair back	_____	_____
Distance from window to floor	_____	_____
Length of your pencil	_____	_____
Width of the room	_____	_____
Length of your foot	_____	_____

The next activity is best done in a group setting where participants can form 3-person teams.

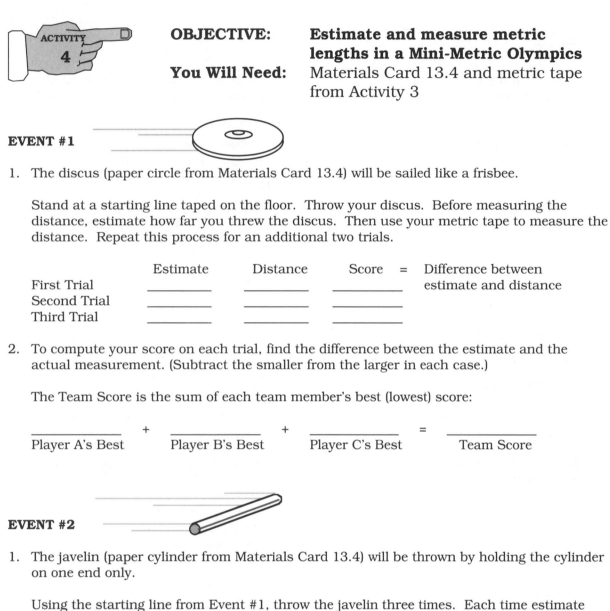

OBJECTIVE: **Estimate and measure metric lengths in a Mini-Metric Olympics**

You Will Need: Materials Card 13.4 and metric tape from Activity 3

EVENT #1

1. The discus (paper circle from Materials Card 13.4) will be sailed like a frisbee.

   Stand at a starting line taped on the floor. Throw your discus. Before measuring the distance, estimate how far you threw the discus. Then use your metric tape to measure the distance. Repeat this process for an additional two trials.

	Estimate	Distance	Score	=	Difference between
First Trial	_____	_____	_____		estimate and distance
Second Trial	_____	_____	_____		
Third Trial	_____	_____	_____		

2. To compute your score on each trial, find the difference between the estimate and the actual measurement. (Subtract the smaller from the larger in each case.)

   The Team Score is the sum of each team member's best (lowest) score:

   _____ + _____ + _____ = _____
   Player A's Best   Player B's Best   Player C's Best   Team Score

EVENT #2

1. The javelin (paper cylinder from Materials Card 13.4) will be thrown by holding the cylinder on one end only.

   Using the starting line from Event #1, throw the javelin three times. Each time estimate the distance, then measure and record the distance of the throw. Compute your score as you did in the first event.

	Estimate	Distance	Score	=	Difference between
First Trial	_____	_____	_____		estimate and distance
Second Trial	_____	_____	_____		
Third Trial	_____	_____	_____		

2. Now compute your Team Score as before:

   _____ + _____ + _____ = _____
   Player A's Best   Player B's Best   Player C's Best   Team Score

EVENT #3

1. The cube put (cube from Materials Card 13.4) is done by laying the cube in the palm of the hand. The cube is then propelled by an upward and outward motion (this is called a put).

    Using the starting line from Event #1, put the cube three times. Each time estimate the distance, then measure and record the distance of the put. Compute your score as in previous events.

	Estimate	Distance	Score	=	Difference between estimate and distance
First Trial	_____	_____	_____		
Second Trial	_____	_____	_____		
Third Trial	_____	_____	_____		

2. Now compute your Team Score as before:

    _____ + _____ + _____ = _____
    Player A's Best   Player B's Best   Player C's Best   Team Score

GO FOR THE GOLD:

Record team scores for each individual event and for the total team score (sum of all three events). The team with the *smallest* score wins.

Recognize GOLD, SILVER, and BRONZE winners for individual events and for the all-around title.

In the next activities you will measure perimeter and
area of two-dimensional shapes.

OBJECTIVE: **Use dot paper to find perimeter and area of geometric shapes**

The non-diagonal distance from one dot to an adjacent dot
on the dot paper will be our unit of linear measure as illustrated:

The perimeter is determined by counting the units around the figure.

Each side has a length of one. The sum of the lengths
of the four sides gives us the perimeter of 4 units.

1. Find the perimeter of each of these figures:

   a.

   b.

   c.

   _____units   _____units   _____units

2. Recall that in Chapter 9 we found distances on a geoboard using the Pythagorean theorem. Apply that theorem where needed to find the perimeter of the following figures.

   a.

   b.

   c.

   _____units   _____units   _____units

3. While linear units are useful for measuring one-dimensional measures such as length, width, height, or perimeter, they are not sufficient for reporting the two-dimensional measure of area.

   For the next activity, our two-dimensional unit will be the smallest square that can be formed on the dot paper with a dot at each vertex, as illustrated:

   1 square unit (written unit^2)

    The area of a figure is determined by counting the number of square units contained within it. The square to the left has an area of 4 square units.

   Area = 4 square units

   Find the area of each of these figures:

   a.

   b.

   c.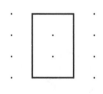

   d.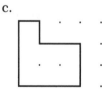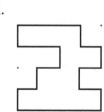

   _____ square units   _____ square units   _____ square units   _____square units

4. Let's look at a method for finding the area of a right triangle.

     To find the area of this triangle, we can draw another congruent triangle as illustrated:

What is the area of the resulting rectangle?_____square units

The area of the triangle is 1/2 the area of the rectangle, or _____square unit.

5. Determine the area of each of these triangles.

a.    b.   c.   d.

_____square units   _____square units   _____square units   _____square units

What special problem is presented by triangle (d) above?

6. Find two different ways to find the area of these polygons.

a.   b. 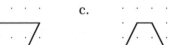   c.   d.

_____square units   _____square units   _____square units   _____square units

7. Find both the perimeter and area of each of these figures.

a.   b. 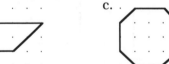   c.   d.

P _____ units   P _____ units   P _____ units   P _____ units

A _____ square units   A _____ square units   A _____ square units   A _____ square units

OBJECTIVE: **Explore relationships between perimeter and area**

You Will Need: Materials Card 13.6

1. Find both the perimeter and area of each of these figures:

    a.   b.   c.   d.

    P _____ units   P _____ units   P _____ units   P _____ units

    A _____ square units A _____ square units A _____ square units A _____ square units

    What do you notice about the perimeters of the four figures?

    What do you notice about the areas of the four figures?

2. Use the dot paper on Materials Card 13.6 to draw examples of all the different rectangles that have an area of 36 square units. Find the perimeter of each rectangle.

    The area of each rectangle is 36 square units; what do you notice about the perimeters?

3. A 6th grade student says that if the perimeters of two rectangles are the same, the areas of these figures must also be the same. How might you respond to this?

    Another student says if areas of two rectangles are equal, then the perimeters are also equal? How might you respond to this?

4. A student confuses finding perimeter and finding area. How could you help the student distinguish between the two attributes?

OBJECTIVE: **Find the area of an irregular shape**

You Will Need: Materials Card 13.7

1. Look at the map of Blackhawk County on Materials Card 13.7. Each square on the grid is equal to 1/100 of a square mile. Estimate the area of the county in square miles. Record your estimate here:_____

2. Now, let's look at a method for improving our estimate of the area.

   First, find the number of squares completely inside the county. Record the number here:_____

   Then, find the number of squares partially inside the county. Record that number here:_____

3. To determine your approximation of the area of Blackhawk County, add the number of squares completely inside the county to 1/2 of the number of squares partially inside the county. The sum is your approximate area in 1/100 square miles.

   _____ + (_____ ÷ 2) ≈ _____
   Squares inside   Squares partially inside   Area in 1/100 square miles

   To convert this to square miles, divide by 100.   Record the quotient:_____

   Quotient = _____ square miles ≈ Area of Blackhawk County

   _____

   The next activity also deals with area, but introduces the concept
   of surface area of three-dimensional objects.

   _____

OBJECTIVE: **Use grid paper to determine surface area**

You Will Need: Materials Card 13.8

We have seen that area is the measurement of a two-dimensional region in a plane or on a flat surface. When we apply this idea to a three-dimensional object, we talk of **surface area** or the sum of the area of all the faces.

Each face of this cube has an area of 1 square unit.

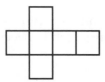

If we open the cube out into a flat pattern (we will call this pattern a **net**), we can see that it has 6 of these 1-square unit faces, or a surface area of 6 square units.

Surface area = 6 square units

1. Cut out figure 1 on Materials Card 13.8. Fold as directed and tape in place to form a rectangular prism like this:

   Count the number of square units on each face. The sum of the areas of the faces is the surface area of this figure.

   What is the surface area of this rectangular prism? _____square units

   Hint: Open the net and lay it flat to count the square units on the surface if you are unsure.

2. Cut out figure 2 on Materials Card 13.8. Fold and tape as directed to form another rectangular prism.

   Your prism should look like this:

   What is the surface area of this prism? _____square units

3. Cut out figure 3 on Materials Card 13.8. First, find the area of the square base (B). Use the method in Activity 5 to find the area of the triangular faces (T_1, T_2, T_3, T_4).
   Record the areas here:

   Area of B = _____ square units   The sum of the areas:
   Area of T_1= _____ square units $B + T_1 + T_2 + T_3 + T_4$ = ____square units
   Area of T_2= _____ square units   This is the surface area of the pyramid
   Area of T_3= _____ square units   formed by this net.
   Area of T_4= _____ square units

   Now, fold and tape your net to form a pyramid like this:

   This pyramid is called a square pyramid.
   Record the surface area here:

                              SA = _____ square units

4. Describe how you could find the surface area of this prism.

   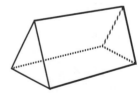

   Draw a sketch of the net for this prism.

The final activities in this chapter will explore the concept of volume. These are also activities using three-dimensional objects.

OBJECTIVE: **Find the volume of prisms**

You Will Need: Materials Card 13.9 and centimeter cubes (optional)

Volume is a measure of the amount of space that a three-dimensional object occupies. We commonly measure volume with cubic units (written u^3) since cubes stack so nicely to fill space.

1. Materials Card 13.9 contains a net for a rectangular prism.

   Hint: Your prism should look like this:

   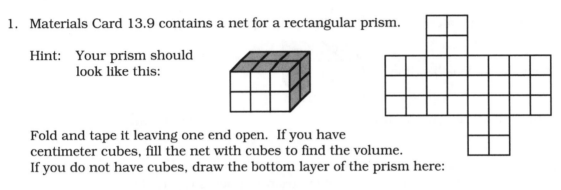

   Fold and tape it leaving one end open. If you have centimeter cubes, fill the net with cubes to find the volume. If you do not have cubes, draw the bottom layer of the prism here:

   How many cubes are in the bottom layer?_____
   How many layers of cubes will this prism contain?_____
   What is the volume of the prism formed by this net? That is, how many unit cubes can be used to "fill" the prism?   V = _____ cubic units

2. If you have cubes, build the following solids. If not, visualize how they are built. How many cubes does it take to make each of these solids? What is the volume of each solid? Hint: Think of taking each solid apart layer by layer. For example:

   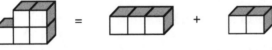

   a.

   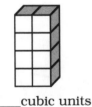

   _____cubic units

   b.

   _____cubic units

   c.

   _____cubic units

   d.

   _____cubic units

   e.

   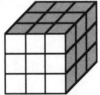

   _____cubic units

   f.

   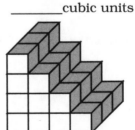

   _____cubic units

OBJECTIVE: **Find surface area and volume of various solids**

You Will Need: Materials Card 13.10
Measuring tape and various boxes

1. Materials Card 13.10 contains nets, or patterns, to make several geometric solids. Cut out the nets along the outer lines and fold them along the solid inside lines. What kind of solid does each net form? Draw a picture below.

   a. Net A   b. Net B   c. Net C   d. Net D

2. Find the surface area of each geometric solid. Explain how. Does it help to flatten out the net again?

   a. Net A   b. Net B   c. Net C   d. Net D

3. Find the volume of each geometric solid. Explain how.

   a. Net A   b. Net B   c. Net C   d. Net D

   Hint: For the solid D, you may want to see how many of them together form a cube.

4. a. Find some three-dimensional objects such as a shoe box, crayon box, or other such box. First estimate what you think the surface area and volume of each object will be. Then find the surface area and volume. Explain how.

   b. How would you find the surface area and volume of an oatmeal container?

The last activity in this chapter requires special materials. It may be done best in a lab setting, but can be accomplished on your own using rice or dry cereal.

OBJECTIVE: **Compare the volumes of a cylinder and a cone**

You Will Need: Materials Card 13.11, rice, tape and scissors

1. Cut out the 2 rectangles on Materials Card 13.11. Roll rectangle A into a cylinder and tape as directed.

Now roll rectangle B into a cone, using point C as the apex (tip) of the cone. Tape the tip only to maintain shape. Place the cone into the cylinder so that the tip of the cone touches the table in the center of the base as illustrated:

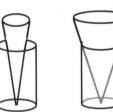

Spread out the cone to fit the top of the cylinder exactly and tape in place inside the cone.

Mark a line all the way around the cone at the top of the cylinder. Remove the cone and tape the outside securely in place. Cut along the mark as illustrated:

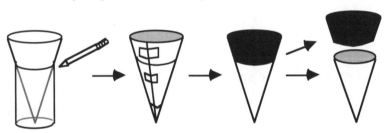

You have constructed a cone that has the same height and radius as the cylinder.

2. Predict how many cones full of rice will fill the cylinder.   _____cones

3. Place the cylinder in a container such as a box lid to catch the spillage.

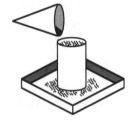

Now fill the cone with rice and pour into the cylinder. Record how many times you must fill the cone and pour it into the cylinder in order to completely fill the cylinder.

_____ cones

Write a ratio that compares the volume of the cone to the volume of the cylinder.
_____ : _____ = Volume of cone : Volume of cylinder

4. Find the volume of the following right circular cylinder and cone.

a.   r = 4 cm

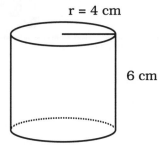

6 cm

b.

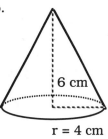

6 cm

r = 4 cm

MENTAL MATH

Draw lines connecting figures whose areas are most nearly the same. You must connect a numbered figure to a lettered figure.

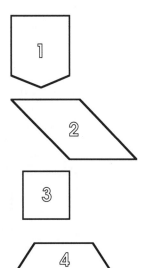

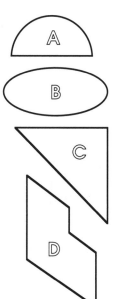

EXERCISES

Where do you send a cat who has lost its tail?

For each shape below, one dimension is missing. Determine the measure of the missing dimension. Find that measure in the set of dimensions listed below. Place the letter that is paired with that dimension on the line or lines at the bottom of the page that match the problem number for which that dimension is a solution.

DIMENSIONS:
    L = 12   O = 3   I = 24   S = 1   A = 4   R = 6   E = 5   T = 27

1. L = 2 units
   W = 2 units
   H = ___ units
   V = 12 unit³

2. L = 2 units
   W = 2 units
   H = 3 units
   V = ___ unit³

3. L = 4 units
   W = 3 units
   H = 1 unit
   V = ___ unit³

4. L = ___ units
   W = 3 units
   H = 4 units
   V = 60 unit³

  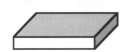 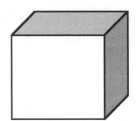

5. L = 4 units
   W = ___ units
   H = 2 units
   V = 8 unit³

6. L = 3 units
   W = 2 units
   H = 4 units
   V = ___ unit³

7. L = 4 units
   W = 2 units
   H = ___ units
   V = 16 unit³

8. L = 3 units
   W = 3 units
   H = 3 units
   V = ___ unit³

   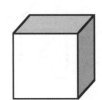

<u> </u> <u> </u>   <u> </u>   <u> </u> <u> </u> <u> </u> <u> </u> <u> </u>   <u> </u> <u> </u> <u> </u> <u> </u> <u> </u>!
   8   1   2   7   4   8   2   6   3   5   8   1   7   4

Milli-Golf

Estimate the distance in millimeters from the tee to hole #1 and record it on the appropriate blank in the score card below. Now use a metric ruler to mark off your estimate from the tee (within the boundaries). Record that as one stroke. If your line ended in the hole, proceed to tee #2. If you missed the hole, estimate from your current position to hole #1 and record a second stroke. Continue until the ball is in the hole, then proceed to tee #2. If you land in a sand trap or water hazard, add one stroke to your score. You must stay within the boundaries for each hole. Continue until you have completed all 6 holes of the **Milli-Golf Course**.

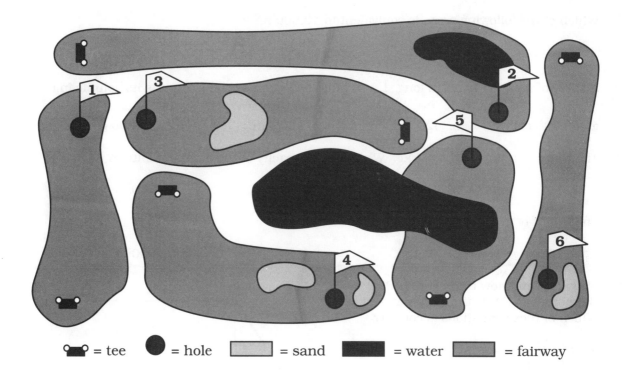

●━● = tee   ● = hole   ▢ = sand   ▮ = water   ▢ = fairway

SCORE CARD:

	Estimate	Strokes	Par			Estimate	Strokes	Par
1.	_____	_____	2		4.	_____	_____	3
	_____					_____		
	_____					_____		
2.	_____	_____	3		5.	_____	_____	4
	_____					_____		
	_____					_____		
3.	_____	_____	2		6.	_____	_____	3
	_____					_____		
	_____					_____		

SELF-TEST

1. Order these:

   (i) 3 m   (ii) 300 mm   (iii) 3 cm   (iv) 0.03 km

   a. iii < ii < i < iv
   c. iv < i < ii < iii
   b. ii < iii < i < iv
   d. None of a, b, or c.

2. Which of the following areas is equivalent to 40,000 m^2 ?

   a. 4 hectares   b. 4 ares   c. 40 km^2 d. None of a, b, or c.

3. A sheet of plywood is 2.4 m long, 1.2 m wide, and 1.5 cm thick. What is its volume in cm^3?

   a. 43,200 cm^3 b. 420 cm^3 c. 43.2 cm^3 d. 420,000 cm^3

4. The water in a jug weighs 4.7 kg. What is the capacity of the jug in milliliters?

   a. 4.7   b. 0.0047   c. 470   d. 4700

5. The length of an average city block is closest to:

   a. 1/10 km   b. 10 km   c. 10 m   d. 1000 cm

6. Suppose you know that figure ABCD is a rhombus and M is the midpoint of side AD. Which of these equations is correct?

   a. $a^2 + (a/2)^2 = h^2$
   b. $a^2 + a^2 = h^2$
   c. $(a/2)^2 + h^2 = a^2$
   d. Not enough information is given.

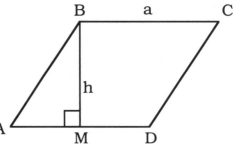

7. Find the area of triangle ABC in square units.

   a. 4
   b. 5
   c. 8
   d. None of a, b, or c.

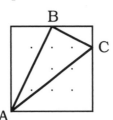

8. If the area of a circle is twice the radius, then the circumference of the circle is:

   a. 4   b. 8   c. 16   d. None of a, b, or c.

9. Imagine cutting out the square corners of this rectangular sheet of paper. Then fold up on the dotted lines to make a box. Which value of x will lead to the box of greatest volume?

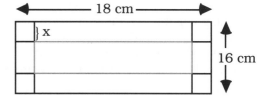

a. $x = 1$ b. $x = 2$
c. $x = 3$ d. $x = 4$

10. The largest possible cone is cut from a wooden rectangular prism 1 by 1 by 2 units. Similarly, the largest possible sphere is cut from a wooden cube 1 by 1 by 1. Which has the larger volume?

a. sphere   b. cone
c. they're equal in volume   d. impossible to determine

SOLUTIONS

Warm-up
Product + Sum

Hands-on Activities
Activity 1
1-3. Answers will vary.
4. One of the longer units is more appropriate because it is less tedious to perform the measurement. Larger units are more convenient for measuring large measures. Smaller units are usually more appropriate for measuring small measures.

Activity 2
1. There are no fractional parts of a span.
2. Different length pencils will give different measures.
3-4. Answers will vary.
5. There is no standard size for a shoe or a pencil, so it is difficult to communicate the measure to someone else.

Activities 3 and 4
Answers will vary.

Activity 5
1. a. 8   b. 12   c. 12
2. a. $6 + 2\sqrt{2}$ b. $\sqrt{2} + 2\sqrt{5}$ c. $1 + 3\sqrt{2} + \sqrt{5} + \sqrt{10}$
3. a. 6   b. 9   c. 7   d. 11   **4.** 2, 1
5. a. 4.5   b. 4   c. 3   d. 2
It is not a right triangle, but it can be divided into two right triangles.

6. a. 6 b. 6 c. 4 d. 1.5

The polygons can be divided into pieces that are rectangles or right triangles and whose areas can be added together. Also the polygons can be surrounded by right triangles to make a rectangle. The area of the polygon can be found by subtracting the areas of the triangles from the area of the rectangle. For example,

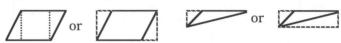

7. a. $8\sqrt{2}$, 8 b. $5 + 2\sqrt{2} + \sqrt{5}$, 5 c. $8 + 4\sqrt{2}$, 14 d. $7 + 3\sqrt{2} + \sqrt{5}$, 7.5

Activity 6

1. 12, 9; 12, 6; 12, 7; 12, 5. The perimeters are all the same. The areas are different.
2. You should have found the following rectangles: 1 by 36, 2 by 18, 3 by 12, 4 by 9, 6 by 6 with perimeters 74, 40, 30, 26, and 24 units respectively. The perimeters are different.
3. Use examples such as in part 1 to demonstrate that while the perimeters stay constant the areas may vary. You might use examples as in 2 to demonstrate that while the perimeters vary, the area can be constant.
4. It might be helpful to ask questions about how long and how much space. Examples such as how much fence surrounds the playground and how much space there is to play in may help explain the difference. Also, refer to the types of units used, such as m and m^2.

Activity 7

The area of Blackhawk County is approximately 5.5 square miles.

Activity 8

1. 10 **2.** 32 **3.** 25, 12.5, 12.5, 12.5, 12.5, 75, 75
4. Find the area of each rectangular face and the area of each triangular base. The sum of the areas is the surface area of the prism.

Activity 9

1. 6, 2, 12 **2.** a. 8 b. 16 c. 27 d. 18 e. 10 f. 30

Activity 10

1. a. triangular prism b. triangular prism c. trapezoidal prism d. square pyramid
2. a. $84u^2$ b. $176u^2$ c. $152u^2$ d. $50 + 25\sqrt{2} \approx 85.4u^2$
Find the area of each of the faces and add them together.
3. a. $36u^3$ b. $140u^3$ c. $96u^3$ d. $125/3 \approx 41.7u^3$
For the prisms, find the area of the base (triangle, trapezoid, etc.) and multiply that times the height. For part (d), three of these make a 5 by 5 by 5 cube.
4. a. Answers will vary b. To find the surface area, you could imagine cutting apart the container, which gives you two circles and a rectangle. To find the volume, you imagine how many cubes could fit in one layer (area of base) and multiply by how many layers (height).

Activity 11

2. Answers may vary. **3.** 3, 1:3 **4.** a. 96π cm^3 b. 32π cm^3

Mental Math

1 to C 2 to D 3 to A 4 to B

Exercises

Where do you send a cat who has lost its tail?

1. 3   2. 4   3. 12   4. 5   5. 1   6. 24   7. 6   8. 27
To a retail store!

Milli-Golf
Answers will vary.

Self-Test

1. a   **2.** a   **3.** a   **4.** d   **5.** a   **6.** c   **7.** b   **8.** a   **9.** c   **10.** c

RESOURCE ARTICLES

Barson, Alan, and Lois Barson. "Ideas." *Arithmetic Teacher* 35 (May 1988): 20-22, 26-29. *Activities building concept of measurement using rulers, scales, and clocks.*

Binswanger, Richard. "Discovering Perimeter and Area with Logo." *Arithmetic Teacher* 36 (September 1988): 18-24. *Explorations developing ideas of perimeter and area.*

Blake, Rick N. "The Spider and the Fly: A Geometric Encounter in Three Dimensions." *Mathematics Teacher* 78 (February 1985): 98-104. *Helping students visualize three-dimensional problems.*

Bright, George. "Ideas." *Arithmetic Teacher* 33 (November 1985): 27-32. *Activities to develop concept of measuring length.*

Clemens, Stanley R. "Applied Measurement — Using Problem Solving." *Mathematics Teacher* 78 (March 1985): 176-180. *A view of the skills needed for proficiency in measurement.*

Cook, Marcy. "Ideas." *Arithmetic Teacher* 36 (April 1989): 27-32. *Activities that involve weight and temperature data.*

Fay, Nancy, and Catherine Tsairides. "Metric Mall." *Arithmetic Teacher* 37 (September 1989): 6-11. *An integrated activity using metric measuring tools and familiar materials.*

Gerver, Robert. "Discovering Pi – Two Approaches." *Arithmetic Teacher* 37 (April 1990): 18-22. *Visual and intuitive introductions to pi.*

Harrison, William R. "What Lies Behind Measurement?" *Arithmetic Teacher* 34 (March 1987): 19-21. *Activities to develop understanding of the concept of a standard unit.*

Hart, Kathleen. "Which Comes First — Length, Area, or Volume?" *Arithmetic Teacher* 31 (May 1984): 16-18, 26-27. *A heirarchy of measurement skills.*

Hawkins, Vincent J. "Applying Pick's Theorem to Randomized Areas." *Arithmetic Teacher* 36 (October 1988): 47-49. *Combines teaching about areas of lattice polygons with Pick's theorem using a game format.*

Hiebert, James. "Why Do Some Children Have Trouble Learning Measurement Concepts?" *Arithmetic Teacher* 31 (March 1984): 19-24. *Research on teaching measurement concepts.*

Jensen, Rosalie. "Multilevel Metric Games." *Arithmetic Teacher* 32 (October 1984): 36-39. *Improvement of skills in comparison, estimation, and linear measurement.*

Kastner, Bernice. "Number Sense: The Role of Measurement Applications." *Arithmetic Teacher* 36 (February 1989): 40-46. *Alternative strategies for teaching the measurement process.*

Kolnowski, Linda W., and Joann King Okey. "Ideas: Area and Perimeter." *Arithmetic Teacher* 34 (April 1987): 28, 32-33. *Activity exploring area and perimeter on dot grid.*

Lindquist, Mary Montgomery. "Estimation and Mental Computation: Measurement." *Arithmetic Teacher* 34 (January 1987): 16-18. *Examples for presenting estimation strategies.*

Lindquist, Mary Montgomery. "Implementing the Standards: The Measurement Standards." *Arithmetic Teacher* 37 (October 1989): 22-26. *Presents activities with pattern blocks to help students develop understanding of attribute being measured.*

Martin, W. Gary, and Joao Ponte. "Measuring the Area of Golf Greens and Other Irregular Regions." *Mathematics Teacher* 78 (May 1985): 385-389. *A stimulating "true-life" problem.*

Miller, L. Diane, and Jim Miller. "Metric Week – the Capitol Way." *Mathematics Teacher* 82 (September 1989): 454-458. *Sequence of activities to increase understanding of metric measures.*

Neufeld, K. Allen. "Body Measurement." *Arithmetic Teacher* 36 (May 1989): 12-15. *Activities exploring relationships between body measurements.*

Shaw, Jean M. "Ideas." *Arithmetic Teacher* 32 (December 1984): 20-24. *Practice in metric measuring skills.*

Shaw, Jean M. "Let's Do It: Student-made Measuring Tools." *Arithmetic Teacher* 31 (November 1983): 12-15. *Students produce their own measuring devices to use.*

Szetela, Walter, and Douglas T. Owens. "Finding the Area of a Circle: Use a Cake Pan and Leave Out the Pi." *Arithmetic Teacher* 33 (May 1986): 12-18. *Several different methods for approximating the area of a circular region.*

Thompson, Charles S., and John Van de Walle. "Let's Do It: Learning about Rulers and Measuring." *Arithmetic Teacher* 32 (April 1985): 8-12. *A developmental sequence of activities that introduce children to linear measurement and the use of rulers.*

Van de Walle, John, and Charles S. Thompson. "Let's Do It: Estimate How Much." *Arithmetic Teacher* 32 (May 1985): 4-8. *Activities designed to help young children learn the basic notion of "about how much."*

Willcutt, Bob. "Triangular Tiles for Your Patio?" *Arithmetic Teacher* 34 (May 1987): 43-45. *Creative spatial problem-solving activities.*

DIRECTIONS IN EDUCATION

Dealing with Diversity - Mathematicians All

American classrooms, like the American culture, are comprised of widely diverse groups of students. In efforts to meet the needs of this diverse population, educators have successively resorted to more narrow subdivisions of students within a classroom. These divisions — or tracks – have created as many problems as they have solved. For example, some students have been routinely scheduled into basic math classes where they will learn, at best, only basic math. In general, these basic skills will only prepare such students to compete against workers in the Third World for Third World wages, yet such placement decisions are frequently made by the intermediate or middle school years. Once relegated to the basic math track, students seldom have the opportunity to participate in "college prep" math courses. While research on tracking consistently shows advantages for gifted students, it is equally consistent in showing disadvantages for every other group of students in our schools.

The problem of tracking is compounded by the fact that women and minorities are more frequently referred to lower tracks in mathematics. In addition, master teachers are often given the opportunity to teach advanced tracks, thus leaving the less experienced or less skilled to teach those students least prepared to understand the concepts to be taught.

Educational trends which are currently at odds with the practice of tracking include mainstreaming of mildly or moderately handicapped youngsters into the regular classroom and the focus on cooperative learning which encourages heterogeneous grouping within the classroom. Increased demands to incorporate cultural awareness and acceptance of differences will further complicate the practice of tracking which currently predominates.

Implications for the classroom teacher:

- As schools move away from tracking in providing for the needs of individual students, classrooms become more heterogeneous. The classroom teacher must assume increased responsibility for assessing and meeting the diverse needs of individual students.

- While vertical acceleration through the sequence of courses or goals has been encouraged by the practice of tracking, enrichment in heterogeneously grouped classrooms may be more appropriately provided through extensions of learning based on a single goal—horizontal enrichment. In that way, individual student needs can be met while allowing the teacher to focus whole group instruction on a single concept.

- When handicapped students or students who speak English as a second language are placed in the mainstreamed classroom, the teacher must learn to work closely with special education consultants and with language tutors in planning for the special needs of these students. Such students are not incapable of learning the required content, they just need different kinds of instructional assistance to achieve their goals.

- As the focus shifts to providing a common core of mathematics instruction for all students, teachers are challenged to:

  - know what comprises the core of mathematics content appropriate for students at that grade level,

  - accept responsibility for the education of a significantly larger fraction of the population,

  - stimulate able students with the excitement and challenge of mathematics while encouraging less able students to set and meet high standards,

  - differentiate instruction by approach and speed, not by varying curricular goals or by advancement to subsequent courses.

As you think about dealing with the diverse population of a mainstreamed classroom, ask yourself:

- Why do able students become more "remedial" when placed in a remedial program?

- What messages are communicated to students who are placed in high level classes? in low level classes?

- How can I provide whole class instruction which meets the diverse needs of my students?

- How can I establish fair and consistent grading practices which provide meaningful feedback to individual students?

To learn more:

Braddock, Jomills Henry, II, and James M. McPartland. "Alternatives to Tracking." *Educational Leadership* 47 (April 1990): 76-79.

Cohen, E.G. *Designing Groupwork: Strategies for the Heterogeneous Classroom.* New York: Teachers College Press, 1986.

Educational Leadership 46 (March 1989). Focus issue on "Dealing With Diversity: Ability, Gender and Style Differences."

Peterson, John M. "Remediation Is No Remedy." *Educational Leadership* 46 (March 1989): 24-25.

14

Geometry Using Triangle Congruence and Similarity

THEME: Exploring Triangle Congruence and Geometric Constructions

WARM-UP

Strategy Review: Make a List.
This strategy, presented in Chapter 1, will be useful in solving these problems.

How many squares of all sizes can you find in this array?

How many triangles can you find?

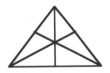

HANDS-ON ACTIVITIES

The first activity of this chapter will help you understand the meaning of congruent triangles and the correspondence between parts.

261

OBJECTIVE: **Recognize correspondences between congruent triangles**

You Will Need: Tracing paper

1. Two triangles are **congruent** if there is a correspondence between vertices such that all corresponding sides are congruent and all corresponding angles are congruent. Visually, that means that they have the same size and shape. Two triangles are given below. Trace △ MTO.

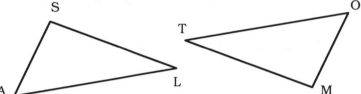

Can you fit the copy of △ MTO on top of △ LAS?

2. When △ MTO fits on top of △ LAS you can identify the correspondence of points. Indicate that correspondence.

   M ↔ ___   T ↔ ___   O ↔ ___

3. In writing a statement of congruence, you want to list the points in corresponding order. Complete these statements:

   △ MTO ≅ △ _____   △ TOM ≅ △ _____   △ MOT ≅ △ _____

4. In the triangles pictured below, identify the correspondence and complete the congruence statements.

   a.   b. 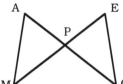   c.

T ↔ __	P ↔ __	S ↔ __
O ↔ __	A ↔ __	A ↔ __
Y ↔ __	M ↔ __	D ↔ __

   △ TOY ≅ △ _____   △ PAM ≅ △ _____   △ SAD ≅ △ _____

The next activities investigate conditions that lead to congruence of triangles.

OBJECTIVE: **Investigate triangle congruence given three sides**

You Will Need: Scratch paper, compass, straightedge, and tracing paper

1. Given below are three segments. Follow the steps below to construct a triangle having sides congruent to these three segments.

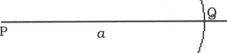

a: _____

b: _____

c: _____

   a. Lay off one side, for example, side a.
      Call this segment $\overline{PQ}$.

   b. Construct an arc the length of b from one endpoint, say P.

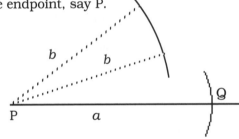

   c. Construct an arc the length of c from the other endpoint, Q.

   d. Where the two arcs meet is the third vertex of the triangle. Complete your triangle.

2. Construct another triangle using these three sides. For example, you might want to use sides in a different order.

3. Trace one of the triangles. Does it fit exactly on top of the other one by some combination of flipping, turning or sliding? Are the triangles congruent?

> Write a sentence that summarizes what you found.

OBJECTIVE: **Investigate triangle congruence given 2 sides, 1 angle**

You Will Need: Scratch paper, compass, straightedge, and tracing paper or protractor from Materials Card 10.4

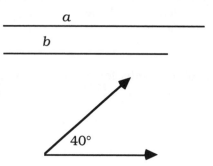

1. Given are two segments and a 40° angle.

    a. Draw a triangle having an angle with the same measure, using a protractor or tracing paper, and putting the segments along the rays of the angle. Connect the endpoints of the segments to find the third side.

    b. Draw another triangle using these given components. For example, switch the segments on the sides of the angle.

    c. Trace one of the triangles. Does it fit exactly on top of the other one? Are they congruent?

2. Using the same angle and segments, follow these steps:

    a. Using a protractor or tracing paper, make a copy of the angle. Call the vertex point A. Extend one side of the angle at least 8 cm.

    b. On the other side of the angle, mark off a segment with the length of *a*. Call its endpoint B.

    c. Set your compass to the length of *b*. From point B swing an arc towards the longer side of the original angle. It should intersect that side in two places. Call one point C and the other D.

    d. You have formed two triangles, Δ ABC and Δ ABD. Are these triangles congruent?

    Write a sentence that summarizes what you found.

OBJECTIVE: **Investigate triangle congruence given 2 angles, 1 side**

You Will Need: Scratch paper, compass, straightedge, and tracing paper or protractor from Materials Card 10.4

1. Given are two angles and one segment.

    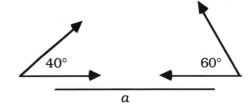

    a. Draw a triangle having one side with the given length, and putting the angles at the endpoints of the segment. The other rays of the angles will meet at the third vertex.

    b. Draw another triangle using these given components. For example, you may want to switch the angles on the ends of the segment.

    c. Trace one of the triangles. Does it fit exactly on top of the other? Are they congruent?

    d. If two triangles have a correspondence of vertices such that two pairs of corresponding angles and the pair of corresponding **included sides** are congruent, are the triangles necessarily congruent?

2. Given are two triangles with two pairs of congruent corresponding angles and a **nonincluded** pair of sides congruent. What other information do you know about these triangles? Are they congruent?

    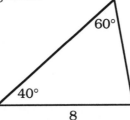

    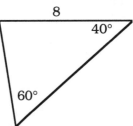

Write a sentence that summarizes what you found.

OBJECTIVE: **Investigate triangle congruence and similarity given 2 angles**

You Will Need: Scratch paper, compass, straightedge, and tracing paper or protractor from Materials Card 10.4

1. Given are two angles. If these two angles were vertex angles of a triangle, what would be the measure of the third angle?

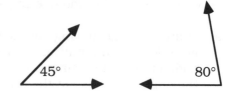

2. Construct a triangle having these vertex angles as follows:

    a. Draw a segment of arbitrary length.
    b. At one end of the segment, draw a 45° angle.
    c. At the other end of the segment, draw the 80° angle.
    d. Extend the sides of the angle until they meet at the third vertex.

3. Construct another triangle using the same angles. For example, select a different arbitrary length. Are the two triangles you have drawn congruent? Explain why or why not.

4. Label the triangles so that corresponding angles are identified as A and D, B and E, and C and F. Is ∠A ≅ ∠D, ∠B ≅ ∠E, and ∠C ≅ ∠F?

    Using a millimeter ruler, measure the lengths of the sides and complete the given ratios:

$$\frac{AB}{DE} = \underline{\quad} =$$
$$\frac{AC}{DF} = \underline{\quad} =$$
$$\frac{BC}{EF} = \underline{\quad} =$$

    Two triangles are **similar** if there is a correspondence between vertices such that all corresponding sides are proportional and all corresponding angles are congruent. Visually, that means that they have the same shape. Are the two triangles you have drawn similar?

> Write a sentence that summarizes what you found.

The next activities explore the construction of regular *n*-gons. These involve applications of the basic construction techniques with compass, straightedge, and Mira.

OBJECTIVE: **Construct regular *n*-gons of the family *n* = 4**

You Will Need: Compass, straightedge, scratch paper

1. Recall that a **square** is any quadrilateral that has four congruent sides and four right angles. Using this definition, apply your construction techniques to construct a square on the scratch paper whose sides are congruent to segment $\overline{AB}$.

   A _____ B

   How many times did you construct a right angle?

2. It can be shown that a rhombus with at least one right angle is a square. Based upon this information, can you refine the construction procedure you used in part 1 above?

3. The diagonals of a square are perpendicular bisectors of each other. Use this fact to construct a square inscribed in the given circle.

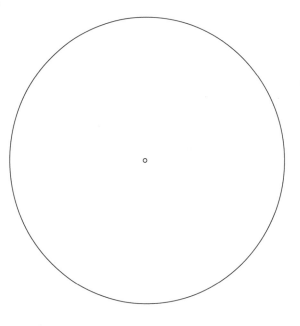

4. Using the square constructed in the previous part, bisect the central angles with other diameters. Connect the consecutive points on the circle (including those found previously).

   What regular *n*-gon does this form?

5. How could you proceed to construct a regular 16-gon?   32-gon?

OBJECTIVE: **Construct regular *n*-gons of the family *n* = 5**

You Will Need: Compass, straightedge, scratch paper

1. The construction of the following regular polygon is accomplished via a series of intermediate constructions. Use great care in each step. Do your work on scratch paper.

    a. Taking AB as a unit length, construct a segment $\overline{CD}$ of length $\sqrt{5}$. Hint: Use the Pythagorean theorem.   A _____ B

    b. Using AB and CD, construct a segment $\overline{EF}$ of length $\sqrt{5} - 1$.

    c. Bisect segment $\overline{EF}$ forming segment $\overline{EG}$. What is the length of segment $\overline{EG}$?

    d. Construct a circle whose radius is AB.

    e. With the compass open a distance equal to EG, make marks around the circle (starting from any point). Connect the consecutive points. What regular polygon did you form?

2. How could you utilize the polygon you just constructed to construct a regular pentagon?

3. How could you construct a regular 20-gon?

The next activities investigate some special construction techniques and outcomes.

OBJECTIVE: **Perform constructions by paper folding**

You Will Need: Several sheets of tracing or wax paper, Mira (optional)

1. To construct the **perpendicular bisector of a segment** $\overline{PQ}$, follow these steps:

    a. Draw segment $\overline{PQ}$ on tracing or wax paper.

    b. Fold the sheet over so that points P and Q are superimposed on each other.

c. While holding those two points between the thumb and a finger of one hand, crease the fold with the thumb and a finger of the other hand.

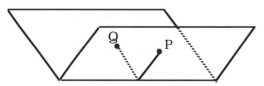

Note: In a similar fashion, this construction can also be performed with a Mira by superimposing the image of point P on point Q.

2. On a sheet of paper, draw an acute triangle. Construct the perpendicular bisectors of each side. These meet at a single point, called the **circumcenter** of the triangle. This point is the center of the **circumscribed circle** that contains all the vertices of the triangle.

Repeat this construction with an obtuse and a right triangle.

Describe where the circumcenter is located for each kind of triangle.

3. To construct the **angle bisector** of angle P by paper folding, follow these steps:

a. Draw an angle RPS on tracing or wax paper.

b. Fold the paper so that the rays PR and PS coincide. Crease the fold.

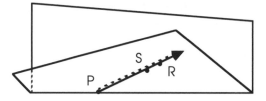

Similarly, fixing the Mira at point P and adjusting it until the rays match bisects an angle with a Mira.

4. Draw an acute triangle and construct the angle bisectors of each of its angles. These meet at a single point, called the **incenter** of the triangle. This point is the center of the **inscribed circle** that is tangent to each of the sides of the triangle.

Repeat this construction with an obtuse and a right triangle.

Describe where the incenter is located for each kind of triangle.

5. To construct the **perpendicular** to a given line *l* passing through a given point P, follow these steps for paper folding:

   a. Draw a line *l* and choose any point P on line *l*.

   b. Fold the paper without creasing it so that the line is superimposed on itself. Slide the paper, keeping the line coinciding with itself, until the fold passes through point P. Crease the fold.

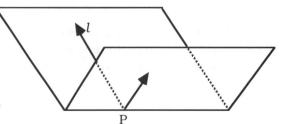

   c. Repeat the process with a point which is not on line *l*.

   Likewise, these constructions can be done by fixing the Mira at point P and pivoting it until the line is superimposed on itself.

6. Draw an acute triangle. Recall that an **altitude** of a triangle is the line through a vertex perpendicular to the opposite side (or the line containing the opposite side). Construct the altitudes from each vertex of the triangle you drew. These meet at a single point, called the **orthocenter** of the triangle.

   Repeat this construction with an obtuse and a right triangle.

   Describe where the orthocenter is located for each kind of triangle.

OBJECTIVE: **Construct the circumcenter, centroid, and orthocenter of a triangle and find the Euler line**

You Will Need: Mira, or compass and straightedge

The triangle given on the next page will be used for each of the following constructions.

Using a Mira for the constructions, instead of a compass and straightedge, will eliminate many extraneous marks. Also, using a different colored pencil or pen for each step may be helpful.

You may also use a copy of the triangle and paper folding and transfer the results onto the triangle shown.

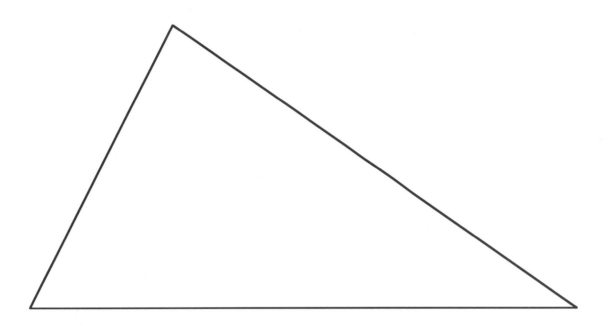

1. Construct the perpendicular bisectors of each side to find the **circumcenter** of the triangle. Label the circumcenter C.

2. The segment connecting a vertex with the midpoint of the opposite side is called a **median** of the triangle. Construct the median from each vertex of the triangle. (Hint: You found the midpoints in part 1 above.) The medians meet at a single point, called the **centroid**. This point is the center of gravity or point of balance of a triangle. Label the centroid D.

3. Construct the altitudes from each vertex to find the **orthocenter** of the triangle. Label the orthocenter O.

4. Connect the circumcenter, the centroid, and the orthocenter. Do these points appear to be collinear? _____ (They should.) The line containing these three points is called the **Euler line**, named for the Swiss mathematician Leonard Euler.

The last activity explores applications of similar triangles.

OBJECTIVE: **Make indirect measurements using similar triangles**

You Will Need: Measuring stick, mirror, and a sunny day (optional)

1. Measure a reasonable distance (1-2 meters) from the base of one wall in your classroom and place the mirror on the floor at that point. Stand beyond the mirror at the point where you can see the image of where that wall meets the ceiling in the mirror.

   a. Record the following distances on the picture below.

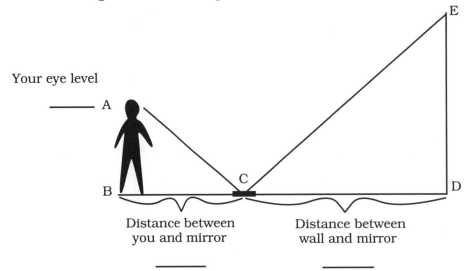

   b. Justify why these two triangles are similar.

   c. Using the similar triangles, find the height of the wall.

   d. If possible, measure the actual height of the wall. How close was your indirect measurement?

2. If conditions permit, go outside for the following activity.

   a. Choose some objects such as a building, flagpole, or tree.

   b. Repeat the process in part 1 to indirectly determine the height of the objects chosen.

3. (Sunny day required.) Choose a partner who is not the same height as you. Find a place where your shadows are visible and measure the following:

        Your height _____   Length of your shadow _____

        Your partner's height _____   Length of your partner's shadow _____

Compute the following ratios:

$$\frac{\text{Your height}}{\text{Partner's height}} = \underline{\quad} = \qquad\qquad \frac{\text{Your shadow}}{\text{Partner's shadow}} = \underline{\quad} =$$

$$\frac{\text{Your height}}{\text{Your shadow}} = \underline{\quad} = \qquad\qquad \frac{\text{Partner's height}}{\text{Partner's shadow}} = \underline{\quad} =$$

What do you observe? What do you think would happen at a different time of day?

4. Choose an object (building, tree, etc...) and measure the following:

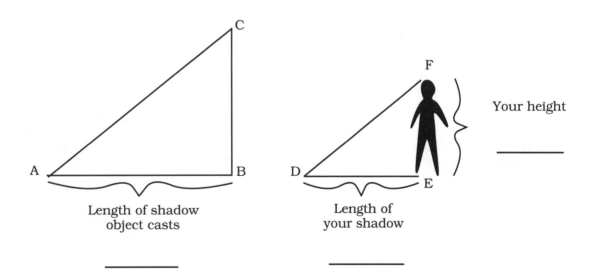

      Length of shadow   Length of
        object casts   your shadow

Justify why these two triangles are similar and use them to find the height of the object.

MENTAL MATH

For each figure below, make one cut that creates two congruent halves. The cut does not have to be straight, but it must be one continuous cut.

For example:

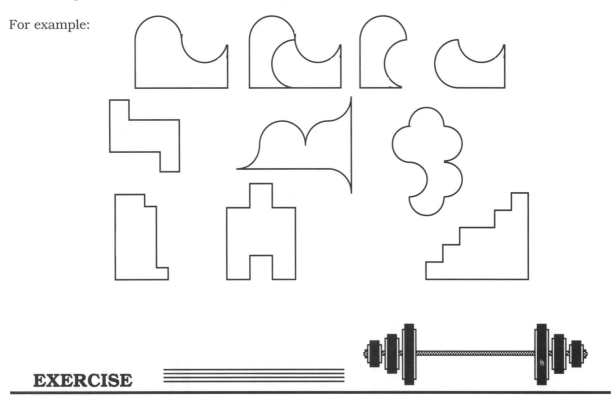

EXERCISE

Treasure Hunt

Given below are the instructions to find the treasure hidden on an exotic island. The only tools you have available are a compass (the kind that draws circles) and a straightedge. Where is the treasure located?

You land at the midpoint of segment AB. The distance from your landing point to point A is one league. From your landing point head straight inland (making a right angle with the shore) for one league. Make a path parallel to the shore and travel eastward for two leagues. Turn toward the north and travel along a path that makes a 60° angle with your previous path. Your stopping point will be where a path through point P intersects your current path at a right angle. Turn and proceed on the path through P for three leagues. Turn toward the north again traveling along a path that makes a 45° angle with your previous path. Travel for three leagues. Turn toward the east traveling along a path that makes a 120° angle with your previous path. Travel for three leagues and start digging.

$\mathcal{P}$

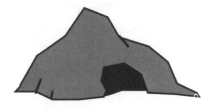

$\mathcal{A}$

$\mathcal{B}$

Constructible Designs

The following designs can be constructed using only compass and straightedge. How many of these designs can you construct? Hint: It may be easier to construct versions larger than those shown.

A.

B.

C.

D.

E.

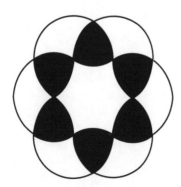

F.

SELF-TEST

1. Which of the following is *not* an appropriate congruence relation for showing that triangles are congruent?

    a. ASA b. SSS c. SAS d. AAA

2. In the diagram at the right, you can say that △ DEF is actually a copy of △ ABC because by construction they

    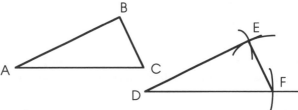

    a. have the same shape.
    b. satisfy the SSS Congruence Property.
    c. have the same size.
    d. satisfy the SAS Congruence Property.

3. Given: Rectangle RSTU with diagonals meeting at point W. Which of the following statements could be shown to be true?

    (i) △ RUT ≅ △ STU   (ii) △ RWU ≅ △ SWT   (iii) △ RWS is isosceles

    a. only i and ii   b. only i and iii   c. only ii and iii   d. i, ii, and iii

4. Given: Kite ABCD with diagonal $\overline{BD}$.
    In order to show that the diagonal divides the kite into two congruent triangles, each of the following statements is *justifiable* and *useful except*

    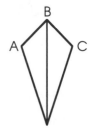

    a. ∠ A ≅ ∠ C b. $\overline{AB}$ ≅ $\overline{CB}$ c. $\overline{BD}$ ≅ $\overline{BD}$ d. $\overline{DA}$ ≅ $\overline{DC}$

5. Given the figure at the right, complete the following statement:
    △ LMN ≅ _____

    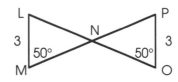

    a. △ OPN
    b. △ PON
    c. △ NOP
    d. Insufficient given information.

6. Which of the following points associated with a triangle is the center of the circle that contains all three vertices of the triangle?

    a. centroid   b. circumcenter   c. incenter   d. orthocenter

7. Which of the following regular polygons cannot be constructed with a compass and straightedge?

    a. 36-gon   b. 85-gon   c. 60-gon   d. 64-gon

8. To construct the circle inscribed in a given triangle, each of the following construction steps would be applied *except*

   a. perpendicular bisector
   c. angle bisector
   b. perpendicular to a line through a point not on the line
   d. circle

9. Given $\overline{UV} \parallel \overline{WX}$, find $\overline{WX}$.

   a. 12
   c. 18
   b. 20
   d. 16

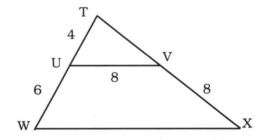

10. At a certain time of day, a flagpole casts a shadow 21 meters long on horizontal ground. At the same time, a vertical pole 4 meters high casts a shadow 6 meters long. How tall is the flagpole?

   a. 10 meters
   b. 11.6 meters
   c. 14 meters
   d. 31.5 meters

SOLUTIONS

Warm-up
14 squares   16 triangles

Hands-on Activities
Activity 1
1. Yes
4. a. J, Y, O, JYO
2. S, L, A
   b. P, E, G, PEG
3. SLA, LAS, SAL
   c. M, D, A, MDA

Activity 2
3. Yes, Yes
   If two triangles have a correspondence of vertices such that all three pairs of corresponding sides are congruent, then the triangles are congruent (SSS Congruence Property).

Activity 3
1. c. Yes, Yes
2. d. No
   If two triangles have a correspondence of vertices such that two pairs of corresponding sides and the pair of corresponding angles are congruent, then the triangles are congruent if the angle is the included angle between the two sides (SAS Congruence Property). If the given angles are opposite one pair of sides, the triangles are not necessarily congruent.

Activity 4

1. c. Yes, Yes   d. Yes
2. The unmarked angles are both 80° (since the sum of the three angles of a triangle is 180°). Yes, based upon the result of part 1.
   If two triangles have a correspondence of vertices such that two pairs of corresponding angles and a pair of corresponding sides (included or nonincluded) are congruent, then the two triangles are congruent (ASA Congruence Property and AAS Congruence Property).

Activity 5

1. 55°
2. No, the triangles are not congruent (unless the same length was chosen).
3. Yes. Answers may vary, but the ratios should be equal. Yes.
   If two triangles have a correspondence of vertices such that two pairs of corresponding angles are congruent, then the triangles are similar (AA Similarity Property).

Activity 6

1. One, two, three or four
2. You should be able to construct a square by only constructing one right angle. Construct the angle first and mark off lengths on two sides of the angle. With the same compass setting, construct arcs from these endpoints that meet to form the fourth vertex.
3. Construct any diameter. Then construct another diameter perpendicular to the first one. Connect the endpoints of these diameters to form a square.
4. An octagon
5. Bisect central angles of a regular octagon; bisect central angles of a regular 16-gon.

Activity 7

1. a. Construct a right triangle with sides of length 2 and 1.
   b. Subtract length AB from CD   c. $(\sqrt{5} - 1)/2$ e. A decagon
2. Connect every other vertex of the decagon.
3. Bisect central angles of a regular decagon.

Activity 8

2. The circumcenter of an acute triangle is inside the triangle. For an obtuse triangle, it is outside. The circumcenter of a right triangle is the midpoint of the hypotenuse.
4. The incenter is located inside the circle for all triangles.
6. The orthocenter falls inside an acute triangle and outside an obtuse triangle. The orthocenter of a right triangle is the vertex of the right angle.

Activity 9

4. Yes

Activity 10

1. Because the angle of incidence is the same as the angle of reflection ($\angle$ BCA $\cong$ $\angle$ DCE) and assuming you and the wall are both perpendicular to the floor ($\angle$ B $\cong$ $\angle$ D), the two triangles are similar by the AA Similarity Property.
3. The ratios of corresponding sides are equal. Also, corresponding ratios of sides within the triangles are equal. At a different time of day, the length of the shadows would be different but their ratio would be the same.
4. Since you are measuring the shadows at the same time of day, the angle of incidence of the sun would be the same ($\angle$ A $\cong$ $\angle$ D). Assuming you and the object form the same angles with level ground, the triangles would be similar by the AA Similarity Property.

Mental Math

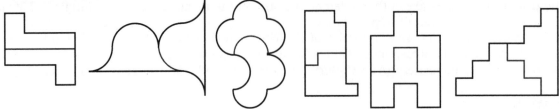

Exercises

Treasure Hunt
    Look in the thatch roof of the hut.

Self-Test

1. d **2.** b **3.** d **4.** a **5.** b **6.** b **7.** a **8.** a **9.** b **10.** c

RESOURCES ARTICLES

Brown, Susan A. "Drawing Altitudes of Triangles." *Mathematics Teacher* 78 (March 1985): 182-183. *Introducing altitudes of triangles on graph paper.*

Ellington, Bee. "Star Trek: A Construction Problem Using Compass and Straightedge." *Mathematics Teacher* 76 (May 1983): 329-332. *Students perform a series of constructions to find Spock, who is lost in space.*

Horak, Virginia M., and Willis J. Horak. "Let's Do It: Using Geometry Tiles As a Manipulative for Developing Basic Concepts." *Arithmetic Teacher* 30 (April 1983): 8-15. *Using tiles to help children construct and visualize basic geometric shapes.*

Lappan, Glenda, and Ruhama Even. "Similarity in the Middle Grades." *Arithmetic Teacher* 35 (May 1988): 32-35. *Discusses research and implications for teachers.*

Roberti, Joseph V. "Some Challenging Constructions." *Mathematics Teacher* 79 (April 1986): 283-287. *A game of geometric solitaire.*

Yeshurun, Shraga. "An Improvement of the Congruent Angles Theorem." *Mathematics Teacher* 78 (January 1985): 53-54. *A proof involving similar triangles.*

Yeshurun, Shraga, and David C. Kay. "An Improvement on SSA Congruence for Geometry and Trigonometry." *Mathematics Teacher* 76 (May 1983): 364-367, 347. *Discussions of investigations involving the SSA theorem.*

DIRECTIONS IN EDUCATION

Parental Involvement - Partnership With Parents

Parents are a precious resource for encouraging student participation and achievement in mathematics. Schools must find meaningful ways in which to involve parents in the learning process. This involvement may take various forms. Parents may participate directly in the schools in the design of curriculum or in delivery of instruction either as paid classroom assistants or as volunteers. Parents may actively participate in the linking of home and school activities by being aware of assignments and topics currently under study, by providing opportunities to link that study to the child's world, or by setting expectations for achievement in school. In addition, parents may participate indirectly by providing a mathematics enriched environment in the home to promote learning about mathematics beyond the school setting. Parents have hopes and dreams for their children. It is the task of the teacher to help parents see the classroom as a place where those dreams are enhanced and supported. Involved parents can provide for continuity of experiences as children move from classroom to classroom, from school to school, or from town to town.

Parental involvement in the schools is enhanced by:

- Clear statements about the nature of volunteer work asked of the parent.

- Allowing parents to work with children rather than giving them mundane paperwork tasks such as cutting or correcting.

- Keeping open lines of two-way communication.

- Sharing news of student successes as well as areas requiring further attention.

- Providing resources which parents can use at home to enrich and extend classroom learning.

- Recognizing and rewarding parental involvement either informally or formally. Personal thank you notes, certificates or a recognition ceremony at school are ways to demonstrate that parents are appreciated in your classroom.

- Pointing out to parents negative attitudes or stereotypes about mathematics which may be unconsciously transmitted to children.

- Providing information to parents which will enable them to feel more knowledgeable as they work with their students. Parents, like teachers, do not wish to seem uninformed in front of their children.

- Sharing information about the use of instructional techniques which may be unfamiliar to parents. It is always easier to support something when it is better understood.

Advantages of parental involvement:

- Misconceptions about schools which may appear in the media can be corrected.

- Parental self-esteem is enhanced, thus contributing to the enhancement of student self-esteem.

- Consistent expectations of school and home encourage student understanding of and compliance with those expectations.

- Parents can better anticipate and support future growth and development of mathematical understanding.

- Positive attitudes toward mathematics can be linked with pleasant experiences within the family through games and other social activities which promote mathematical understanding.

- Parental support of the schools will be communicated in their places of work and in the community at large.

- Teachers form strong partnerships with parents which foster positive home/school relationships and reduce confrontational situations.

As you think about involving parents in your classroom, ask yourself:

- What do parents consider to be "meaningful" involvement in their child's classroom?

- How can I clarify for parents the opportunities for involvement in my classroom?

- How can I encourage more parental involvement in my classroom?

To learn more:

Comer, James P. *Maggie's American Dream.* New York: New American Library, 1988.

National Association for the Education of Young Children. *Developmentally Appropriate Practice in Early Childhood Programs Serving Children From Birth Through Age 8, Expanded Edition.* Sue Bredekamp, Editor. Washington, DC: NAEYC, 1987.

Walter G. Secada. "Parental Involvement in a Time of Changing Demographics." *Arithmetic Teacher* 37(December 1989): 33-35.

Stenmark, Jean K., Virginia Thompson, and Ruth Cossey. *Family Math.* Berkeley, CA: University of California — Berkeley, 1986.

15 Geometry Using Coordinates

THEME: Using Coordinates in Geometry

Strategy Review: Identify Subgoals.
This strategy, presented in Chapter 14, will help solve the given problem.

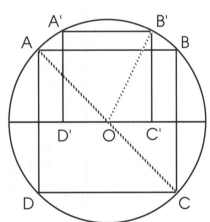

The area of the square ABCD inscribed in circle O is 30 cm². What is the area of square A'B'C'D' inscribed in a semicircle of circle O?

HANDS-ON ACTIVITIES

The first activities of this chapter will help you become familiar with a coordinate system in the plane.

OBJECTIVE: **Illustrate a coordinate system on a square lattice**

1. In previous chapters you have worked with a geoboard or with a square lattice. The points in an array like the one pictured can also be identified using coordinates.

    First, number the columns from left to right.

    Then, number the rows beginning with the bottom row.

    A point can be identified by giving its column number and its row number, in that order.

    For example, point A has coordinates (2, 5).

    Find the coordinates of the following points.

    a. B   b. C   c. D   d. E

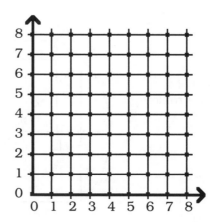

2. Connecting the dots in each row and column yields the grid pattern to the right. The grid could be extended to include more points as illustrated.

    a. Plot the points A (2, 1), B (6, 1), C (6, 2), D (5, 3), E (5, 6), F (4, 8), G (3, 6), H (3, 3), and I (2, 2).

    b. Connect A to B, B to C, ... , and I to A. What type of polygon have you drawn?

3. Point A has coordinates (0, 5).

    We could extend the grid to the
    left and label it with integers.
    Then we see point B has coordinates
    (-3, 6).

    A similar extension of the
    grid allows us to find coordinates
    for points such as C and D.

    What are the coordinates of
    points C and D?

    C = (,   )   D = (,   )

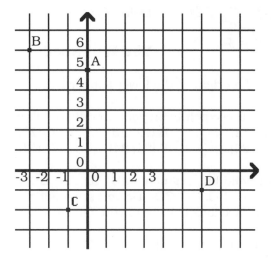

4. The grid system we now have is called the **Cartesian coordinate system**, in honor of the
    mathematician René Descartes.

    The two darkened lines that are
    perpendicular to each other are
    called the **axes** (singular is axis).
    Here we call the horizontal line
    the **x-axis** and the vertical line
    the **y-axis.** They meet at the point
    called the **origin**, which has
    coordinates (0, 0).

    a. Plot the points A (5, 2), B (3, -1),
        C (-2, 5), D (1, -4), E (-3, -4),
        and F (-6, -2).

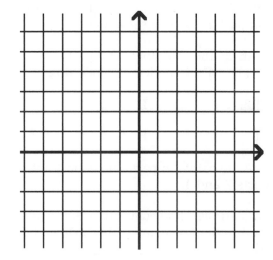

    b. The axes divide the plane into 4 regions, called **quadrants**. These are numbered I to
        IV, counterclockwise, beginning in the upper right-hand region. Identify the quadrant
        that each of the points A through F is in.

    c. In quadrant I all coordinates are positive. What do the coordinates of all the points in
        quadrant II have in common? in quadrant III? in quadrant IV?

OBJECTIVE: **Practice plotting points**

You Will Need: Materials Card 15.2 or graph paper

1. Place the origin at the lower left corner.

2. Locate these points on your coordinate plane.
    A (12, 12)   B (12, 20)   C (20, 20)   D (20, 12)
    E (16, 24)   F (24, 24)   G (24, 16)   H (16, 16)

    Make solid line segments $\overline{AB}$, $\overline{AD}$, $\overline{AH}$, $\overline{BE}$, $\overline{EF}$, $\overline{EH}$, $\overline{DG}$, $\overline{FG}$, $\overline{GH}$. Make dashed line
    segments $\overline{BC}$, $\overline{CF}$, $\overline{CD}$. Do you see a cube? _____
    Which face looks closer to you, face ABCD or face EFGH?

3. Divide each coordinate in A, B, C, D, E, F, G, H by 2 to get new points A', B', C', D', E', F',
    G', H'. Complete the following.

    A' (6, 6)   B' (,   )   C' (,   )   D' (,   )

    E' (,   )   F' (,   )   G' (,   )   H' (,   )

4. Locate A', B', C', D', E', F', G', H' on your graph. Make similar solid and dashed lines as you
    did in part 2. Do you see a cube? _____

5. Now divide the coordinates in A', B', C', D', E', F', G', H', by 2 to get points A", B", C", D",
    E", F", G", H". Complete the following.

    A" (3, 3)   B" (,   )   C" (,   )   D" (,   )

    E" (,   )   F" (,   )   G" (,   )   H" (,   )

6. Locate the points in part 5 on your graph. Make similar solid and dashed lines as you did
    in parts 2 and 4.

7. Draw a straight line connecting B, B', and B". Draw another line connecting C, C', and C".
    Draw another line connecting D, D', and D". Extend your three lines so that they intersect.
    Do they meet at the origin? _____

8. Turn your paper half-way around. What do you see? Would the title "The Shrinking Cube"
    be appropriate for this activity?

9. Can you draw another cube that lines up with the three you have drawn and is smaller
    than all the others? Draw it.

The next activities explore the concepts of **distance** and **slope**
in the Cartesian coordinate system.

OBJECTIVE: **Develop the idea of distance in the plane**

1. a. Points A and B are shown
        to the right on a portion of a
        square lattice. What are their
        coordinates?
            A (,)   B (,)

    b. Form a right triangle with segment
        $\overline{AB}$ as the hypotenuse. Draw the
        vertical line through A and the
        horizontal line through B. Name the
        point where these lines intersect
        point C. What are the coordinates
        of point C?   C (,)

    c. What is the length of segment $\overline{AC}$? of $\overline{BC}$?

    d. Use the Pythagorean theorem to find the length of segment $\overline{AB}$; AB = _____

2. On the following coordinate grid, points A and B are given with their coordinates.

    a. Point C is located at the
        intersection of the horizontal
        line through A and vertical line
        through B. What are the
        coordinates of C? _____

    b. What is the distance
        between A and C? _____
        between B and C?_____

    c. Use the Pythagorean theorem to find
        the distance between A and B.

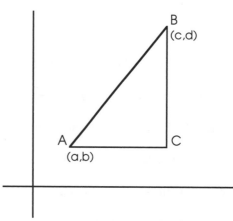

Summarize: If A is the point (a, b) and B is the point (c, d), then the distance
from A to B is

This result is known as the **coordinate distance formula**.

OBJECTIVE: **Investigate the slope of a line**

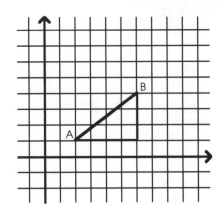

1. The **slope** of a line segment $\overline{AB}$ is defined as the ratio of rise/run where rise is the vertical change from A to B and run is the horizontal change from A to B.

   Imagine that segment $\overline{AB}$ is a road up a hill.

   a. What is the vertical change from A to B? _____

   b. What is the horizontal change from A to B? _____

   c. What is the ratio of rise/run?

2. Sometimes, the 'rise' may be negative.

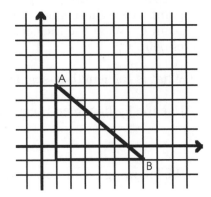

   a. What is the vertical change from A to B? _____

   b. What is the horizontal change from A to B? _____

   c. What is the slope of segment $\overline{AB}$? _____

3. On the grid to the right are points A and B with their coordinates (a, b) and (c, d), respectively.

   a. What is the vertical change from A to B? _____

   b. What is the horizontal change from A to B? _____

   c. What is the slope of segment $\overline{AB}$? _____

   d. What is the vertical change from B to A? _____

   e. What is the horizontal change from B to A? _____

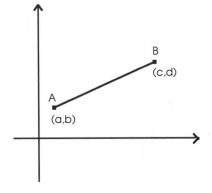

   f. What is the slope of the segment $\overline{BA}$? _____

   g. Compare your results in parts (c) and (f). What to you observe?

   Summarize: If A is the point (a, b) and B is the point (c, d), then the slope of line segment $\overline{AB}$ (where $a \neq c$) is

   This result is known as the **slope formula** for a line segment.

4. A line l is given on the grid to the right. Points A (-4, -1), B (0, 1), C (2, 2), and D (6, 4) are on the line l. Find the slopes of segments $\overline{AB}$, $\overline{AC}$, and $\overline{BD}$. What is the slope of line l?

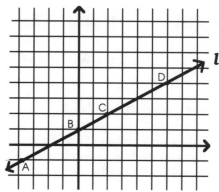

5. The following pairs of lines are parallel. Find the slope of each line and explain how the slopes of parallel lines are related.

a.

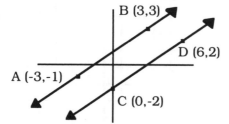

Slope of $\overset{\leftrightarrow}{AB}$ ____   Slope of $\overset{\leftrightarrow}{CD}$ ____

b.

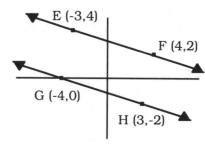

Slope of $\overset{\leftrightarrow}{EF}$ ____   Slope of $\overset{\leftrightarrow}{GH}$ ____

The following pairs of lines are perpendicular. Find the slope of each line and explain how the slopes of perpendicular lines are related. Hint: Consider their product.

c.

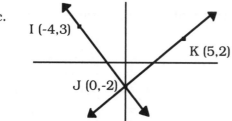

Slope of $\overset{\leftrightarrow}{IJ}$ ____   Slope of $\overset{\leftrightarrow}{JK}$ ____

d.

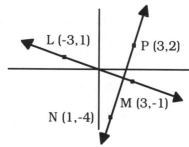

Slope of $\overset{\leftrightarrow}{LM}$ ____   Slope of $\overset{\leftrightarrow}{NP}$ ____

> Summarize:
> If two nonvertical lines are parallel, then their slopes are _____ .
>
> If two lines, neither of which is vertical, are perpendicular, then the product of their slopes is _____ .

The final activity explores the relationship between points in the plane and algebraic equations.

OBJECTIVE: **Investigate equations of lines geometrically**

You Will Need: A straightedge

1. Consider the equation $y = 2x - 3$.

    a. We want to find points of the form (x, y) that satisfy this equation. For the points below, an x-coordinate has been chosen. By substituting x into the equation, find the corresponding y-coordinate.

    (0,)   (2,)   (4,)   (1,)   (3,)   (-1,)

    b. On the coordinate grid to the right, plot the points you found in part (a). Connect these points to form a line.

    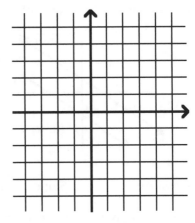

    What is the slope of this line? _____
    Does that number appear in the equation? _____ Where? _____

    What is the y-coordinate of the point where the line crosses the y-axis? _____ This is called the **y-intercept**. Does this value appear in the equation? _____ Where? _____

    c. Repeat parts (a) and (b) with the equation $y = -(2/3)x + 4$.

    d. In general, the equation of a nonvertical line may be written in the form $y = mx + b$.
    What does the value of m represent? _____
    What does the value of b represent? _____

2. a. On the coordinate grid to the right, graph the following points: (0, 0), (1, 2), (2, 4), (3, 6), (-1, -2), (-2, -4), and (-3, -6).

    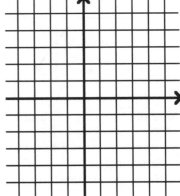

    b. Connect the points to form a straight line. What do you observe about the x- and y-coordinates of the points on this line?

    c. If (x, y) is a general point on this line, express the relationship you found as an equation.

    Note: Any line in the plane can be represented by an algebraic equation. However, not all equations will be as easy to find as the example here.

3. On the coordinate grid to the right, graph the vertical line through (3, 2).

   Does this line have a slope? _____
   Does it have a *y*-intercept? ____
   What do you observe about the *x*-coordinates of the points on this line? _____

   Write an equation to express this.

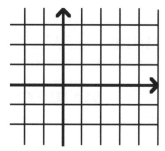

Summarize:
A nonvertical line can be represented by an equation of the form $y = mx + b$.
What does m represent? _____
What does b represent? _____

A vertical line has no slope. A vertical line through the point (a, b) can be represented by the equation _____ .

MENTAL MATH

Identify the line or circle on the graph that is described below.

   A. $y = 2x + 1$

   B. $x = -2$

   C. $(x - 3)^2 + (y - 2)^2 = 13$

   D. $y = (-2/3)x + 1$

   E. $(x + 3)^2 + (y + 2)^2 = 4$

   F. a line parallel to $y = (1/4)x + 5$

   G. a line whose slope is zero

   H. a line perpendicular to $y = (-2/3)x - 3$

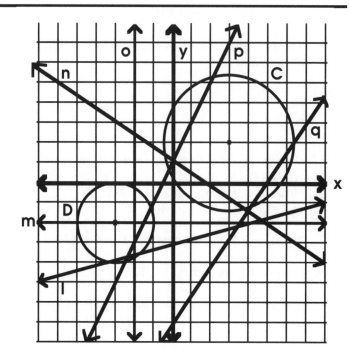

EXERCISES

SYMMETRY THROUGH COORDINATES

A. 1. Graph the points and form △ ABC.
   A(3, 5)   B(4, 1)   C(2, -1)

2. Multiply each *x*-coordinate by -1.
   A'(, 5)   B'(, 1)   C'(, -1)

3. Graph △ A'B'C'.

4. The two triangles *together* have
   what kinds of symmetry?

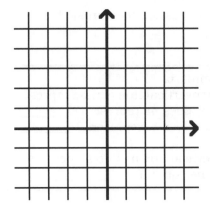

B. 1. Graph the points and form quadrilateral ABCD.
   A(-2, 4)   B(2, 5)   C(5, 1)   D(-4, 0)

2. Multiply each *y*-coordinate by -1.
   A'(-2,   )   B'(2,   )   C'(5,   )   D'(-4,   )

3. Graph quadrilateral A'B'C'D'.

4. The two quadrilaterals *together* have what kinds
   of symmetry?

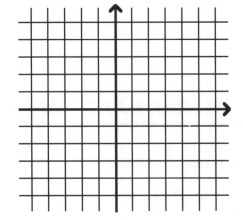

C. 1. Graph the following points and form segments
   $\overline{HI}$, $\overline{IJ}$, . . . , $\overline{NH}$.
   H(0, 4)   I(1, 2)   J(3, 2)   K(1, 0)
   L(-1, 0)   M(-3, 2)   N(-1, 2)

2. Multiply all coordinates by -1 to form H', I', J', . . . , N'.

3. Graph the segments $\overline{H'I'}$, $\overline{I'J'}$, ..., $\overline{N'H'}$.

4. The resulting figure has what kinds of symmetry?

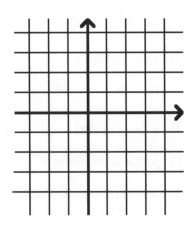

GEOMETRIC TRAINING

Dave likes to build model trains. However he has not completed the one pictured below. Follow the directions given to complete his model.

1. For a window, draw the rectangle whose sides are on the lines $x = -1$, $y = 2$, $x = -8$, $y = 7$.

2. For the top, draw the parallelogram whose sides are on lines $y = 8$, $y = 10$, $y = -2x + 8$, $y = -2x - 18$. Hint: To find one corner, determine where the lines $y = 8$ and $y = -2x + 8$ intersect.

3. For the back wheel, shade the region between the circle $(x + 4)^2 + (y + 6)^2 = 25$ and the circle $(x + 4)^2 + (y + 6)^2 = 16$.

4. For the front wheel, shade the region between the circle $(x - 9)^2 + (y + 7)^2 = 16$ and the circle $(x - 9)^2 + (y + 7)^2 = 9$.

5. For the smokestack, draw the trapezoid whose sides are on $y = 4$, $y = 6$, $y = -2x + 22$, $y = 2x - 18$ and the rectangle whose sides are on $x = 8$, $x = 12$, $y = 6$, $y = 8$. Look for intersection points.

6. For the cowcatcher, draw the right triangle with the vertex of the right angle at (15, -11), one vertical leg, and the hypotenuse on the line $y = (-3/2)x + 17.5$. Again, look for intersection points.

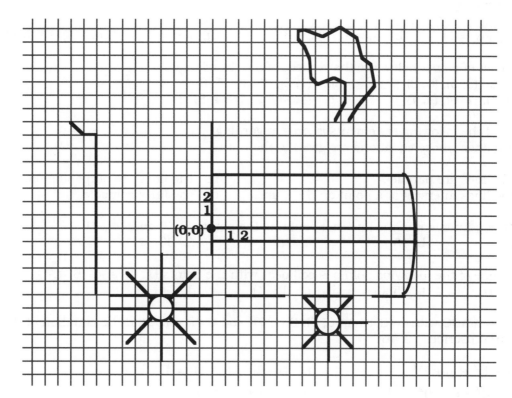

SELF-TEST

1. The distance from the origin to the point A (-3, 4) is

   a. 25   b. 5   c. $\sqrt{7}$ d. None of a, b, or c.

2. The equation of the vertical line through (6, -4) is

   a. $y = -4$ b. $y + 6 = 0$ c. $x - 6 = 0$ d. $x + 6 = 0$

3. An equation of the line passing through the point (-4, 5) with slope -3/2 is

   a. $3x + 2y = -2$ b. $2y - 2x = 3$ c. $2y - 3x = 2$ d. $3x - 2y = -2$

4. If the points A (-1, 1) and B (5, -7) are the endpoints of the diameter of a circle, find the equation of the circle.

   a. $(x - 2)^2 + (y + 3)^2 = 25$ b. $(x + 3)^2 + (y + 4)^2 = 100$

   c. $(x + 2)^2 + (y - 3)^2 = 5$ d. $(x - 2)^2 + (y + 3)^2 = 49$

5. The equation of the line passing through the point (-2, 3) that is perpendicular to the line $3x + y = 0$ is

   a. $3y + x = 11$ b. $y = (1/3)x + 3$ c. $3y + x = 7$ d. $3y - x = 11$

6. Which set of points below are the vertices of a right triangle?
   a. (1, 2), (3, 5), (6, 3)   b. (1, 5), (3, 7), (5, 9)
   c. (3, 1), (2, 6), (4, 7)   d. (4, -3), (2, 1), (4, 8)

7. Which of the following statements is *true* regarding the two lines whose equations are given to the right? $2x - y + 1 = 0$ $-2x - y + 1 = 0$

   a. The lines are parallel.   b. The lines are perpendicular.
   c. The lines intersect at a point on the y-axis.   d. The lines coincide.

8. Find the y-intercept of the line that contains the points (2, 7) and (4, -1).
   a. -15   b. 15   c. 23   d. 30

9. Which one of the following points is collinear with the points (1, -2) and (6, 1)?
   a. (4, -1)   b. (5, 0)   c. (12, 4)   d. (-4, -5)

10. Given is $\triangle$ ABC with vertices A (-3, 5), B (1, 7), and C (5, -1). Find the equation of the circle that circumscribes $\triangle$ ABC.

   a. $(x + 1)^2 + (y + 2)^2 = 5$ b. $(x - 2)^2 + (y - 1)^2 = 41$

   c. $(x - 1)^2 + (y - 2)^2 = 25$ d. None of a, b, or c.

SOLUTIONS

Warm-up

A subgoal would be to find the radius of the circle.

$$AD^2 + DC^2 = (2r)^2 \qquad (B'C')^2 + (OC')^2 = (OB')^2$$
$$2AD^2 = 4r^2 \qquad (B'C')^2 + ((1/2)B'C')^2 = r^2$$
$$2(30) = 4r^2 \qquad (5/4)(B'C')^2 = 15$$
$$15 = r^2 \qquad (B'C')^2 = 12 \qquad \text{The area is 12 cm}^2.$$

Hands-on Activities

Activity 1

1. a. (4, 5) b. (3, 2) c. (5, 1) d. (1, 3)   **2.** b. A 9-gon resembling a rocket
3. C (-1, -2), D (6, -1)
4. b. A in I, C in II, E & F in III, B & D in IV   c. A negative x-coordinate, positive y-coordinate; negative x- and y-coordinates; positive x-coordinate, negative y-coordinate

Activity 2

2. You should. EFGH
3. B' (6, 10), C' (10, 10), D' (10, 6), E' (8, 12), F' (12, 12), G' (12, 8), H' (8, 8)
4. You should.   **5.** B" (3, 5), C" (5, 5), D" (5, 3), E" (4, 6), F" (6, 6), G" (6, 4), H" (4, 4)
7. Yes

Activity 3

1. a. A (2, 5), B (5, 1)   b. (2, 1)   c. 4, 3   d. 5

2. a. (c, b)   b. $c - a$, $d - b$ c. $\sqrt{(c-a)^2 + (d-b)^2}$

$\sqrt{(c-a)^2 + (d-b)^2}$

Activity 4

1. a. 3 units   b. 4 units   c. 3/4   **2.** a. -5 units   b. 6   c. -5/6
3. a. $d - b$ b. $c - a$ c. $(d - b)/(c - a)$ d. $b - d$ e. $a - c$ f. $(b - d)/(a - c)$
  g. The results are equal. It does not matter which endpoint is used first, as long as you are consistent in the numerator and denominator.
  $(d - b)/(c - a)$
4. 1/2, 1/2, 1/2   The slope of l is equal to the slope of any line segment of l, here 1/2.
5. a. 2/3, 2/3   b. -2/7, -2/7   The slopes are equal.
  c. -5/4, 4/5   d. -1/3, 3   The product of the slopes is -1.
  equal, -1

Activity 5

1. a. -3, 1, 5, -1, 3, -5   b. 2 It is multiplying the x.   -3 It is added to the x-term.
  c. The slope is -2/3. The y-intercept is 4.   d. slope; y-intercept

2. b. The y-coordinate is 2 times the x-coordinate.   c. $y = 2x$

3. No; no, always equal to 3; $x = 3$
Slope; y-intercept, $x = a$

Mental Math

   A. p   B. o   C. Circle C   D. n   E. Circle D   F. l   G. m   H. q

Exercises

Symmetry Through Coordinates
   A. Reflection symmetry in the y-axis   B. Reflection symmetry in the x-axis
   C. Reflection symmetry in the x-axis and y-axis, rotation symmetry in the origin

Self-Test
1. b   **2.** c   **3.** a   **4.** a   **5.** d   **6.** a   **7.** c   **8.** b   **9.** d   **10.** c

RESOURCE ARTICLES

Burger, William F. "Graph Paper Geometry." In *Mathematics for Middle Grades* (1982 NCTM Yearbook). Reston, VA: National Council of Teachers of Mathematics, 1982. *Collection of introductory coordinate geometry activities.*

Cangelosi, James S. "A 'Fair' Way to Discover Circles." *Arithmetic Teacher* 33 (November 1985): 11-13. *Discovering the attributes of circles.*

Hastings, Ellen H., and Daniel S. Yates. "Microcomputer Unit: Graphing Straight Lines." *Mathematics Teacher* 76 (March 1983): 181-186. *Investigations involving slope.*

Kroll, Diana L. "Ideas." *Arithmetic Teacher* 33 (December 1985): 27-32. *Activities to develop the coordinate system.*

Smith, Robert F. "Let's Do It: Coordinate Geometry for Third Graders." *Arithmetic Teacher* 33 (April 1986): 6-11. *Developing children's ability to name and locate coordinates.*

Terc, Michael. "Coordinate Geometry – Art and Mathematics." *Arithmetic Teacher* 33 (October 1985): 22-24. *Early experience with plotting coordinate points.*

Tucker, Benny F. "Secret Codes and Systems of Equations." *Mathematics Teacher* 79 (April 1986): 256-258. *Finding solutions to systems of equations graphically.*

Vissa, Jeanne M. "Coordinate Graphing: Shaping a Sticky Situation." *Arithmetic Teacher* 35 (November 1987): 6-10. *Uses stickers as part of interesting activities to introduce coordinate graphing.*

DIRECTIONS IN EDUCATION

Recommendations of the NCTM Standards – Math for the 21st Century

In an effort to ensure that all students possess a suitable and sufficient mathematics background to become productive citizens in a future that will be characterized by complex information and technology, the National Council of Teachers of Mathematics has prepared a direction-setting document called *Curriculum and Evaluation Standards for School Mathematics*. The Standards provide both the recommendations for changes and the rationale behind those recommendations.

What are the Curriculum and Evaluation Standards?

- The Curriculum Standards are a framework for curriculum development which attempts to create a logical network of relationships among identified topics of study.

- The Evaluation Standards provide for assessment in three distinct categories: 1) assessment strategies for the curriculum standards themselves; 2) assessment strategies which may be used by classroom teachers to improve instruction; and 3) assessment strategies which may be used to determine the quality and effectiveness of a mathematics program.

- The reasons for the development of the Standards are: 1) to ensure quality; 2) to indicate goals; and 3) to promote change. The goals are designed to meet both societal needs and individual student needs.

What are the new societal goals required for the 21st century?

- **Mathematically literate workers.** Mathematical expectations for future workers in industry include:

  - The ability to set up problems with the appropriate operations.
  - Knowledge of a variety of techniques to approach and work on problems.
  - Understanding of the underlying mathematical features of a problem.
  - The ability to work with others on problems.
  - The ability to see the applicability of mathematical ideas to common and complex problems.
  - Preparation for open problem situations, since most real problems are not well formulated.
  - Belief in the utility and value of mathematics.

- **Lifelong learning.** Rapidly changing technology requires workers capable of retraining and flexibility.

- **Opportunity for all.** Mathematics, a critical filter for employment and full participation in our society, must become accessible to all.

- **An informed electorate.** Citizens must have the ability to read and interpret complex, and sometimes conflicting, information to participate in decision making in a technological society.

What are the new goals for students?

- **Learning to value mathematics.** Students should have numerous, varied learning experiences which help them to see the role of mathematics in society and its relationship to other fields.

- **Becoming confident in one's own ability.** Activities which are relevant to students' lives and which promote success and self-reliance help students to view math as a common, familiar human activity.

- **Becoming a mathematical problem solver.** It is through problem solving that students discover and apply the power and utility of mathematics. Skilled problem solvers become productive citizens.

- **Learning to communicate mathematically.** Students need to learn the symbols and terms of mathematics and to use them in reading, writing and talking the language of mathematics. Communication of mathematical ideas promotes clarification, refinement, and consolidation of their thinking.

- **Learning to reason mathematically.** Students should be able to make conjectures, gather evidence, and build an argument to support a theory. Good reasoning should be valued as much as the students' ability to find correct answers.

As you think about implementing the NCTM Standards, ask yourself:

- Do I fully understand the Standards and their implications for classroom instruction?

- Does my mathematical background indicate attainment of the goals for students?

- How can I help my students to be prepared for life in the 21st century?

- Can I effectively use assessment strategies to improve my classroom instruction?

- Do I know the components of an effective mathematics program?

To learn more:

National Council of Teachers of Mathematics. *Curriculum and Evaluation Standards for School Mathematics.* Reston, VA: The Council, 1989. Each section provides information about the need for change, the rationale for such change and implications for curriculum and instruction. An executive summary of the Standards is also available from NCTM.

16

Geometry Using Transformations

THEME: Using Geometric Transformations

WARM-UP

Strategy Review: Use Symmetry.
This strategy is presented in Chapter 16 of the text.

Imagine that you are looking in a mirror and you see a clock behind you. What time does the real clock show for the following *mirror images*?

A.

B.

C.

HANDS-ON ACTIVITIES

A **geometric transformation** is a 1-1 correspondence between points in the plane. The first few activities will investigate some basic transformations and their properties.

OBJECTIVE: **Investigate translations and their properties**

You Will Need: Tracing paper

1. A **translation** is a transformation associated with a sliding motion of a specified distance and direction, without any turning. The distance and direction can be indicated with an arrow or **directed line segment**. Follow the given steps to translate the indicated point.

   a. The arrow indicates a translation.
   Extend the arrow by drawing a dashed line $\overleftrightarrow{AB}$.

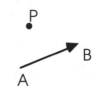

   b. Lay a piece of tracing paper on the figure and trace the dashed line, point A (the tail of the arrow), and the point P you want to translate.

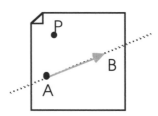

   c. Slide the tracing paper until point A is at the head of the arrow (on top of point B). Be sure that the dashed line is still on top of itself.

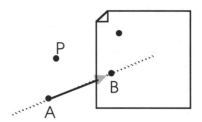

   d. With your pencil, press an indentation through the tracing paper at point P. Remove the tracing paper and at the mark, label the point P'. The point P' is the translation image of point P.

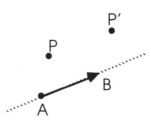

2. Using tracing paper, find the images of points X, Y and Z under the translation indicated by the directed line segment $\overrightarrow{AB}$. Mark these points X', Y' and Z' respectively.

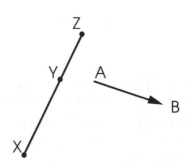

a. Draw the segment with endpoints X' and Z'. Is the point Y' on segment $\overline{X'Z'}$? (It should be!)

b. Translate $\overline{XZ}$ by using tracing paper. How does its image compare to $\overline{X'Z'}$?

c. Choose the *most complete* way of finishing the following statement: The translation image of a segment is a
    A. segment.
    B. segment congruent and parallel to the original segment.
    C. segment congruent to the original segment.
    D. segment parallel to the original segment.

3. For the translation indicated by $\overrightarrow{AB}$, use tracing paper to find the images of the given ray, line, angle and triangle.

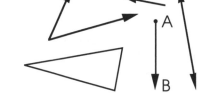

Complete the following: The translation image
of a ray is a _____ ,
of a line is a _____ ,
of an angle is an _____ ,
and of a triangle is a _____ .

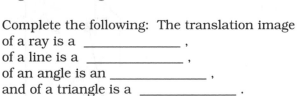

How do the measures of the angle and its image compare?

How do the size and shape of the triangle and its image compare?

What is the relationship between the line and its image?

4. Finding images with tracing paper provides a good model of transformations. Imagine that the tracing paper is a copy of the plane. As you move the tracing paper, not only does P correspond to its image P', but each point of the plane corresponds to a unique point.

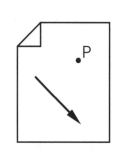

Are there any points that correspond to themselves after a translation, that is, points that do not move?

Summarize the properties of translations that you have found.

OBJECTIVE: **Investigate rotations and their properties**

You Will Need: Tracing paper

1. A **rotation** is a transformation associated with a turning motion through a specified **directed angle** around a fixed point, called the **center**. Follow the steps given next to rotate point P.

   a. The given angle and point C determine the rotation. Here the angle is drawn with its vertex at the center C.

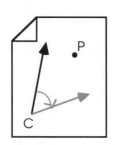

   b. Lay a piece of tracing paper on top and trace the initial side of the angle and the point P.

   c. Fix the center C with your pencil point and turn the tracing paper until the traced initial side of the angle coincides with the terminal side of the original angle.

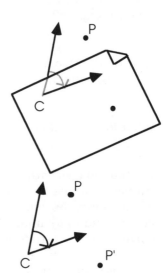

   d. With your pencil, press an indentation through the tracing paper at point P. On your original sheet of paper, mark the image point P'.

2. Using tracing paper, find the images of points X, Y and Z under the rotation indicated with center O and the given directed angle. Label these points X', Y' and Z'.

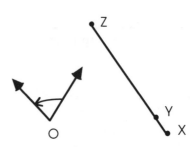

a. Draw the segment with endpoints X' and Z'. Is point Y' on this segment?

b. Rotate $\overline{XZ}$ by using tracing paper. How does its image compare to $\overline{X'Z'}$?

c. Describe the rotation image of a segment as completely as possible.

3. Using tracing paper, find the images of the given figures under the rotations indicated.

   a. Is the image of a line a line, the image of a ray a ray, and the image of an angle an angle?

   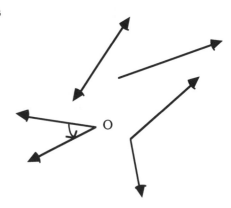

   How do the measures of the angle and its image compare?

   b. Is the image of a triangle a triangle?

   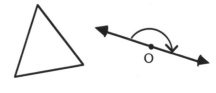

   How do the triangle and its image compare with regard to size and shape?

4. Tracing paper serves as a good model for finding images of the rotation transformation.

   Are there any points that remain fixed under a rotation?

   Summarize the properties of rotations that you have found.

OBJECTIVE: **Investigate reflections and their properties**

You Will Need: Tracing paper

1. A **reflection** is a transformation that gives a 'mirror' image across a line, called the **reflection line**. Follow the steps given next to find the reflection image of point P, which is not on the reflection line, and the point Q, which is on the reflection line.

   a. The given line determines a reflection. Mark a reference point, R, on the line.

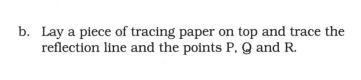

   b. Lay a piece of tracing paper on top and trace the reflection line and the points P, Q and R.

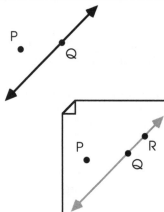

   c. Turn the tracing paper over so that it is face down. Be sure that the copy of the reflection line and the reference point each coincide with the original line and reference point.

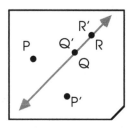

   d. Using your pencil, make an imprint through the tracing paper at points P and Q. Mark the image points P' and Q' on the original sheet of paper.

2. Using tracing paper, find the reflection images of P, Q and R across the line l. Label these points P', Q' and R'.

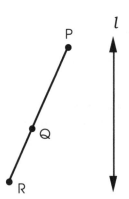

   a. Draw the segment with endpoints P' and R'. Does this segment contain Q'? (It should!)

   b. Reflect $\overline{PR}$ by using tracing paper. How does the image of $\overline{PR}$ compare with $\overline{P'R'}$?

   c. Describe the reflection image of a segment as completely as possible.

3. In each part use tracing paper to find the images of the given figures under the reflections in line *l*.

a.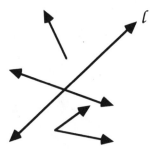

b.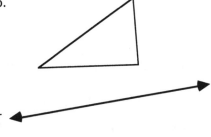

c. Is the image of a line a line, the image of a ray a ray, and the image of an angle an angle?

How do the measures of an angle and its reflection image compare?

How do a triangle and its reflection image compare?

4. Finding images with tracing paper also models the reflection transformation.

Are there any points that correspond to themselves under a reflection; that is, are there any fixed points?

> Summarize the properties of reflections that you have found.

OBJECTIVE: **Investigate glide reflections and their properties**

You Will Need: Tracing paper

1. A **glide reflection** is a transformation that combines a translation and a reflection where the reflection line is parallel to the translation direction. Follow the steps given next to find the glide reflection image of a point P.

   a. The given line l and the directed line segment $\overrightarrow{AB}$ determine a glide reflection. Notice that $l \parallel \overrightarrow{AB}$. Mark a reference point on the reflection line and extend $\overrightarrow{AB}$ by drawing a dashed line $\overleftrightarrow{AB}$.

   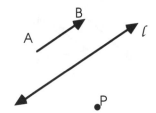

   b. Lay a piece of tracing paper on top. Trace the dashed line and points A and P.

   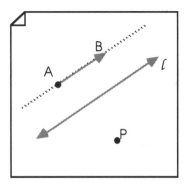
   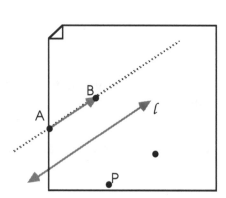

   c. Slide the tracing paper until point A is on top of point B. Be sure that the dashed line is still on top of itself.

   d. Trace the reflection line and the reference point.

   e. Turn the tracing paper over so that it is face down. The reflection line and reference point should coincide with the original line and point.

   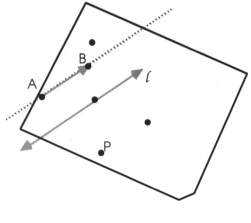

   f. Mark the image point P'.

   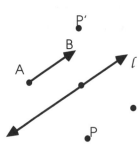

2. Repeat the glide reflection in part 1, except do the reflection first, followed by the translation. How do the images of parts 1 and 2 compare?

3. Perform the following glide reflections that are determined by the line l and the arrow $\overrightarrow{AB}$.

a.

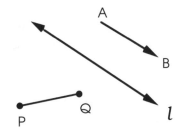

b.

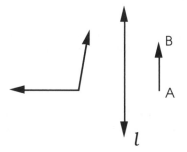

How does a segment compare to its image in length?

How does an angle compare to its image in angle measure?

c. How does a triangle compare to its image in size and shape?

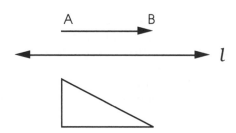

Summarize the properties of glide reflections that you have found.

OBJECTIVE: **Investigate magnifications and their properties**

You Will Need: Compass and straightedge

1. A **magnification** is a transformation that 'stretches' or 'shrinks' the plane away from or toward a specific point. Follow the steps given next to find the magnification image of point P.

    a. The **center** point O and a **scale factor** k determine a magnification. Here, let $k = 2$.

    b. Draw ray $\overrightarrow{OP}$.

    c. Measure $\overline{OP}$ and copy that segment such that P is one endpoint. Thus, OP' = 2·OP.

    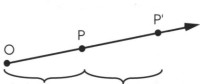

    d. Mark the resulting image point P'.

2. Using the technique from part 1, find the magnification images of points P, R and S where point O is the center and the scale factor k is 3. Label these image points P', R', and S' respectively.

    a. Does the segment $\overline{P'S'}$ contain R'?

    b. How do the lengths of $\overline{PS}$ and $\overline{P'S'}$ compare?

    c. How else are $\overline{PS}$ and $\overline{P'S'}$ related?

3. Using the technique described in part 2, magnify ∠ABC where O is the center and $k = 2$.

 a. Is the resulting figure also an angle? (It should be!)

 b. How do the measures of the two angles compare?

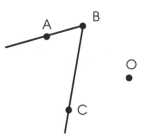

4. Draw the magnification image of △ABC where O is the center and $k = 1/2$.

 a. Is the resulting figure also a triangle? (It should be!)

 b. How do the sizes and shapes of the two triangles compare?

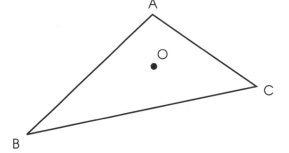

Summarize the properties of magnifications that you have found.

The last activity looks at the relationship between translations, rotations, and reflections.

OBJECTIVE: **Investigate combinations of reflections**

You Will Need: Tracing paper or Mira, straightedge, compass, and protractor

1. Lines *p* and *q* are parallel. Draw the reflection image of △ ABC across line *p*. Label the result △ A'B'C'.

   Draw the reflection image of △ A'B'C' across line *q*. Label the result △ A"B"C".

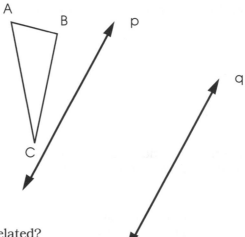

   a. Are the points A, A' and A" collinear? Test with a straightedge. Is the same true for the points B, B', and B", and the points C, C', and C" ?

   b. How are segments $\overline{AA''}$, $\overline{BB''}$, and $\overline{CC''}$ related?

   c. What single transformation will map △ ABC onto △ A"B"C"?

   d. Compare the lengths of segments $\overline{AA''}$, $\overline{BB''}$, $\overline{CC''}$, and the distance between lines *p* and *q*. What did you find?

   e. Describe the transformation you found in part (c) as completely as possible.

2. Lines *p* and *q* intersect at point M. Draw the reflection image of △ ABC across the line *p*. Label the result △ A'B'C'.

   Draw the reflection image of △ A'B'C' across the line *q*. Label the result △ A"B"C".

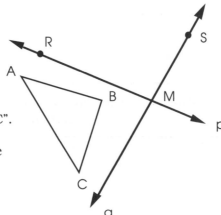

   a. Do the points A, A' and A" lie on a circle with center M? Is the same true for points B, B', B" and C, C', C"?

b. What single transformation will map △ ABC onto △ A"B"C"?

c. Compare the measures of ∠ AMA", ∠ BMB", and ∠ CMC" and the measure of ∠ RMS. What do you find?

d. Describe the transformation you found in part (b) as completely as possible.

MENTAL MATH

Given below are patterns that can be folded together to make a cube. Match each of the patterns on the left with its respective cube on the right.

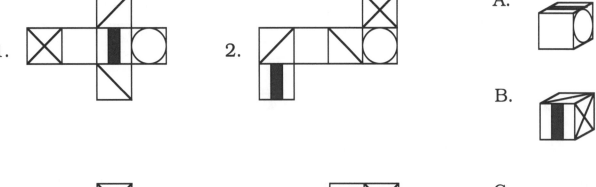

1. 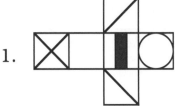   2.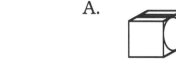

A.

B.

3. 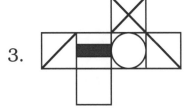   4.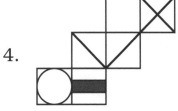

C.

D.

EXERCISES

FANCY "FREEZING"

The one-dimensional strip patterns given below are called **frieze patterns.** Imagine that they extend indefinitely to the left and right. Each one has translation symmetry; that is, sliding it to the right or left a certain distance maps it onto itself. Identify the other symmetries of these frieze patterns, if they exist. Note: No two of these patterns are equivalent, i.e. have the same list of symmetries.

A.   **B.**

C.   **D.**

E.   **F.**

G.

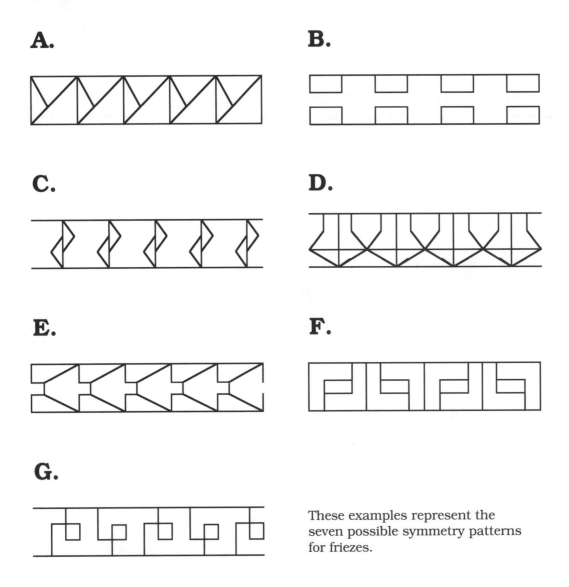

These examples represent the
seven possible symmetry patterns
for friezes.

FOLDING PATTERNS

A sheet of paper is folded in half the long way, then in thirds as shown below.

While folded, a hole is punched through all thicknesses. The paper is then unfolded and spread out. The dashed lines represent the creases.

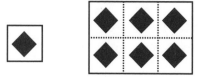

In each case below, the folded version is given on the left. Select the correct pattern for the spread-out paper on the right.

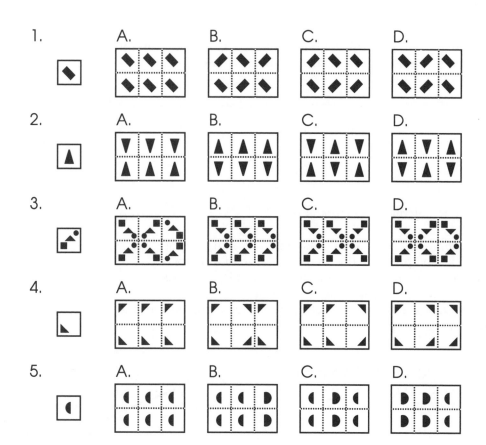

1.   A.   B.   C.   D.

2.   A.   B.   C.   D.

3.   A.   B.   C.   D.

4.   A.   B.   C.   D.

5.   A.   B.   C.   D.

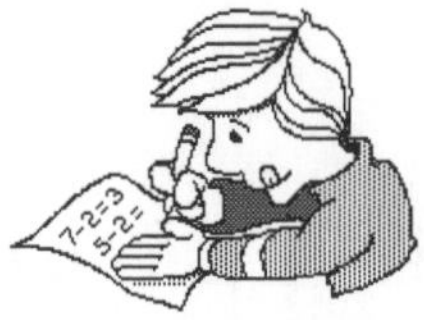

SELF-TEST

1. Which triangle below has orientation opposite from that of this triangle?

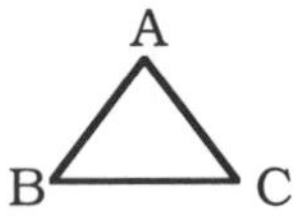

a. 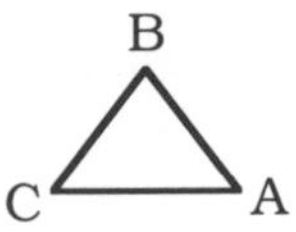

b. 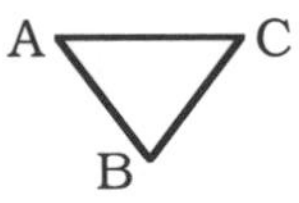

c. 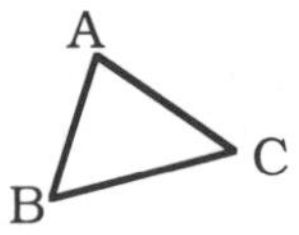

d. 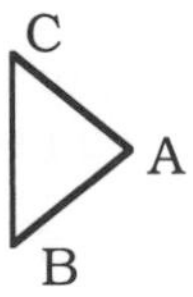

2. Which transformation will map Δ PQR to Δ P'Q'R'?

a. Translation
b. Rotation
c. Reflection
d. Glide reflection

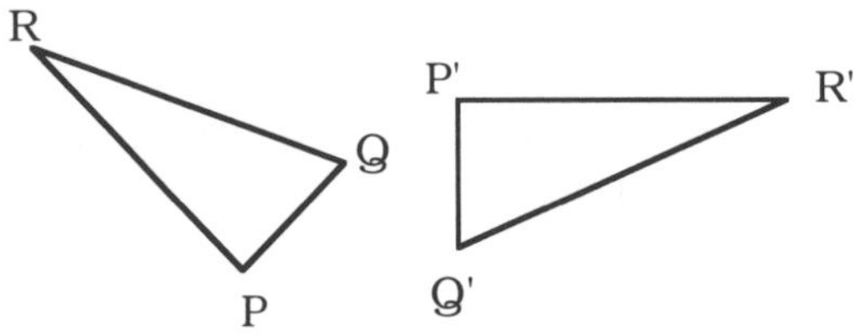

3. Which of the following transformations does not map the given infinite tessellation to itself? (Points E and F are midpoints of their respective sides.)

a. S_{AB} b. M_{BD}

c. $R_{C,180°}$ d. M_{EF} followed by S_{CD}

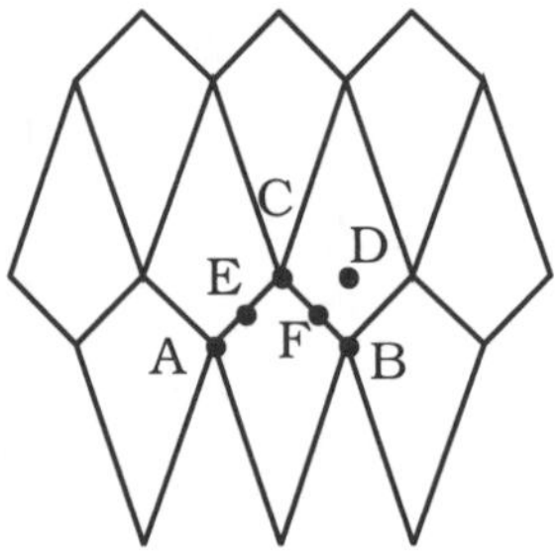

4. Which of the following statements is *true* ?

a. Translations and reflections preserve the orientation of a figure.
b. Magnifications preserve the shape and size of a figure.
c. If two polygons are congruent, then there exists a translation, rotation, reflection, or glide reflection that maps one to the other.
d. If two polygons are similar, then there exists a translation, rotation, reflection, or glide reflection that maps one to the other.

5. Given that $\Delta ABC \sim \Delta EDC$, what is the scale factor of the magnification involved in mapping Δ ABC to Δ EDC?

a. 2/3 b. 3/2 c. 2/5 d. 5/2

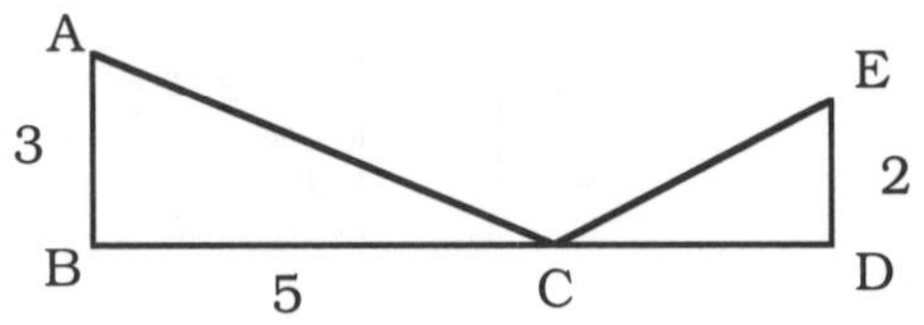

6. Each of the following is a property of an isometry *except* which one?

    a. An isometry maps a segment to a segment of the same length.
    b. An isometry maps an angle to an angle with the same measure.
    c. An isometry maps a line to a line parallel to the original line.
    d. An isometry maps parallel lines to parallel lines.

7. Triangle $\triangle$ ABC is congruent to $\triangle$ A'B'C' and $\overline{AB} \| \overline{A'B'}$. Point P is the midpoint of $\overline{AA'}$ and point Q (different from P) is the midpoint of $\overline{BB'}$ and $\overline{PQ} \perp \overline{AA'}$. Which of the following statements is necessarily true?

    a. A translation maps $\triangle$ ABC to $\triangle$ A'B'C'.
    b. A reflection maps $\triangle$ ABC to $\triangle$ A'B'C'.
    c. A glide reflection maps $\triangle$ ABC to $\triangle$ A'B'C'.
    d. Either a translation or a reflection maps $\triangle$ ABC to $\triangle$ A'B'C'.

8. Triangles $\triangle$ ABC and $\triangle$ A'B'C' are congruent and have the same orientation. The perpendicular bisectors of $\overline{AA'}$ and $\overline{BB'}$ intersect. Which transformation will map $\triangle$ ABC to $\triangle$ A'B'C'?

    a. Translation   b. Rotation   c. Reflection   d. Glide reflection

9. Which of the following does *not* map every line l to a line l' such that $l \| l'$.

    a. Reflection   b. Translation   c. Rotation of 180°   d. Magnification

10. Triangle $\triangle$ A'B'C' is the image of $\triangle$ ABC under $R_{P,180°}$ followed by $R_{Q,180°}$. Which single transformation maps $\triangle$ ABC to $\triangle$ A'B'C'?

    a. Translation in the direction of $\overrightarrow{PQ}$ with distance PQ.
    b. Rotation of 180° about the midpoint of $\overline{PQ}$.
    c. Reflection in the perpendicular bisector of $\overline{PQ}$.
    d. Translation in the direction of $\overrightarrow{PQ}$ with distance 2·PQ.

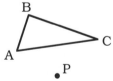

SOLUTIONS

Warm-up
8:00, 4:30, 10:20

Hands-on Activities

Activity 1
2. b. They are the same segment.   c. B
3. Ray, line, angle, triangle; They are equal. They are the same. They are parallel.
4. No
A translation maps a segment to a segment parallel and congruent to it, a line to a line parallel to it, an angle to a congruent angle, a ray to a ray, and a triangle to a congruent triangle.

Activity 2
2. a. Yes
b. The image of $\overline{XZ}$ is $\overline{X'Z'}$.
c. It is a segment with the same length.
3. a. Yes; They are equal.
b. Yes; They have the same size and shape.
4. Yes, the center point.
A rotation maps segments to congruent segments, angles to congruent angles, rays to rays, lines to lines, and triangles to congruent triangles.

Activity 3
2. b. The image of $\overline{PR}$ is $\overline{P'R'}$.
c. It is a segment with the same length.
3. c. Yes; They are equal. They have the same size and shape.
4. Yes, each point on the reflection line.
A reflection maps segments to congruent segments, lines to lines, angles to congruent angles, rays to rays, and triangles to congruent triangles.

Activity 4
2. They are the same point.
3. a. They have the same length.
b. They have the same measure.
c. They have the same size and shape.
A glide reflection maps segments to congruent segments, lines to lines, rays to rays, angles to congruent angles, and triangles to congruent triangles.

Activity 5

2. a. Yes
   b. P'S' = 3PS
   c. They are parallel.
3. b. They are the same.
4. b. They are the same shape, but the new sides are 1/2 as long.
   A magnification with scale factor k maps a segment to a segment parallel to it and k times its length, an angle to a congruent angle, a line to a line parallel to it, a ray to a ray, and a triangle to a triangle with the same shape, but with sides k times the length of the original sides.

Activity 6

1. a. Yes; Yes
   b. $\overline{AA''} \parallel \overline{BB''} \parallel \overline{CC''}$ and all are perpendicular to lines p and q.
   c. A translation
   d. $\overline{AA''}$ is twice as long as the distance between lines p and q.
   e. It is a translation in the direction perpendicular to lines p and q with the distance equal to twice the distance between lines p and q.
2. a. Yes; Yes
   b. A rotation
   c. The measures of $\angle AMA''$, $\angle BMB''$, and $\angle CMC''$ are twice the measure of $\angle RMS$.
   d. It is a rotation whose center is the intersection of the lines and whose angle has measure twice the measure of the angle from line p to line q.

Mental Math

1. D   **2.** C   **3.** A   **4.** B

Exercises

FANCY "FREEZING"
   A. Translation only
   B. Rotation, horizontal and vertical reflections
   C. Rotation
   D. Vertical reflection
   E. Horizontal reflection
   F. Vertical reflection, glide reflection
   G. Glide reflection

FOLDING PATTERNS
   1. B   **2.** A   **3.** D   **4.** B   **5.** C

Self-Test

1. d   **2.** b   **3.** c   **4.** c   **5.** a   **6.** c   **7.** d   **8.** b   **9.** a   **10.** d

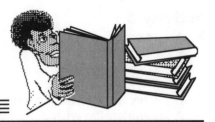

RESOURCE ARTICLES

Bidwell, James K. "Using Reflections to Find Symmetric and Asymmetric Patterns." *Arithmetic Teacher* 34 (March 1987): 10-15. *Activities exploring the idea of symmetry.*

Brieske, Tom. "Visual Thinking with Translations, Half-Turns, and Dilations." *Mathematics Teacher* 77 (September 1984): 466-469. *Helping students to think visually about algebraic operations and the associated mappings of the plane.*

DeTemple, Duane. "Reflection Borders for Patchwork Quilts." *Mathematics Teacher* 79 (February 1986): 138-143. *Geometric problem solving involving least common multiples and greatest common divisors.*

May, Beverly A. "Reflections on Miniature Golf." *Mathematics Teacher* 78 (May 1985): 351-353. *Application of reflections to miniature golf.*

Sawada, Daiyo. "Symmetry and Tessellations from Rotational Transformations on Transparencies." *Arithmetic Teacher* 33 (December 1985): 12-13. *Using transparencies to explore rotational transformations.*

Sicklick, Francine, Susan B. Turkel, and Frances R. Curcio. "The 'Transformation Game'." *Arithmetic Teacher* 36 (October 1988): 37-41. *An instructional game presenting concepts of reflection, translation, and rotation.*

Thompson, Patrick W. "A Piagetian Approach to Transformation Geometry via Microworlds." *Mathematics Teacher* 78 (September 1985): 465-471. *Developing the ability to apply a system of transformations.*

Woodward, Ernest, and Patsy G. Buckner. "Reflections and Symmetry - a Second-Grade Miniunit." *Arithmetic Teacher* 35 (October 1987): 8-11. *Presents a 5-day series of lessons on symmetry using a Mira.*

DIRECTIONS IN EDUCATION

Professional Growth — The Teacher As Lifelong Learner

Establishing a pattern of continuous professional growth and lifelong learning may be the single most important challenge faced by teachers. Futurists have stated that most of the jobs which will be held by the students of today have not even been thought of yet. As technology continues to expand and to change the way we manage the world, mathematics must continue to expand. Once math teachers taught their students to calculate cords of wood, to compute the number of pecks in a bushel and to do long division such as eight digits into ten digits or more. Today calculators and computers exist which can convert units of measure into equivalent units, which can solve equations and symbolically graph those solutions, and which can perform multiple long division problems in the time needed to complete just one using a paper-and-pencil algorithm. The mathematical skills which were once considered basic for students and teachers are now seen as outdated or as limited in scope. Continuous professional growth can assist teachers in moving ahead to the basics which will be required of students as they move into the world of work.

Components of professional growth which will keep teaching skills current include:

- **Opportunities to keep content area knowledge and skills up-to-date.** College courses, workshops, and specific subject-related professional conferences all provide opportunities to enhance content expertise.

- **Opportunities to keep instructional methodology current and exciting.** In addition to college courses, workshops, and conferences, many districts offer opportunities to enhance instructional techniques. It is essential that teachers take advantage of these opportunities.

- **Opportunities to know and understand the rationale behind change in instructional techniques and/or content.** Journals such as *The Arithmetic Teacher, The Mathematics Teacher* or more general journals such as *Educational Leadership* should be a part of the classroom teacher's regular professional reading. These journals provide a research base and the opportunity to hear from recognized experts in the field.

- **Opportunities to see and experience the use of instructional materials in the classroom.** As new materials are developed — manipulatives, supplemental printed materials, software or hardware, or text related materials — teachers need to explore options for the use of these materials in the classroom. Workshops and conferences provide excellent opportunities to discover new instructional materials.

- **Opportunities to interact with peers in a professional growth environment.** The classroom can isolate teachers from interaction with their peers. Collegial support of peers in your building or district will eliminate some of the feelings of loneliness — of being out on a limb — that teachers experience when they implement change in their classrooms.

- **Understanding that change takes time.** As teachers implement change, they experience the need for more information, the need for more time, and the need for support in their efforts. Teachers need to give themselves time to make a change in their classroom instruction without becoming frustrated by early problems. Self-analysis of the nature of the change needed, the problems encountered and potential solutions to those problems, and of the personal feelings encountered during the change will be helpful. In addition, teachers should seek out peers or supervisors who can provide support for making changes in the classroom.

- **Setting both short-term and long-term goals for professional growth.** Many teachers follow patterns throughout their teaching career which were established in the first three years of teaching. Beginning teachers must project themselves into the mid-years of their career and see how dull a career can be if one does the same things in the same way for thirty years or more. In addition to personal dissatisfaction, the loss of self-esteem which occurs when fellow teachers no longer regard the teacher as current and knowledgeable in the field will make membership in the teaching profession far less rewarding than it can be. Beginning teachers should enter the profession with short-term goals to explore the various professional organizations and to participate in some professional growth opportunity in each of the first three years of teaching. At the end of the three year period, the teacher should establish long-term goals which must then be continually revised to meet changing needs.

As you think about lifelong professional growth, ask yourself:

- Can I name three professional journals which would be of use to me in my teaching?

- Do I know how to obtain memberships in professional organizations?

- What professional conferences or conventions are being held in my geographic area in the next year? Note: *Educational Leadership*, the journal of the Association for Supervision and Curriculum Development, *Education Week* and state education departments usually provide information about such conferences.

To learn more:

Arithmetic Teacher and *Mathematics Teacher*. Published by the National Council of Teachers of Mathematics. 1906 Association Drive, Reston, Virginia 22091.

Educational Leadership. Published by the Association for Supervision and Curriculum Development. 1250 N. Pitt Street, Alexandria, Virginia 22314-1403.

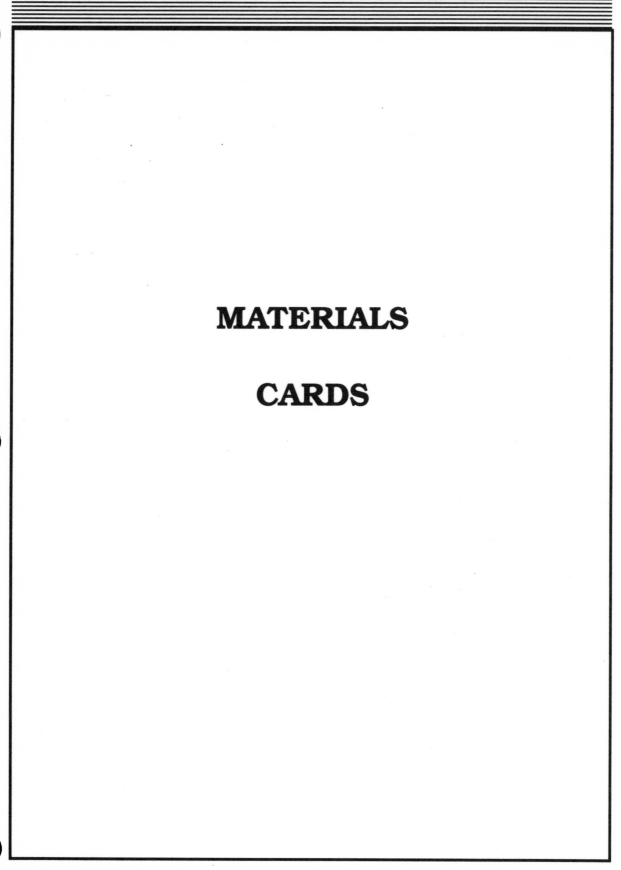

MATERIALS

CARDS

MATERIALS CARD 1.1

You may do this activity by placing the circles over the designated letter or you may construct the towers by following the directions given below.

YOU WILL NEED: 3 paper clips and tape. Straighten one end of a paper clip and insert it through the base at point A. Repeat for points B and C. Bend curved portion of clip flat against the bottom of the base and tape in place. Your finished base should look like this:

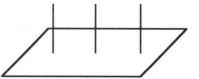

Remove each circle and punch a small hole in the center of each.

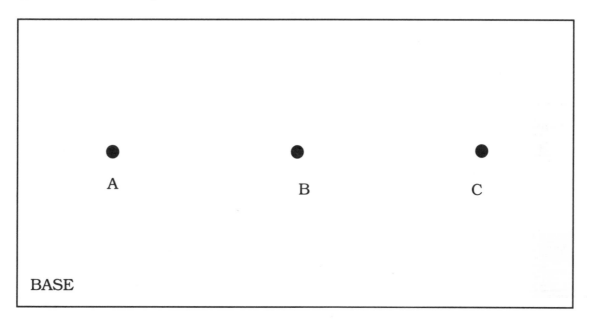

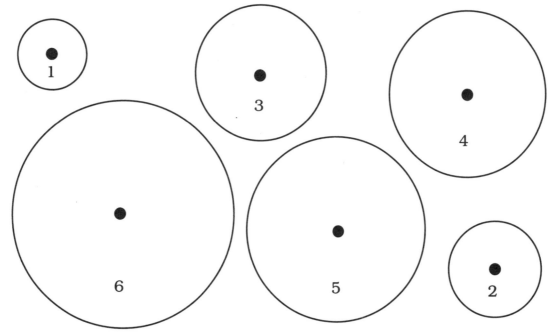

MATERIALS CARD 1.4

Remove each of these pieces.

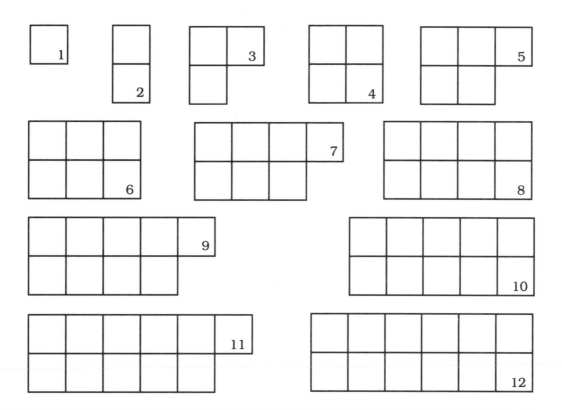

- -

MATERIALS CARD 1.5

Use the following as patterns. Cut several if needed.

2' X 12' hole to be filled

3' X 8' piece of plywood

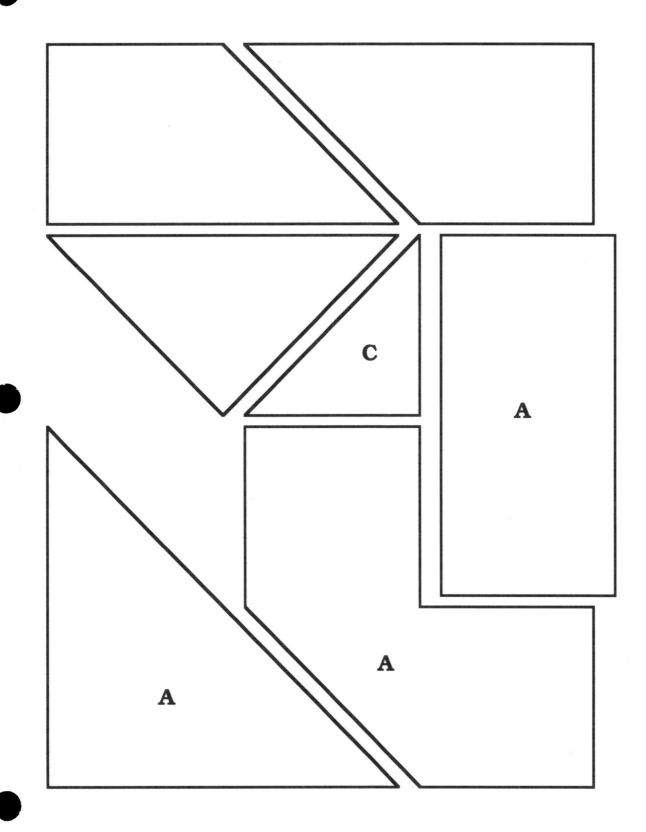

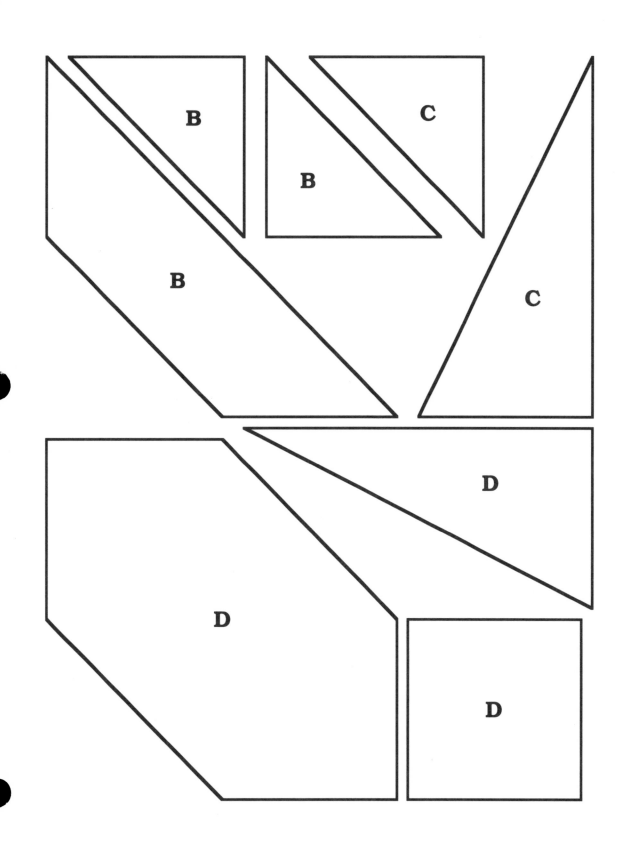

MATERIALS CARD 2.1

Remove the following pieces from the materials card. Save these pieces for use later in the chapter.

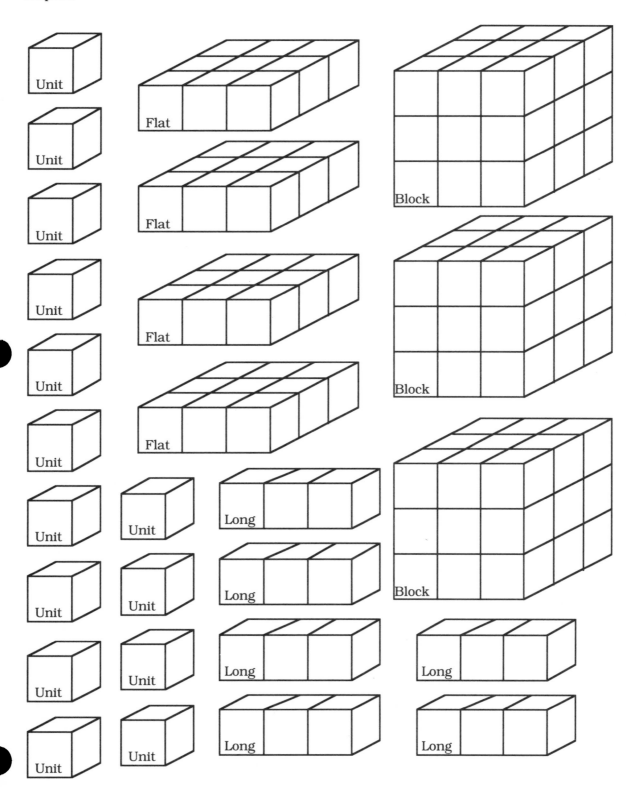

MATERIALS CARD 2.2

Remove from the card. Fold on all heavy
black lines. Put flap A on top
of flap B. Tuck flap C inside the
cube behind flap B. Tuck flap D
in. Tape if necessary.

Save this die for use in
Chapter 11 also.

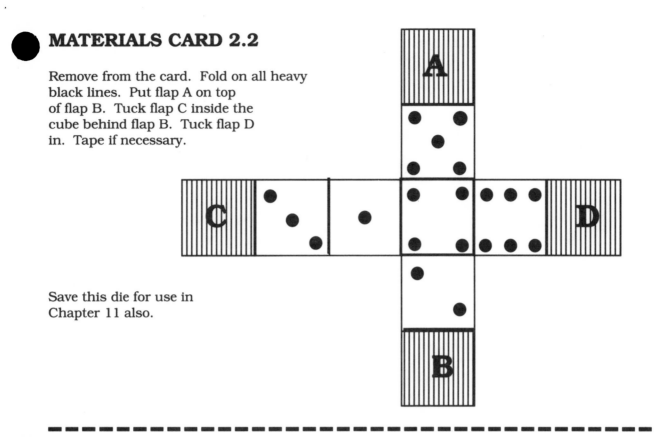

- -

MATERIALS CARD 3.1

Remove these strips
and color them
as labelled.

W = White
R = Red
G = Light Green
P = Purple
Y = Yellow
D = Dark Green
K = Black
N = Brown
E = Blue
O = Orange

Save these
pieces for use
later in this
chapter and
in Chapter 6.

MATERIALS CARD 3.7

Separate into squares.   Save these pieces for use later in this chapter and in Chapter 5.

1	2	3	4	5	6	7	8	9	10
11	12	13	14	15	16	17	18	19	20
21	22	23	24	25	26	27	28	29	30
31	32	33	34	35	36	37	38	39	40
41	42	43	44	45	46	47	48	49	50
51	52	53	54	55	56	57	58	59	60
61	62	63	64	65	66	67	68	69	70
71	72	73	74	75	76	77	78	79	80
81	82	83	84	85	86	87	88	89	90
91	92	93	94	95	96	97	98	99	100

MATERIALS CARD 6.1

Remove the circles and then cut on all solid lines.
Save these pieces for use later in the chapter.

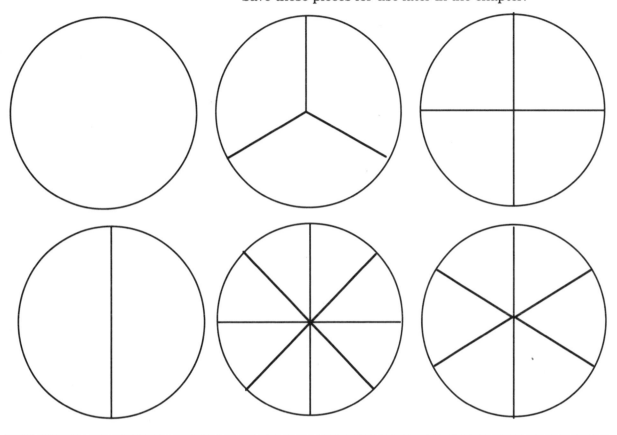

MATERIALS CARD 6.2

Remove the fraction strips on this and the next card. Separate them at the heavy dark lines.
Save these strips for use later in the chapter.

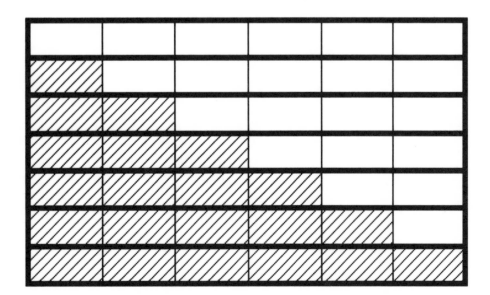

MATERIALS
CARD 6.4

Remove the Tangram Puzzle
and separate on all of the solid
lines. You will have 7 pieces.

Save these pieces for use in
Chapter 12.

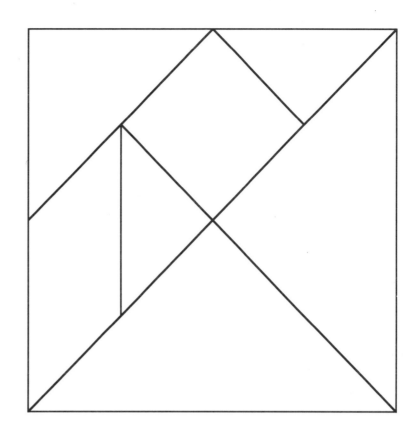

MATERIALS CARD 6.8

Remove the pattern. Fold on all heavy black lines.
Put flap A on top of flap B. Tuck flap C
inside the cube behind flap B. Tuck
flap D in. Tape if necessary.

A

1/2

| C | 2/3 | 1/8 | 1/3 | 1/6 | D |

1/4

B

MATERIALS CARD 7.1

Use the circle as a decimal point marker.
Save these for use later in the chapter.

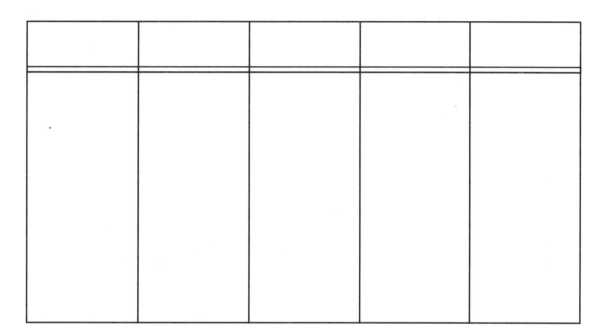

MATERIALS CARD 7.7

Separate into squares.

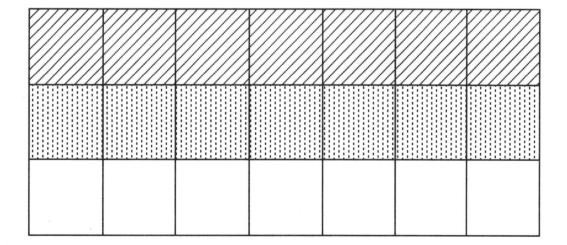

MATERIALS CARD 7.8

Separate into single triangles, rhombuses, trapezoids, and hexagons.

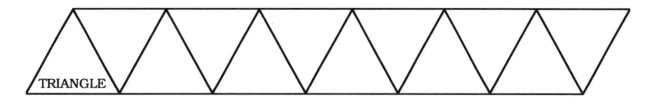

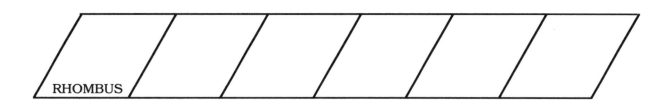

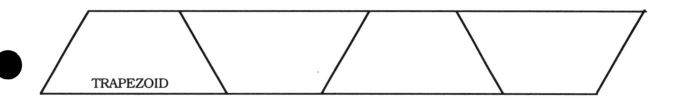

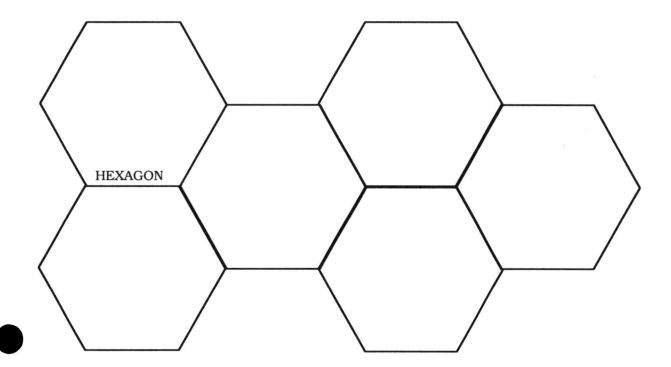

MATERIALS CARD 7.9

Cut into strips and tape the flap marked X under the next strip each time to construct a meter strip.

Save your meter ruler to use again in Chapter 13.

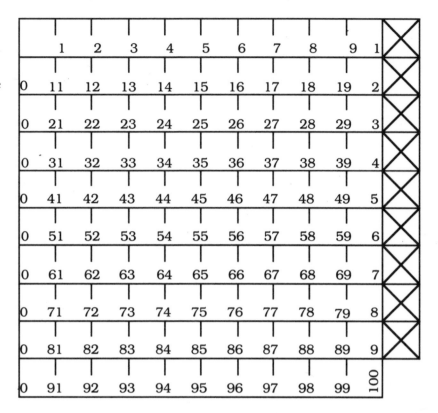

MATERIALS CARD 8.1   Remove these chips. Save for use later in the chapter.

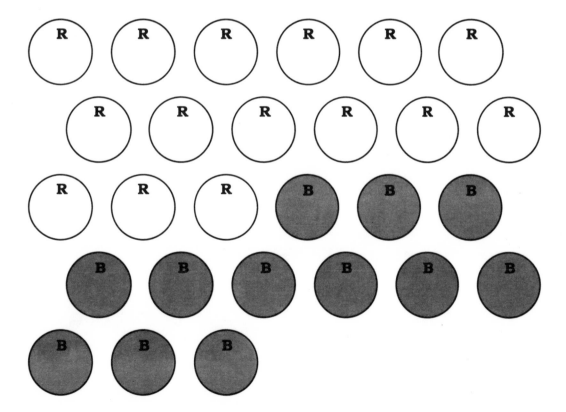

MATERIALS CARD 9.2

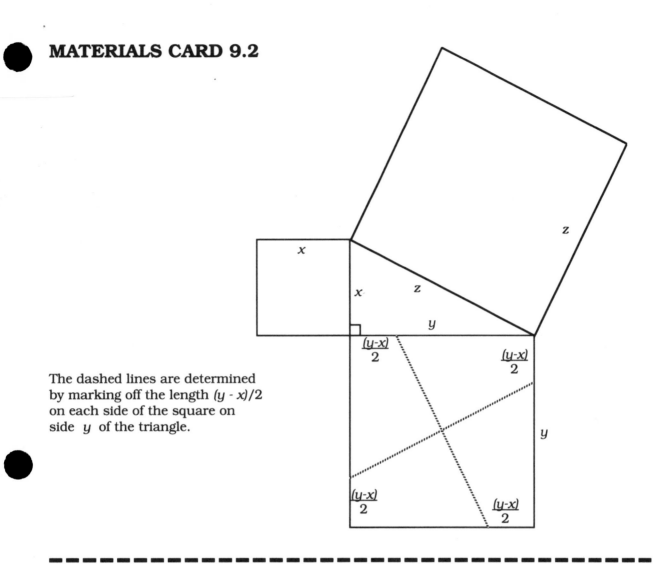

The dashed lines are determined
by marking off the length $(y - x)/2$
on each side of the square on
side y of the triangle.

- -

MATERIALS CARD 9.3

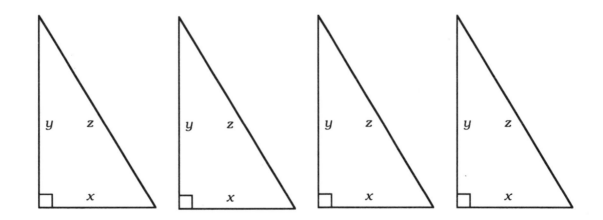

MATERIALS CARD 10.4

Save this protractor
for use in Chapter 14.

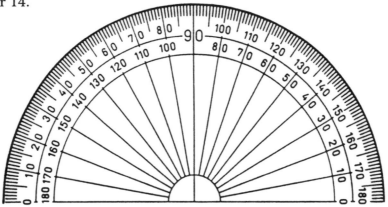

MATERIALS CARD 11.1

Remove these cubes.

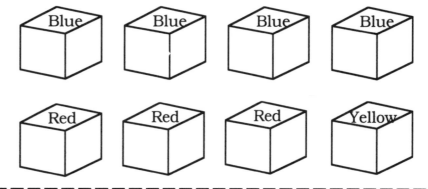

MATERIALS CARD 11.2

Place the pencil point at the center of the
disk through the end of a paper clip or
safety pin as illustrated.

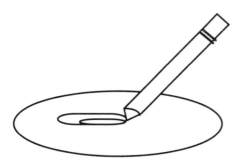

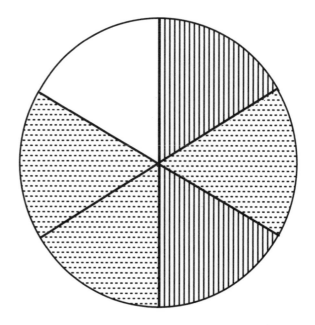

MATERIALS CARD 11.7

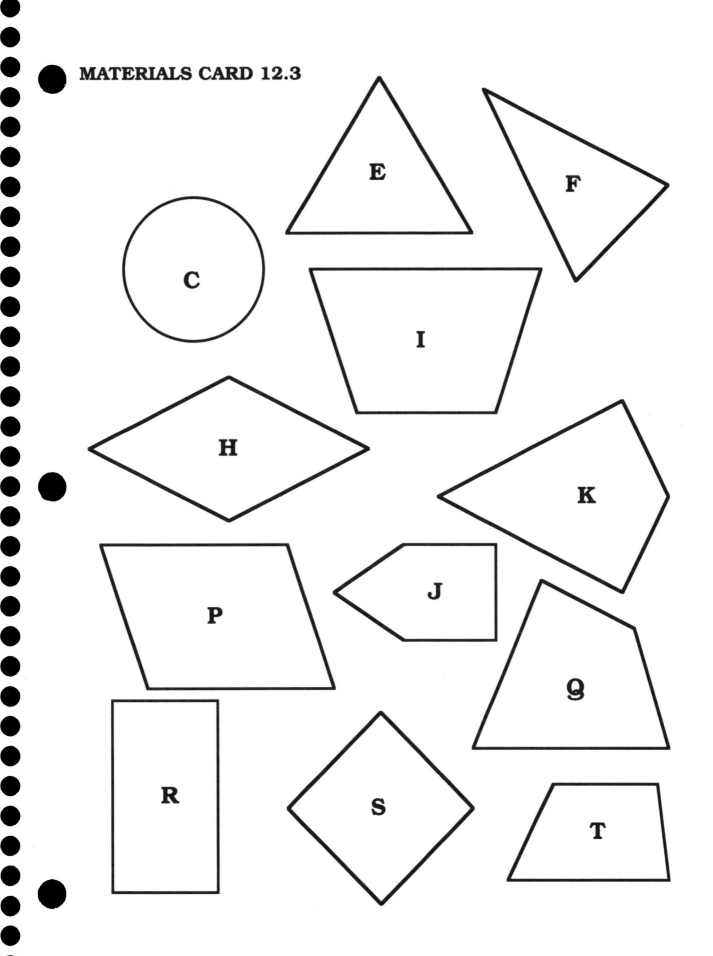

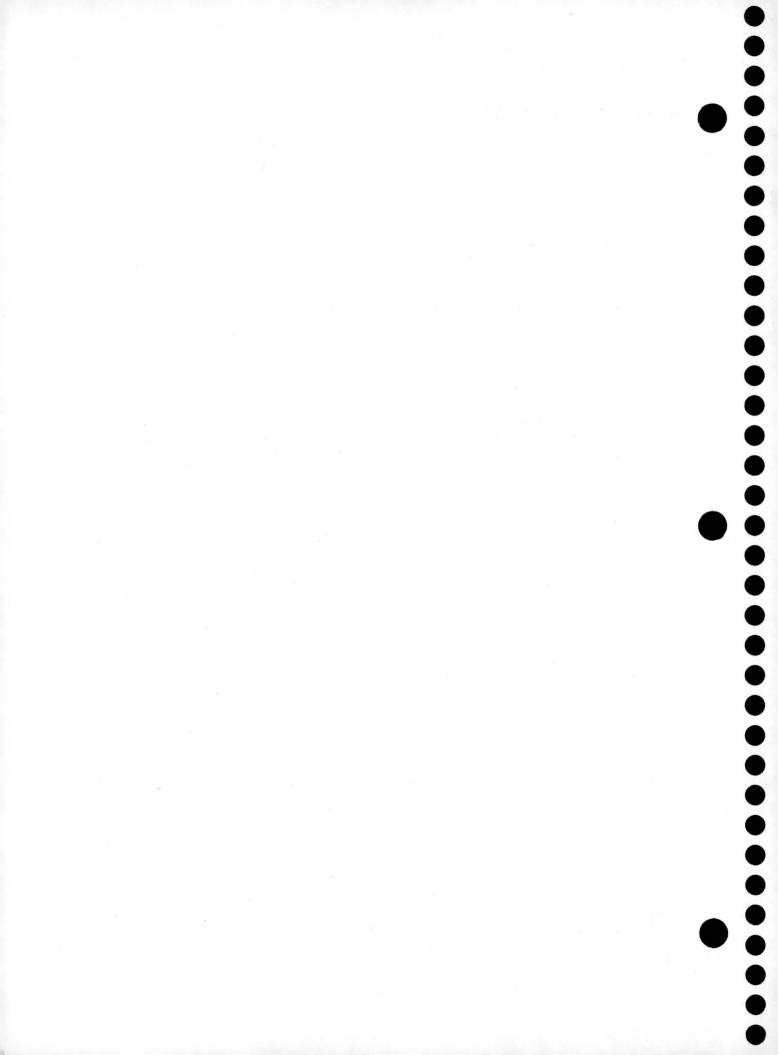

MATERIALS CARD 12.8

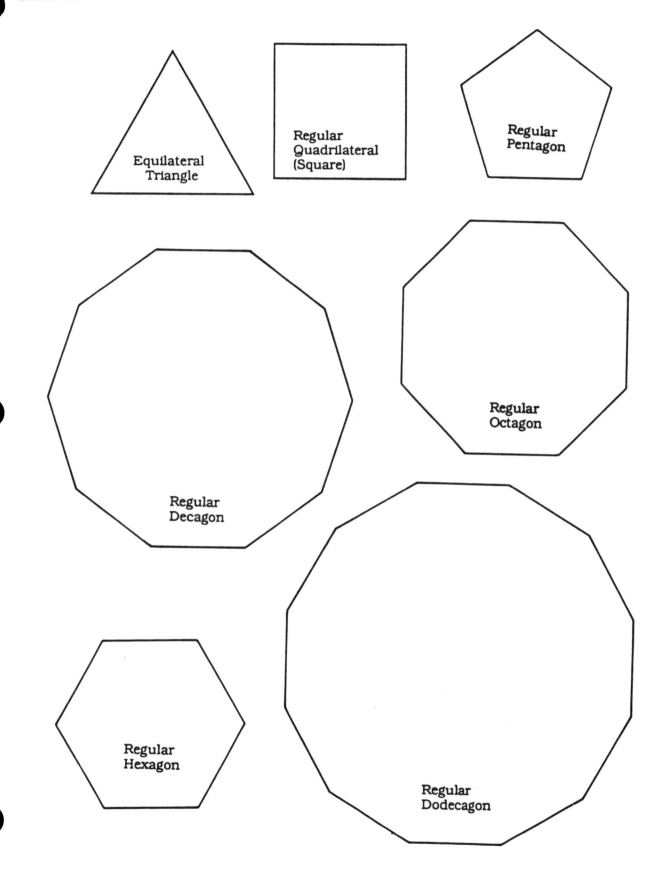

MATERIALS CARD 12.9

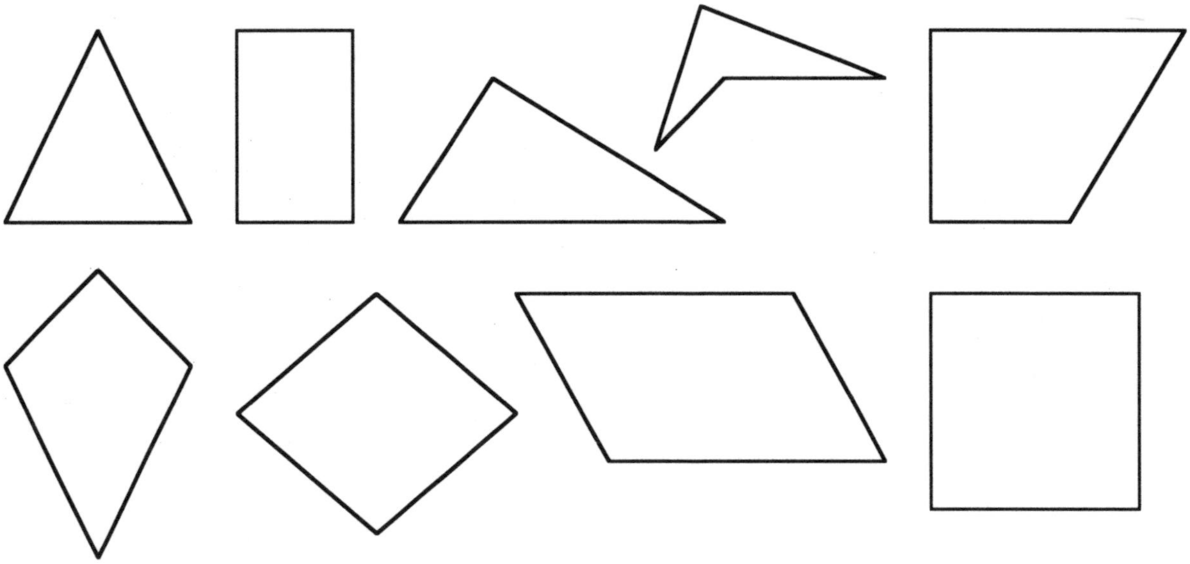

MATERIALS CARD 12.10

Use these circles as patterns.
Make the number of copies indicated.
Fold along dotted lines and put
together with paper clips or tape --
flaps on outside!

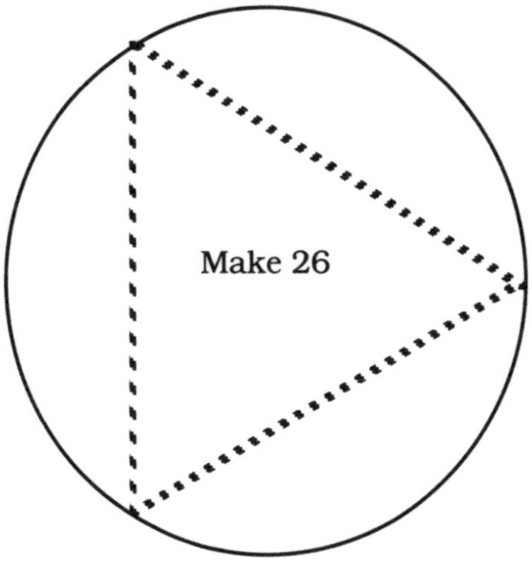

Make 26

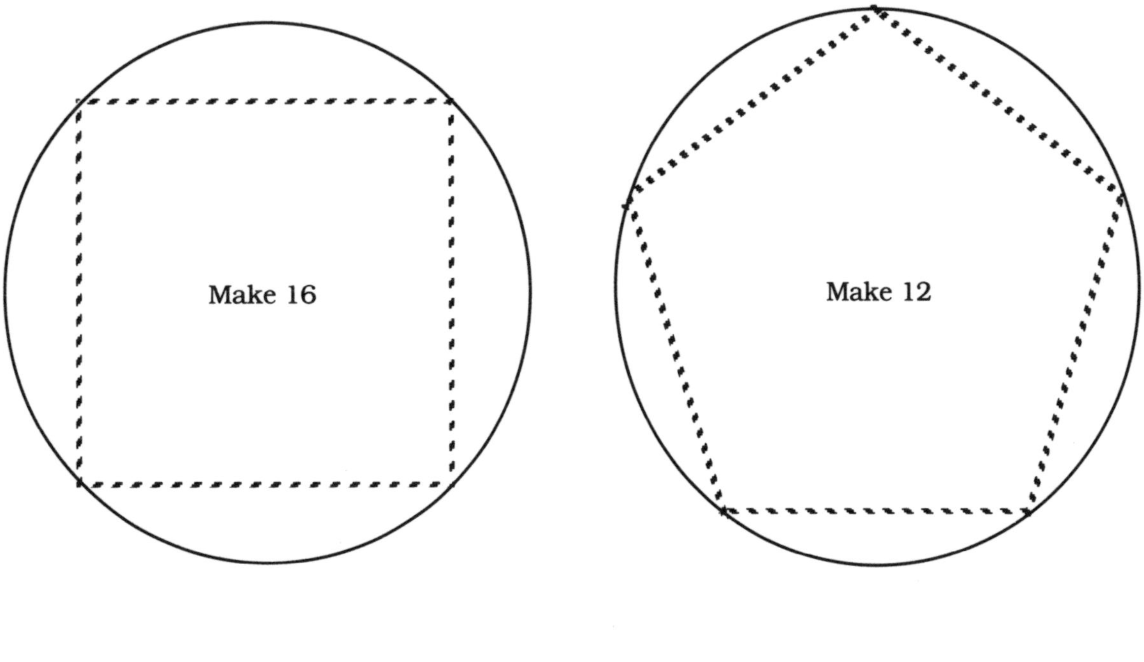

Make 16

Make 12

MATERIALS CARD 13.4

Remove each figure; fold the cube and tape in place. Roll the rectangle into a long cylinder and tape in place.

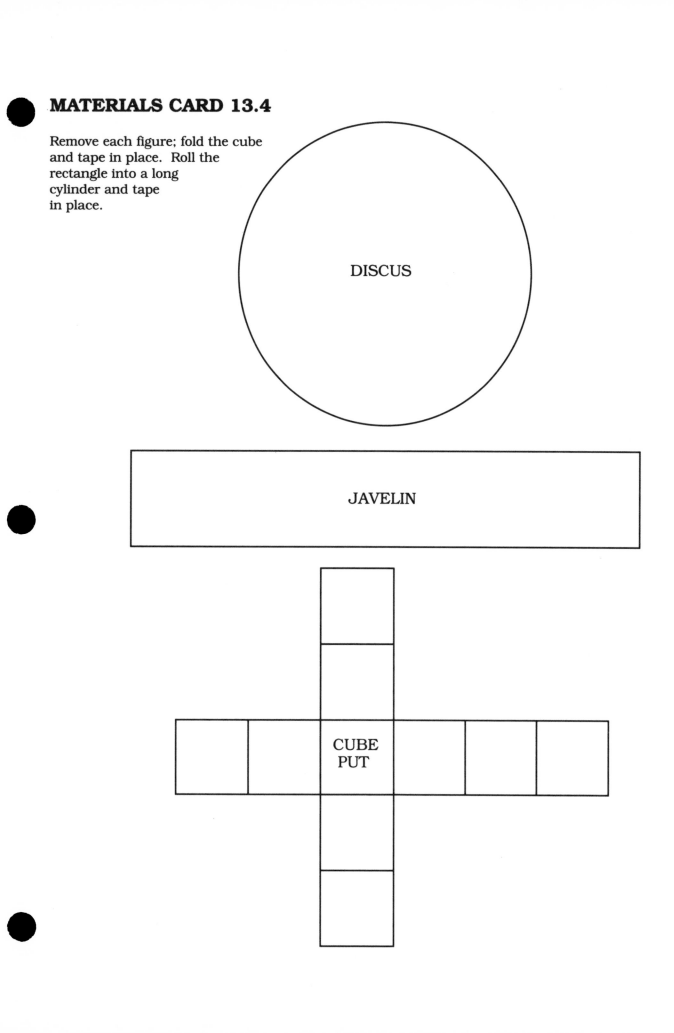

DISCUS

JAVELIN

CUBE
PUT

MATERIALS CARD 13.6

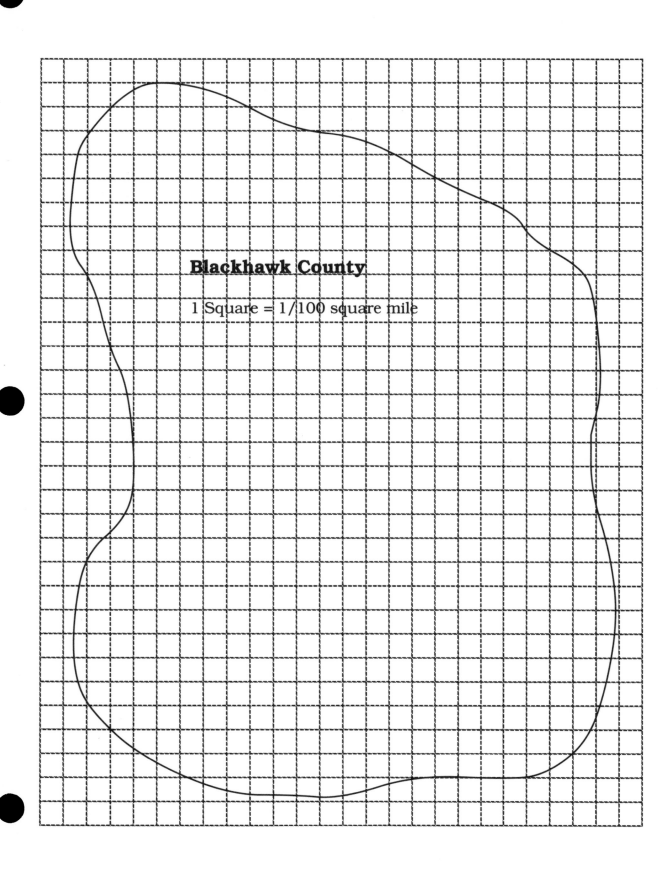

Blackhawk County

1 Square = 1/100 square mile

MATERIALS CARD 13.8

Remove each figure and fold on the solid lines so that the grid paper becomes the outside of the box. Tape in place.

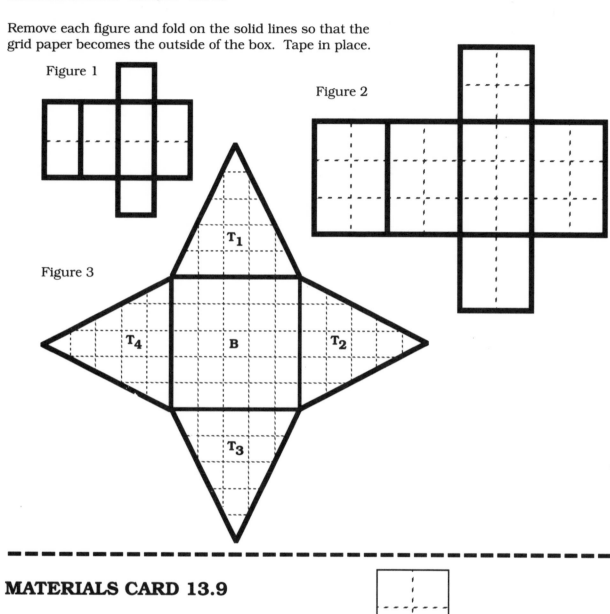

Figure 1

Figure 2

Figure 3

T_1

T_4 B T_2

T_3

MATERIALS CARD 13.9

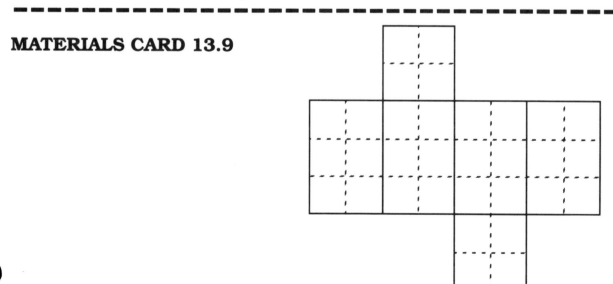

MATERIALS CARD 13.10

A

B

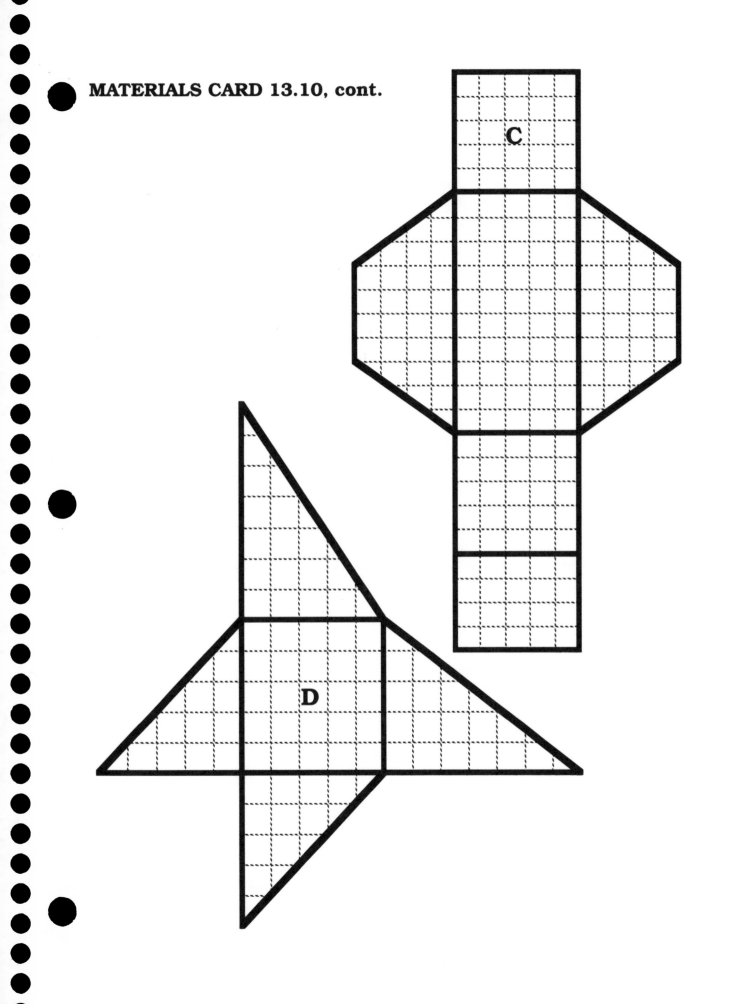

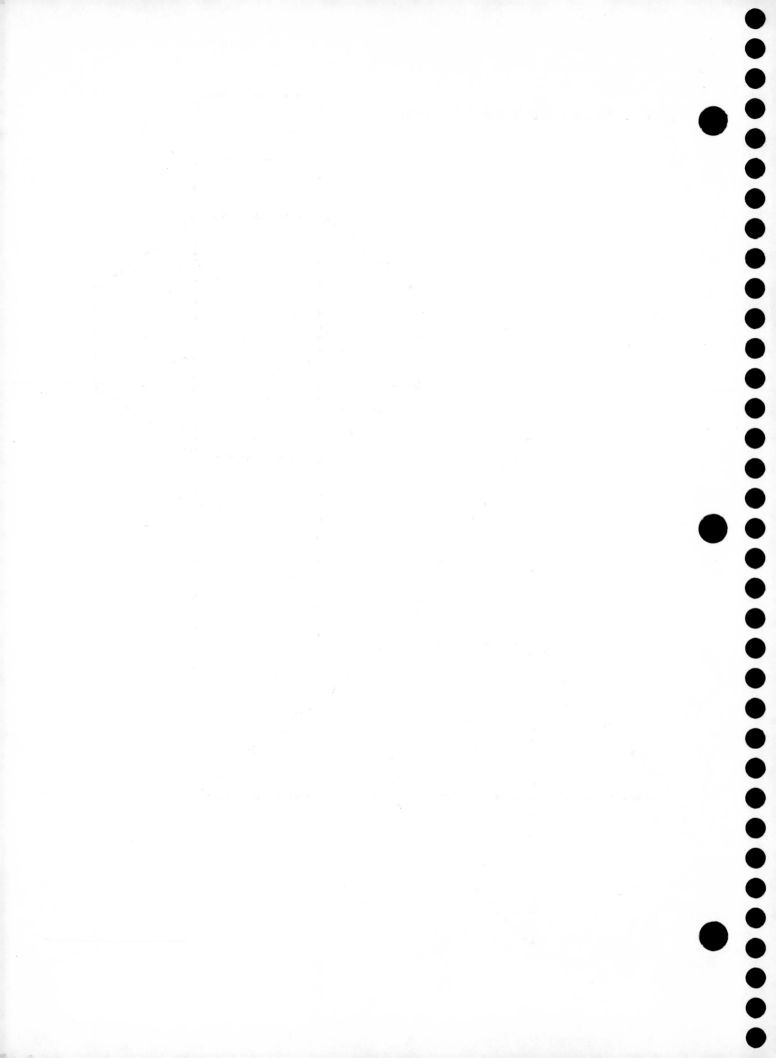

A

Overlap and tape securely.

B

C Apex of cone

MATERIALS CARD 15.2

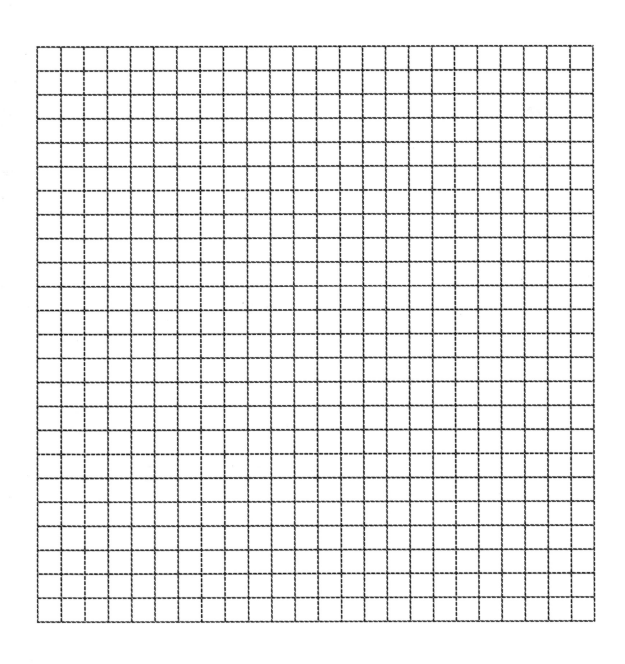